Black Metafiction

Self-Consciousness in
African American Literature

By Madelyn Jablon

University of Iowa Press ⚏ Iowa City

University of Iowa Press, Iowa City 52242
Copyright © 1997 by the University of Iowa Press
Printed in the United States of America

Preliminary versions of chapters 1, 3, 4, and 6 appeared as "Black
Metafiction: Self-Consciousness in African-American Literature," in
Arkansas Review: A Journal of Criticism (Spring 1994); "The African-
American *Künstlerroman*," in *Diversity: A Journal of Multicultural
Issues* (Spring 1994); "The Art of Influence in Toni Morrison's *Tar
Baby*," in *Middle Atlantic Writers Association Review* (June 1995);
and "'Making the Faces Black': The African American Detective
Novel," in *Changing Representations of Minorities East and West*,
edited by John Rieder and Larry E. Smith (Honolulu: University of
Hawaii Press, 1996).

Printed on acid-free paper

Library of Congress Cataloging-in-Publication Data
Jablon, Madelyn
Black metafiction: self-consciousness in African American literature /
by Madelyn Jablon.
p.   cm.
Includes bibliographical references and index.
ISBN 0-87745-560-0
1. American fiction—Afro-American authors—History and
criticism.   2. Afro-Americans in literature.   3. Self-consciousness
in literature.   4. Experimental fiction, American—History and
criticism.   5. American fiction—20th century—History and
criticism.   I. Title.
PS374.N4J33   1997
813.009'896073—dc20   96-38809
                                                                CIP

02 01 00 99 98 97   C   5   4   3   2   1

FOR DENNIS

Contents

> > > > > > > > > >

Acknowledgments

I am grateful to the faculty of the Department of English at the State University of New York at Buffalo for inciting and nurturing my interest in literature. In particular, I wish to thank Robert Newman for his steadfast enthusiasm, William Fischer for his patience, and Neil Schmitz for introducing the students of English 326 to the practitioners and theorists of metafiction. The conversation that began in that class many years ago continues here.

Many of the ideas for this book germinated during two summer seminars. First among them was the 1991 Faculty Resource Network Summer Seminar at New York University. I am indebted to Jeffrey Sammons, Margaret Washington, and the participants in the seminar for the opportunity to defend the enterprise of literary theory. The second summer seminar was organized by Bernard Bell. The Pennsylvania State University 1994 Summer Seminar on Theory and Culture was vital to this project. The workshop on literary criticism and vernacular theory conducted by Houston Baker, Jr., helped me to formulate my ideas on culture and theory. Houston Baker's responses to excerpts from the manuscript encouraged me long after the seminar ended.

I must also express heartfelt gratitude to the community of friends and family who encouraged me to persist, upsets and setbacks notwithstanding. I want to thank Brian Striar for sound, practical advice at crucial stages of the book's development. Gratitude for friendship that inspires and sustains belongs to a family of friends in Rehoboth Beach, a resort on the northern shore of the Delmarva Peninsula. I owe special thanks to "slower lowers" Legba (Keith Fitzgerald) and his cohorts at the Back Porch Café, Barbara and Stephen Crane of Browserabout Books and Café, and Bagelmeister Peter Wise of Pierre's Pantry. Thanks are owed my father, Michael Jablon, for an inherited predisposition for imagining the world as a better place, and my mother, Evelyn Goldstein Jablon, for admonishing a bored second grader: "Read!" Most important, I must thank Montana, Louie-Louie, the Brothers and the Sisters, and my husband, Dennis Mertz, a steadfast believer in dreams I had long ago given up for lost. I could not have done this without him and his luck, but that's another story entirely.

Black Metafiction

Introduction

> Chappie was so happy that he was beside himself.
> He had sent a letter to the campus
> deconstructionists, informing them of their
> termination. The letters said you're fired. Those
> who believed that the words "you're fired" meant
> exactly that could finish the semester. Those who
> felt that the words only referred to themselves
> would have to leave immediately.
>
> —Ishmael Reed, *Japanese by Spring*

Theories of Metafiction: Black and White

In recent years scholars of African American literature have sent out a plea for theories that issue from the genre. *Afro-American Literary Studies in the 1990s*, edited by Houston A. Baker, Jr., and Patricia Redmond, is testimony to this. In this collection of essays, the leading critics in the field discuss the shortcomings of imposing structuralist, poststructuralist, psychoanalytic, and feminist theories on black texts. Although some theoretical frameworks seem more relevant than others, theories with origins extrinsic to the genre are regarded as problematic at best and dangerous at worst. The suggested alternative is an inductive method of investigation. Instead of imposing theory on texts, critics begin with an analysis of the works themselves and extrapolate a theory from them. Henry Louis Gates, Jr., a critic whose reputation was founded on the deconstruction of black texts, has joined the chorus of voices that are demanding new theories. In Gates' contribution to the collection "Canon-Formation, Literary History, and the Afro-American Tradition: From the Seen to the Told," he says: "I once thought our most important gesture to *master* the canon of criticism, to *imitate* and *apply* it, but I now believe that we must turn to the black tradition itself to develop theories of criticism indigenous to our literatures" (25).

One could argue that the impulse to uncover the theory in texts, to work inductively, is a consequence both of discoveries made in the study of black texts and of the study of theories extrinsic to them, but what is important here is this recent development in African American literary theory. Scholars of African American literature have shifted their focus from theory to text. One consequence of this is a return to "oppositional criticism," what Gates describes in *Loose Canons* as a "wacky packs" version of literary history:

> The dilemmas of oppositional criticism haunt the fractured
> American academic community. The 1980s witnessed not only a
> resurgence of what I'll call the New Moralism, but the beginning
> of its subsidence. Seventies-style Hermeneutics killed the author;
> eighties-style Politics brought her back. The seventies sponsored
> a hedonistic vocabulary of free-play, *jouissance*, the joys of in-
> determinacy. The eighties brought back a grim-faced insistence
> on hidden moral stakes. . . . we lost facts, and we got back ethics:
> a trade-in but not necessarily an upgrade. (181–183)

Gates suggests that the trend toward inductive criticism is a reaction to work done in the 1970s and 1980s, when critics such as himself created a renaissance in the field of African American literary theory by envisioning the canon through poststructuralist theory. However, interpreting the advent of inductive criticism as a reaction to structuralist theory is only a partial explanation for the current state of affairs. The widespread interest in multiculturalism, the advent of postcolonialism, and the recognition of the political dimension of all theory—even that which seems exempt from it—have also contributed to the shift. Gates is alluding to these influences when he says: "Back in the 1930s, a magazine editor wondered aloud if there was a typewriter at *The Partisan Review* with the word *alienation* on a single key. Right now I'm on the lookout for a typewriter that has *counterhegemonic cultural production* on a single key" (187). Not surprisingly, Gates warns of the difficulties of our current position: ethics has its limitations as a means of evaluating and understanding literature, and so too does this new divide in the bastions of theory.

This is especially evident to those whose interests situate them with a foot in each camp. From this vantage point, we see scholars of African American literature in the position of trying to reinvent theory and theorists whose ignorance of black literature and its traditions makes their work suspect. Examples of both abound. In their discussions of metafiction, theorists such as Robert Scholes, Patricia Waugh, and Linda Hutcheon omit reference to the tradition of self-consciousness in black fiction. Similarly, scholars such as Henry Louis Gates and Houston Baker, Jr., scholars whose discussion of self-consciousness is grounded in the black literary tradition, provide only cursory treatment of theories generated externally. In 1985, Gates said that he had applied white theories to black texts and that his next task was to uncover theories endemic to the black vernacular. In 1988, he said his objective was to use white theories and to modify them through their application to black texts.[1] These are both valid approaches, and they can occur simultaneously. Baker's application of phenomenology and Deborah McDowell's and Mae Henderson's experiments with dialogics demonstrate how both disciplines are enriched by these kinds of ventures: critics make discoveries about black literature at the same time that they revise and enrich theories generated in other contexts.[2] That is an aim of this study. Gates and Baker have laid the groundwork for the endemic research. Hutcheon and Waugh have developed theories that omit discussion of black literature and the tradition of self-consciousness in African American literature. This study is a vernacular revision of their theories and a contribution to the body of scholarship that employs intrinsic and extrinsic theories improvisationally.

In the preface to *The Signifying Monkey*, Gates explains that his aim is to "show how the black tradition has inscribed its own theories of its nature and function within elaborate hermeneutical and rhetorical systems" (xvi). In the same paragraph, he notes that he has "borrowed liberally" from Western critical arguments (xiv). As Gates seems to acknowledge, the very premise of his study—looking for a theory intrinsic to the African American vernacular—borrows from Western critical arguments. Although his search takes him to Africa, it is grounded in contemporary theories founded on the study of Western literature.

Nevertheless, Gates begins with a study of the African Esu-Elegbara and African American Signifying Monkey to demonstrate the self-consciousness inherent in the black vernacular. Gates says, "The black tradition has inscribed within it the very principles by which it can be read. Ours is an extraordinary self-reflexive tradition, a tradition exceptionally conscious of its history and the simultaneity of its canonical texts" (xxiv). Gates traces this self-consciousness from the eighteenth-century African American autobiography of James Albert Ukawsaw Gronniosaw through Alice Walker's novel *The Color Purple*. He shows how writing becomes a focus of eighteenth-century narratives and how these episodes are read by later generations of writers who re-inscribe them in the canon. Metafiction is a by-product of the contemporary writer's dialogue with literary predecessors.

Responding to canonical texts is one of several ways in which metafiction is present in the vernacular. While some texts demonstrate metafictionality through the suggestion of a relationship with a literary forerunner, others do so through self-contemplation and the contemplation of vernacular metafictional traditions. Zora Neale Hurston fits squarely in this tradition. Essays such as Hurston's "Characteristics of Negro Expression" provide evidence of an aesthetic that is indeed self-conscious.[3] Her autobiography, *Dust Tracks on a Road*, also demonstrates a self-conscious concern with writing. Like its relative, the *künstlerroman*, it describes the development of an artist. Hurston recalls games played with corn-husk dolls and journeys on an imaginary horse—vital contributions to the growth of her literary imagination. Gates, Baker, and others have referred to the metafictional attributes of *Their Eyes Were Watching God*.[4] Discussions of silence and speech, metaphor, the vernacular, free indirect discourse, and the foregrounding of the act of storytelling classify this work as an example of metafiction, a work that "talks out loud" about itself and its invention. Indeed, it seems possible to argue that the subject of artistic invention is a thread running through the fabric of Hurston's entire oeuvre.

While scholars of African American literature cite Hurston's work in discussions of vernacular traditions of self-consciousness, her name is not mentioned in Linda Hutcheon's *Narcissistic Narrative*, the most comprehensive discussion of metafiction to date. Like Robert Scholes' *Fabulation and Metafiction*, Hutcheon's study acknowledges the work of Ishmael Reed and Clarence Major as metafiction but omits discussion of the tradition of self-consciousness in African American literature that is present in endemic theories.

Nevertheless, Hutcheon, like Gates, points out that self-reflexivity is not the stronghold of a few postmodern writers. Like James Mellard and Robert Alter, Linda Hutcheon and Patricia Waugh regard self-consciousness as a characteristic of the narrative, one that predates postmodernism.[5]

Theorists of African American literature and theorists of Western literature also agree that self-consciousness is as old as the storytelling tradition itself. Hutcheon envisions it as a part of Aristotle's poetics, a mimesis of process that is overshadowed by a mimesis of product in the nineteenth century. Waugh says it pre-dates or shares its genesis with the novel: "Although the *term* metafiction might be new, the *practice* is as old (if not older) than the novel itself: metafiction is a tendency or function inherent in all novels" (5).

Like Gates, Hutcheon predicates her work on the foundation of myth, but whereas Gates makes use of African and African American myths, Hutcheon founds her theory on the Greek myth of Narcissus, which she interprets as an allegory of the history of narrative and evidence that narcissism is "the original condition of the novel" (8). Hutcheon's reading of Ovid focuses on the roles of Echo and Narcissus. Like novelistic language, Echo can neither speak autonomously nor be silenced, and her demise signifies language's succumbing to the service of reality: "When formal realism was seen as the accepted goal of fiction, the novel . . . seemed to refuse to give independent power to (or even pay attention to) its medium, language" (11). According to Hutcheon, the romantic concern with the creative process is allegorized by Narcissus' fascination with his own reflection, and the death of the novel is portrayed by Narcissus' death.[6] Echo's survival is indicative of the remaining postmodern obsession: a fascination with language and linguistic codes, verbal process as the focal point of fiction (14).

The similarities in the theories of Hutcheon and Gates are noteworthy. Although Hutcheon commences with a study of Western comparative literature and Gates commences with a study of African and African American works, both begin their investigations with the discussion of myths: Narcissus and Esu-Elegbara or the Signifying Monkey. Both read these myths as allegories about the nature of art and artistic production. Both decode the myths to reveal a history or tradition of self-consciousness and a system of classification: Hutcheon classifies the different kinds of self-conscious fiction; Gates, the different forms of signifyin(g).[7] The final chapters of both studies are devoted to discussions of specific examples.

Baker has also theorized about black metafiction, but he begins by noting that self-consciousness is ancillary to African American history. Regarding the text as a metaphor for the self, Baker suggests that literary self-consciousness mirrors a self-consciousness that originated during slavery. Like its author, the black text is conscious of its origins and its participation in the community and canon.

In *Workings of the Spirit*, Baker begins by reminding us that African culture survived and proved most durable when it produced no material product, no evidence that could be seized and destroyed by slaveowners: "Africans uprooted from ancestral soil, stripped of material culture and victimized by the brutal contact with various European nations were compelled not only to maintain their cultural heritage at a *meta* (as opposed to material) level but also to apprehend the operative metaphysics of various alien cultures. Primary to their survival was the work of *consciousness*, of nonmaterial counterintelligence" (38). Baker advances this argument by comparing African American intellectual discourse with theoretical discourse: "Theory's relentless tendency is to go beyond the tangible in search of *metalevels* of explanation. A concern for metalevels, rather than tangible products, is also a founding condition of Afro-American intellectual discourse" (38). For Baker, the connection between African American intellectual discourse and theory provides a historical explanation for the self-consciousness in African American literature.

It is helpful to become familiar with the history of the term "metafiction" before continuing. Scholars credit William Gass with the invention of the term. In *Fiction and the Figures of Life,* he defines "metafiction" as "fiction which draws attention to itself as artefact to pose questions about the relationship between fiction and reality" (25). Waugh uses this definition as a foundation for her own, one that emphasizes the social and cultural dimensions of the term.[8] In the chapter "Metafiction and the Contemporary Avant-garde," she observes the political dimension of metafiction by noting that "metafiction sets up an opposition to . . . the language of the realistic novel" and the view of reality it sustains (11). She underscores the political significance of this maneuver by arguing that metafiction is not a refusal to confront "reality" but an insistence that such a confrontation must commence with the redefinition of the term and a renewed awareness of the language used to describe it:

> The metafictional novel thus situates its resistance *within* the form of the novel itself. Saussure distinguished between *langue* and *parole*: between the language system (a set of rules) and any act of individual utterance that takes place within the system. Each metafictional novel self-consciously sets its individual *parole* against the *langue* (the codes and conventions) of the novel tradition. Ostentatiously "literary" language and conventions are paraded, are set against the fragments of various cultural codes, not because there is nothing left to talk about, but because the formal structures of these literary conventions provide a statement about the disassociation between, on the one hand, the genuinely felt sense of crisis, alienation and oppression in contemporary society and, on the other, the continuance of traditional literary forms like realism which are no longer adequate vehicles for the mediation of this experience. Metafiction thus converts what it sees as the negative values of outworn literary

conventions into the basis of a potentially constructive social criticism. It suggests, in fact, that there may be as much to be learnt from setting the mirror of art up to its own linguistic or representational structures as from directly setting it up to a hypothetical "human nature" that somehow exists as an essence outside historical systems of articulation. (11)

Waugh envisions a "spectrum" of metafiction. At one end are novels that "take fictionality as a theme to be explored" (18). In the center are examples of new realism, "texts that manifest the symptoms of formal and ontological insecurity but allow their deconstructions to be finally recontextualized or 'naturalized' and given a total interpretation" (19). At the other end are those fictions that "posit the world as a fabrication of competing semiotic systems which never correspond to material conditions" (19). Waugh employs these distinctions to conclude that "much British fiction fits into the first half of the spectrum, though problematically, and much American fiction into the other half, though with the same proviso" (19). Although Waugh's "spectrum of metafiction" is helpful in distinguishing among techniques of metafiction (thematic, ontological, linguistic), her definition suggests that mimetic fiction serves as a norm, and her spectrum characterizes a work in relation to this standard. Metafiction that is thematic, such as the *künstlerroman*, is placed closest to non-self-conscious literature. Metafiction that is linguistic is viewed as most remote. This hierarchy seems arbitrary, since inverting or reversing the spectrum provides an equally workable model. This method is also contrary to the ideas that give rise to the invention of metafiction, ideas that question the very distinctions that Waugh tries to impose. Finally, Waugh regards thematic, ontological, and linguistic metafiction as distinct categories, but many works exhibit more than one such category. Hutcheon's paradigm is susceptible to many of the same criticisms, although her system of classification is much more complex.

The theory that Hutcheon presents in *Narcissistic Narrative* is a modification of Jean Ricardou's horizontal and vertical representational cross. Hutcheon explains Ricardou's theory as "structured on two types of self-reflexiveness, or to use his term, autorepresentation—vertical and horizontal. The vertical variety is *inter*dimensional, operating between the 'fiction' (what is said) and the 'narration' (how it is said). Horizontal autorepresentation is *intra*dimensional" (21). Hutcheon notes that Ricardou fails to make "the distinction between texts which are self-conscious about their *diegetic* or narrative process and those which are *linguistically* self-reflexive" (22). To compensate for this omission, she creates four categories: overt and covert forms of diegetic and linguistic narcissism (154).

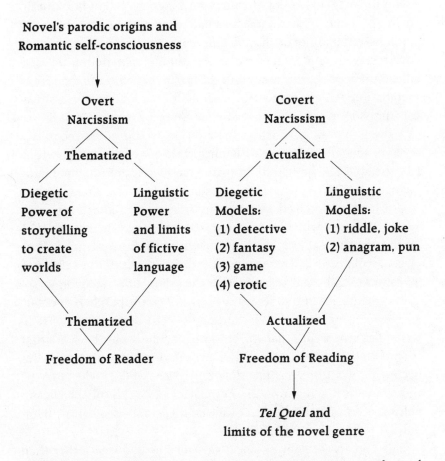

Novel's parodic origins and Romantic self-consciousness

Overt Narcissism

Thematized

Diegetic Power of storytelling to create worlds

Linguistic Power and limits of fictive language

Thematized

Freedom of Reader

Covert Narcissism

Actualized

Diegetic Models: (1) detective (2) fantasy (3) game (4) erotic

Linguistic Models: (1) riddle, joke (2) anagram, pun

Actualized

Freedom of Reading

***Tel Quel* and limits of the novel genre**

The first pair of terms, "overt" and "covert" narcissism, is derived from Ricardou's model. Overt narcissism is interdimensional. It operates between the diegetic and the linguistic levels and can be perceived as a theme of the work. On the other hand, covert narcissism is intradimensional and results in *actualized* metafiction. Rather than describe the life of an artist, metafiction thematized, it enacts the life of the artist. Both classifications, thematized and actualized, can be manifested diegetically and linguistically. Covert narcissism of the diegetic variety is exemplified by parody, the detective story, fantasy, game structure, and the erotic. This class of metafiction "makes the reader aware of the fact that he, too, is actively engaged in creating a fictional universe" (28). The covert linguistic variety is exemplified by riddles, jokes, puns, and anagrams (34). While Hutcheon may seem to be an overzealous hairsplitter who establishes categories based on minor or obscure differences, her discussions of overt, covert, diegetic, and linguistic classifications of metafiction are valuable. Moreover, the discussions of the origin, evolution, and future of metafiction, which serve as the scaffold for her system of classification, provide an informative reading of literary history.

A discussion of theories of metafiction would not be complete without reference to Mikhail Bakhtin's theory of dialogism, which has already been applied to African American literature, producing favorable results. A cursory view of some of the terminology, such as is provided by Michael Holquist in *Dialogism: Bakhtin and His World*, suggests why. Such terms as "dialogism," "heteroglossia," "intertextuality," and "polyphony" point to Bakhtin's critique of the Hegelian dialectic and his recognition of the "*multiplicity* in human perception" (22). His insistence that the self be understood in its social context leads him to regard the self as a "multiple phenomenon" and being as "co-being" (29). Building on Einstein's theory of relativity, Bakhtin argues that "all meaning is relative in the sense that it comes about only as a result of the relation between two bodies occupying *simultaneous but different* space, where bodies may be thought of as ranging from the immediacy of our physical bodies to political bodies and to bodies of ideas in general (ideologies)" (Holquist 20–21).

This revision of subject-object relations as dialogue rather than dialectic has its correlative in African American aesthetics. It exists in black music as synchrony and counterpoint. Dissatisfaction with viewing subject and object as a dialectic is evident in Toni Morrison's

Beloved and *Tar Baby*, where "point of view," a key term in dialogism, explodes to accommodate a multitude of perspectives. Such novels do not conclude with the suggestion of synthesis but remain polyphonic, unwilling to compromise the chorus of voices into a performance by one. Deborah McDowell observes this aspect of the dialogic in Toni Morrison's *Sula*:

> The novel invokes oppositions of good/evil, virgin/whore, self/ other, but moves beyond them, avoiding the false choices they imply and dictate. As Hortense Spillers puts it eloquently, when we read *Sula*, "No Manichean analysis demanding a polarity of interest—black/white, male/female, good/bad [and I might add, positive/negative, self/other]—will do." The narrative insistently blurs and confuses these and other binary oppositions. ("The Self and the Other" 80)

Mae Henderson makes use of Bakhtin's concepts of polyphony and heteroglossia in her essay "Speaking in Tongues," which illustrates the aspects of dialogism that make it "an exercise in social theory" (Holquist 37). Bakhtin believes that social environment has a greater influence than genetics: "The child was conceived not as an isolated entity making its lonely way through the maze of a preprogrammed cognitive design, but as an organism tied to a community of others: 'the true direction of the development of thinking is not from the individual to the socialized, but *from the social to the individual*'" (80). This idea provides the foundation for his ideas on language—his use of the term "utterance" (rather than "parole") to stress its social aspect (61) and his understanding of speech as a primary, and writing as a secondary, activity.

Bakhtin's emphasis on the social and the verbal helps to highlight two important elements in the African American cultural tradition: community and the spoken word. Bakhtin's understanding of time is also congruent with its significance in black culture. Like G. F. W. Hegel and Georg Lukács, Bakhtin perceives the development of the human species as comparable to the development of an individual's increasing self-consciousness, but according to dialogism, "this sequence *has no necessary telos built into it*. It is a narrative that has the appearance of being developmental only from a present point of view" (76). Bakhtin questions linear time and history as a progression of steps or stages toward a state of enlightenment, wisdom, or vision. Novels such as Charles Johnson's *Middle Passage* and Cyrus Colter's *Night Studies* emphasize personal and collective memory and the continuous interplay of past and present as an alternative to chronological linear time. Such reconfigurations of the past as Morrison's "rememory" and Alice Walker's "dream memory" are also consistent with Bakhtin's philosophy of time and history.

The political implications of the denial of *telos* are noteworthy. Although this passage appears in the context of a discussion of the development of the novel, it reveals Bakhtin's view of the historical process: "Instead of a teleology whose course is a movement from one unitary state to another, Bakhtin's historical masterplot opens with a deluded perception of unity and goes on to a growing knowledge of ever-increasing difference and variety that cannot be overcome in any uniting synthesis" (Holquist 76).

Dialogism is especially relevant to a study of black metafiction because both dialogue and self-consciousness play important roles in Bakhtin's work. They are evident in his ideas of "existence as a dialogue" or the idea that we must appropriate the vision of others to see ourselves: "In order to forge a self, I must do it from outside, I author myself" (29), for "only from a position outside something can it be perceived in categories that fix it in time and place" (31). This definition of self-consciousness as the result of an interplay between self and others has its corollary in black literature and in novels like *Sula*, which pursue the subject of self-consciousness through the maze of relationships that make up Sula's experiences.

Unlike Hutcheon and Gates, who deconstruct myths to discover theories, Bakhtin reads literature as a metaphor for existence. His pursuit of literary theory originates in an interest in psychology and philosophy. The result of his efforts to understand existence, the self, and the self's relationship with that which is not the self produces an *architectonics* or system of organization, which provides insight into psychology, philosophy, and literature.

Baker's poetics resembles Bakhtin's because both posit a one-to-one correspondence between text and subject. Bakhtin accomplishes

this through his use of metaphors derived from the field of literature. Baker accomplishes it through references to history. Literary
self-consciousness reflects the conditions of a human subject, both
would also agree. Because Bakhtin's interest is psychology, not literature, however, he perceives the novel as a recapitulation of the various dialogues that constitute the experience of the individual. In
other words, like Baker, he equates metafiction with the psychology of self-consciousness, but his definition of self-consciousness
is complicated by an understanding of consciousness as a matrix
of dialogues that are constantly changing and constantly affecting
each other. If metafiction were introduced into Bakhtin's architectonics it would be manifest in a dialogic self-consciousness or a two-
sided mirror that permits one to look at one's self and elsewhere
simultaneously.

This is not an exhaustive discussion of theories of metafiction.
Several important representatives of such theories are excluded.
Many of them, such as Robert Scholes, are included in discussion
of other theorists. Peter Burger's and Renato Poggioli's theories of
the avant-garde are also omitted, since they would propel us deeper
into the realm of literary theory and further away from the kind of
textual analysis or inductive research that the contributors of *Afro-
American Literary Studies in the 1990s* request. It is also not my
intention to provide an extensive comparison of the various theories,
citing the advantages and disadvantages of each and choosing the one
best suited for the study of African American literature. It is my purpose to refer to theories when they assist in the discussion of particular works or when a reading calls for the recasting of a theory. Before
commencing, it will be helpful to understand the history of African
American literary theory and the biases that impeded the study of
black metafiction.

The History of African American Literary Theory

Before the 1980s, a rigorous antiformalism inhibited the study of
black metafiction. This antiformalism was a consequence of the
misapplication of the sociohistorical critical model. Although this
model provided the foundation for the study of African American lit-

erature by asserting a connection between literature and society, an eagerness to counter formalism resulted in scholars' using this approach to disassociate social and artistic concerns in literature.

The legitimate application of social criticism involves the user in an analysis of literature as a cultural artifact: because literature is a product of a given society, it provides information about that society's customs, values, history, and language, as well as insight into the function it assigns to literature. Within this framework, both the absence and the presence of a manifest political content are deemed significant because they provide information about the cultural milieu that produced the literature. This perspective encourages the critic to explore the social and historical corollaries of all literary phenomena, even those that are not motivated by a specific political ideology.

The value of this critical model rests in the assertion of a connection between a community and its literary artifacts. It contrasts with formalist criticism, which severs the link joining literature and culture by defining literature as autotelic, analyzable independent of its social milieu. However, in an effort to defend against attacks made by formalists, attacks that threaten the very foundation of the study of African American literature, overzealous critics decried all manifestations of formalism. This resulted in limiting the applicability of this critical method, making it antagonistic to the analysis of the cultural implications of formalist innovations and inept at analyzing the social and historical conditions that gave rise to such innovations.

The following passage from Donald B. Gibson's *Politics of Literary Expression* demonstrates the consequences of antiformalism. Encumbered by the form/content, aesthetics/politics antithesis that is the outgrowth of a criticism founded on an antiformalist foundation, he develops this formula for interpreting the significance of a writer's concern with form:

> A clear relationship between form and value emerges when we consider social involvement. The greater the writer's commitment to the idea that literature is its own end, the greater his or her concern for the formal aspect of writing. Conversely, the greater the writer's social commitment, the less attention he or

she is likely to give matters of form. Consequently, considerations of form are significant, for a writer's social values are often expressed by his or her handling of form. The question is never whether a writer gives attention to form, but the extent to which the writer's effort is directed toward form. The complexities come in describing accurately the relative value that a writer places on form in relation to the character of the content of his or her writing. Hence the intent is not to establish simple categories. (11)

Gibson suggests that "attention to form" is significant because it identifies writers with negligible "social commitment." Aesthetic concerns are important because they point to the relative absence of political ones and they assert no significance outside this diametrical framework. Besides being untrue—many writers express interest in both—an additional problem with this theory appears in the final sentence of this passage. The "relative degrees of attention" that must be assessed in the application of this formula undercut the categories that provide the terms of its premise. Of greater significance than the faulty logic is its exemplification of the formalistically qualified sociohistorical critical model. In its recognition of the mutually exclusive, antagonistic categories of politics and aesthetics, it divests art of social and political concerns. The correct application of social criticism would direct an interpretation of the writer's foremost interest in aesthetics as a significant statement in its own right: it might be read as illustrative of the important role that aesthetics and form play in shaping consciousness, or as a commentary on Western aesthetics.[9] Nevertheless, it is important to recognize that the aesthetics/politics dualism that was central to the critical analysis and evaluation of much African American literature foreclosed the possibility of interpreting aesthetics for its historical and political relevance.

In spite of its limitations, the sociohistorical approach to literature played an important role in legitimating the study of black literature. Assertions of the importance of theme and content provided an alternative to new criticism, which exalted form and artistic innovation and thereby discouraged the study of formalistically conventional literature produced by writers of realism and naturalism. By focusing on content and minimizing the importance of form, African American sociohistorical criticism inverted the priorities of new criticism and consequently functioned as a "separatist" theory that advocated the study of black literature on the basis of its difference from Anglo-American literature.

As a result, an aversion to formal innovation became rooted in the sociohistorical approach to African American literature. Within this context, black writers who demonstrated an interest in artistic concerns such as those suggested by literary self-consciousness or metafiction were criticized for undercutting the most important justification for the study of black literature: content that expressed the need for political reform. This explains the long-standing bias against formal innovation and the large body of prescriptive criticism that warned writers not to be distracted from the serious business of politics by the trivial interest in art.

This ideology provided part of the foundation for the Black Arts Movement of the 1960s, a movement that asserted, according to Larry Neal, "a radical reordering of the western cultural aesthetic" (Scott 306). A closer look at some of the actual mandates of this new aesthetic, however, causes one to question whether they functioned to reorder or to reinforce the Western cultural aesthetic implicit in literary realism.

Addison Gayle, Jr., a leading spokesperson for the Black Aesthetic, defines it as "a means of helping black people out of the mainstream of americanism," yet his specifications for a literature intended to accomplish this are an enumeration of the conventional literary techniques that help to define mainstream America. Even his prescription for a didactic literature—one that teaches—can be understood to lie within the bounds of this tradition: "to evaluate the life and culture of the black people it is necessary that one live the black experience in a world where substance is more important than form, where the social takes precedence over the aesthetic, where each act, gesture, and movement is political" (xi–xii).

This definition of protest fiction subsumes all the criteria of the established literary tradition, among which are that literature bear a mimetic relationship to reality; that it reflect "experience," "life," and "culture," rather than itself; and that it subordinate form to "substance" or content. Excluded from this definition are works that provide a critique of a society through the rejection of these conventions, works that question that ideology underlying realism through self-study—works wherein the political content is articulated by the innovative use of form. The explication of such innovations required the attentiveness to form that characterized the work of the new critic, but the critics of African American literature refused to acknowledge the politics implicit in formal innovation. The results of this refusal are evident in the postulation of two schools of writers: the school of Richard Wright and the school of Ralph Ellison.

Larry Neal's "And Shine Swam On," the afterword to the black nationalist primer, *Black Fire*, illustrates the use of this distinction. In this essay, he applauds Wright's presentation and analysis of the psychological effects of racism on both the oppressed and the oppressors. He says that Wright's treatment of this issue suggests his affinity with Marcus Garvey, W. E. B. Du Bois, and Malcolm X. He contrasts Ellison's writing with Wright's by suggesting that it is less "pertinent" to the lives of contemporary readers. Neal says that though *Invisible Man* is "interesting to read," it has little bearing on the world as the "New Breed" sees it: "Contemporary black youth feels another force in the world today. We know who we are, and we are not invisible, at least not to each other. We are not Kafkaesque creatures stumbling through a white light of confusion and absurdity. The light is black (now get that) as are most of the meaningful tendencies in the world" (652).

Immediately following this passage is a quote from Frantz Fanon's *The Wretched of the Earth*. It reiterates Neal's condemnation of Ellison's use of the "Kafkaesque," the formal innovation associated with white literature. It says, "Let us waste no time in sterile litanies and nauseating mimicry" (652). This serves as the conclusion of Neal's discussion of Ellison. It chastises Ellison for "aping" white writers, mimicking their style, superimposing it on a subject that requires a different means of expression—but readers familiar with Ellison and Wright know that this is an equally accurate description of Wright's work. In "How Bigger Was Born," Wright discusses writers who have influenced his work. He says, "This association with white writers was the life preserver of my hope to depict Negro life in fiction, for my race possessed no fictional works dealing with such problems, had no background in such sharp and critical testing of experience, no novels that went with a deep and fearless will down to the dark roots of life" (xvi). "How Bigger Was Born" is, in part, an acknowledgment of Wright's debt to white writers, but Neal excludes mention of it because, like most black nationalists, he views literary realism as the "naturalized" Black Aesthetic.

Readers familiar with *Invisible Man* know that it, like *Native Son*, studies the psychological effects of racism. The narrator's "invisibility" is one of these effects. As such, it is one of the best realistic descriptions of the black man's feelings of nonexistence and of its causes. Readers familiar with *Invisible Man* know, too, that it, like *Native Son*, expresses the need for radical and immediate change. Neal omits discussion of these aspects of Ellison's work. His focus is restricted to the style of the novel. He thinks that because it is innovative, it is white, and because it is white, it is unable to articulate the political sentiments of the black nationalist. Like Gibson and many other spokespeople of the Black Arts Movement, he believes that "realistic" literature is the vehicle of change. Because the Ellison school oversteps the boundaries set forth in Gayle's definition of the Black Aesthetic, this group of writers was criticized for rejecting the "radical separatist ethnicism" of the Black Arts Movement in favor of an assimilationist politics articulated by the employment of Western aesthetics. It is equally reasonable, however, to identify the Wright school as proponents of the assimilationist politics espoused in the use of established literary conventions and to identify the Ellison school as motivated by a more radical politics, as expressed by its disregard for established literary conventions. For this second group of writers, a renunciation of convention functions as a critique of the society that engages them: it does not reflect the subordination of politics to aesthetics but serves instead as a recognition of the very political issues implicit in aesthetic theory.

The Black Arts Movement identified realism as the only mode of fiction through which social commentary could be voiced. It rejected all others as incapable of conveying the message of protest; they were to be regarded as the products of a racist society, and black writers engaging them were to be condemned as conscripts in their own demise. A didactic literature propagandizing militant ideology described the role that art was to play in the war to end the discrimination against and oppression of black Americans. Examples of literature that fits this prescription are included in *Black Fire*. Although the poetry and drama in this anthology suggest that the movement wasn't opposed to technical innovation, they also demonstrate that the field of experimentation was limited to the realistic rendering of black life—its language, its culture, its history. Moreover, any innovative techniques were to be used to convey the politics of the black nationalist movement. This becomes even more apparent when one examines the short stories in the anthology. They included transcriptions of black English—one technical innovation of the Black Arts Movement—but none transgresses the boundaries of literary realism and none conveys a message other than the propagandistic one.

In the collection of essays *The Dark and Feeling*, Clarence Major criticizes Gayle's prescription for social realism. He argues that "the novel *not* deliberately aimed at bringing about freedom for black people has liberated as many minds as has the propaganda tract" (25). He says, "The social realist can never suggest that 'hidden system of organization'—the unconscious experience and its interplay with one's conscious life—because he has never touched it. But it is present in all life and therefore should be in art" (19). Although the inability to portray the unconscious was one limitation of social realism, there were additional reasons for some writers' rejection of realism as a viable means of achieving social reform.

Writers familiar with the history of realism in literature understood that although such art might be radical in content, its formal modes of perception are the conventional and reactionary ones of the white middle class (Graff 16). Writers sensitive to the ontological and epistemological foundations of realism saw them as ancillary to political domination and exploitation. In *Literature against Itself*, Gerald Graff addresses this issue: "the distinction between ourselves and what we perceive turns 'other' into an alien thing ripe for domination and manipulation. In a parallel fashion, civilization turns both nature and human beings into manipulable things through technological mastery on one hand and colonialism and exploitation on the other" (64). The epistemology also served to perpetuate racial oppression because it presupposed an unalterable reality, and "acknowledging the reality principle is synonymous with reconciling oneself to the established order as if it were an eternal law of nature" (Graff 65).

In their disavowal of realism, those of the Ellison school succeeded in demonstrating that objectivism was not the exclusive proprietor of truth but an arbitrary construct, a fiction employed by Western civilization in the dispensation of meaning and value. Alternate definitions of knowledge and reality existed in black culture and black history, and if these could be viewed outside the established framework, they would appear equally valid and would point to the reconstruction of society along new lines. This perspective called for the creation of a radical aesthetic that could describe systems of thought not founded on Western logic, on Western definitions of knowledge and reality, or on the Western literary conventions in which these are made manifest and proliferate. Because "radical reform requires the shattering of the realist sensibility," these writers engaged avant-garde literary techniques as a means of instituting social change (Graff 66).

This aversion delayed the study of metafiction, which was regarded as formalist innovation, an invention of elite white postmodernists. It was thought to represent the pinnacle of self-interest and support of the status quo. To many critics, black metafiction was not "serious" literature, but as trivial and solipsistic as only white writers sequestered safely within the halls of academe could afford to be. In their efforts to find a place for African American literature, scholars in that field overlooked the connection between stylistic innovation and radical politics. This explains why such studies were not done and why experimental writers such as Clarence Major were excluded from the canon. The inductive study of black literature leads to acknowledging formal innovation as an integral part of the African American literary tradition. As a result, experimental writers who participate in this tradition are recognized as concurring with many of the personal and political ideals of the Black Arts Movement. When critics were able to recognize innovation as part of African

American literary history, they were able to revise their vision of the past and discover the legacy of black metafiction.

The Roots of Black Metafiction: The Legacy

Black literature has always theorized about itself. The legacy of African American metafiction can be traced at least as far back as 1789 and the publication of *The Interesting Narrative of the Life of Gustavis Vassa, the African As Written by Himself*. In *The Signifying Monkey*, Gates traces African American theorizing to its African roots. He deconstructs the myths of the African Esu-Elegbara and the African American trickster, the Signifying Monkey, to demonstrate that black literature, oral and written, is extremely self-conscious, aware of itself as artifice, as fabulation, and in relation to existing literary or aesthetic traditions. Building on this foundation, Gates develops his theories of "signifyin(g)" and "the speakerly text": "Signifyin(g) is black double-voicedness, because it always entails formal revision and an intertextual relation and because of Esu's double-voiced representation in art, I find it an ideal metaphor for black literary criticism, for the formal manner in which texts seem concerned to address their antecedents. Repetition, with a signal difference, is fundamental to the nature of signifyin(g)" (51).

The culmination of this investigation is a discussion of Alice Walker's *The Color Purple* as a revision or "(re)writing" of Zora Neale Hurston's *Their Eyes Were Watching God*. In this concluding chapter, Gates focuses his investigation of theory in literature on a study of narrative voice—more particularly, the development of the narrative voice in fiction by women. Although he talks briefly about the technical innovations in *The Color Purple*, such as the revitalization of the epistolary form, he reads the novel not as a broad theoretical statement—for what it says about art and artistic creation—but rather as a direct response to Hurston's novel. Whereas Gates analyzes Equiano's narrative for what it says about literature and creativity, he reads Walker's novel as if it were the transcripts of a private phone conversation between Hurston and Walker. This is especially evident in the conclusion of his discussion when he observes that Walker "has written a letter of love to her authority figure,

Hurston" (244). He suggests that Celie's relationship to Shug Avery is a rewriting of Janie's relationship to Tea Cake and that Walker's relationship to Hurston resembles Celie's relationship to Shug: "Like Janie, Celie is married to a man who would imprison her, indeed brutalize her. Unlike Janie, however, Celie is liberated by her love for Shug Avery, the "bodaciously" strong singer with whom she shares the love that Janie shared with Tea Cake. It is Shug Avery, I shall argue, who stands in this text as Walker's figure for Hurston herself" (244).

Although one can argue with Gates' reading of *The Color Purple* (as does Deborah McDowell, who says it is much more a response to Frances E. W. Harper's *Iola Leroy* than to Hurston's *Their Eyes Were Watching God*) and his almost exclusive emphasis on revision as the way African American literature theorizes,[10] *Signifying Monkey* lays the groundwork for an appreciation of the legacy of self-consciousness in African American literature. Gates' chapter "Reading of the Tradition" provides the groundwork upon which any subsequent theory must stand. Here he explains "the trope of the talking book." Citing the scene in which Equiano speaks to the book, raising it to his ear to hear its answer, Gates formulates the thesis of textual self-consciousness and literary theorizing in fiction: "Equiano's usage amounts to a fiction about the making of fiction" (158). Although this evidence of self-consciousness in eighteenth-century African American literature is an important discovery, the foundation on which it rests reveals both the strength and the shortcomings of Gates' analysis. His interpretation of this scene and his assumptions concerning the widespread influence of *The Narrative* are questionable.

The focus on the book, allowing it greater significance than other symbols of Western culture, the timepiece or the portrait, is problematic. Gates also circumvents the celebration of Western culture in *The Narrative*, instances when Equiano acts and speaks on its behalf, such as when he decides not to return to Africa. Notwithstanding, Gates says that Equiano's narrative becomes the "prototype of the nineteenth century slave narrative" and that writers such as Frederick Douglass, William Wells Brown, and Harriet Jacobs imitate it (152–153). William L. Andrews, author of *To Tell a Free Story*, differs. He says that Equiano is more "sensibly" viewed as an "Anglo-African" writer,

> whose writing differs from his African American contemporaries who had to accept the readership their editors and amanuenses created for them. In Equiano's story we find an optimistic conviction that African and English cultural values and semantic fields could be made to intersect in a complementary fashion. The white-edited narratives of African born James Gronniosaw and Venture Smith suggest the irreconcilability of African and American cultural values and perspectives. (59)

Andrews reads *The Narrative* as atypical, and this raises questions about the influence that Gates attributes to it, but regardless of the reading of particular scenes and the extent of Equiano's influence on nineteenth-century African American writers, later writers do seem to make their concerns with writing a part of their work, and, as Gates points out, all these writers portray the slaves' arduous journey to freedom with a simultaneous journey from orality to literacy (153). All come to connect reading and writing with freedom and equality. It is important to note, however, that these writers are responding to white canonical works as well as to black ones—just as Wright did—and that they are responding to the conventions of Western literature and the history of autobiography. Although we can stretch the margins of Gates' theory of signifyin(g) to include discussion of African American literature's response to Western literary conventions because we can include that under the rubric of revision (though Gates focuses his discussion of revision on black texts), there is much more self-consciousness that remains outside these margins even when they have been stretched to include all imaginable forms. Revision is only one of the many ways that literature theorizes about itself, and it is useful to keep the other forms in front of us as we survey African American literature.

One of the most easily recognized types of metafiction and one central to the African American literary tradition is the *künstlerroman*, or the portrait of the life of the artist. Many eighteenth-century and nineteenth-century African American autobiographies can be seen as part of this tradition because they combine fiction and fact. The autobiographies of Harriet Wilson, Frederick Douglass, and Booker T. Washington exemplify this tradition, even though these writers may not have seen themselves as artists and the telling of their stories as fiction. The weaving of fact and fiction that makes the African American *künstlerroman* is exemplified in James Weldon Johnson's *The Autobiography of an Ex-Coloured Man*, a book that signifies on the autobiographical tradition of African American literature and Saint Augustine's and Rousseau's romantic visions of artistic sensibility. The protagonist of Johnson's autobiography must choose between two artistic traditions: the Western tradition, which includes classical music, and the African American tradition, which features ragtime. The novel describes his efforts to synthesize these traditions in his transcription of black musical themes into classical compositions. Rewriting African American music so it can be appreciated by those whose are accustomed to Western classical music makes the protagonist of Johnson's novel feel he is making an important contribution to the advancement of the race, but witnessing a lynching makes him forsake his project to cross the color line:

> I finally made up my mind that I would neither disclaim the black race nor claim the white race; but that I would change my name, raise a mustache, and let the world take me for what it would; that it was not necessary for me to go about with a label of inferiority pasted across my forehead. All the while I understood that it was not discouragement or fear or search for a larger field of action and opportunity that was driving me out of the Negro race. I knew that it was shame, unbearable shame. Shame at being identified with a people that could with impunity be treated worse than animals. For certainly the law would restrain and punish the malicious burning of live animals. (190–191)

The Autobiography of an Ex-Coloured Man signifies on African American, Anglo-American, and European literary traditions. It is not, as Gates suggests by his use of the term, a revision of African American aesthetic traditions only. The ex-coloured man believes he has forsaken his heritage when he reneges on his project of musical transcription to cross the color line, "selling his birthright for a mess of pottage" (211). The irony of this confession makes this artist's lack of self-consciousness amusing, for what he has failed to accomplish as a musician he has succeeded in accomplishing as a writer. *The Autobiography* is the synthesis of aesthetic traditions that the protagonist has attempted to marry in his music. Moreover, it fulfills the ambition that inspired his work as a composer: making African American culture appreciable to Western readers.

Also under the heading of African American *künstlerroman* are novels about artists who never produce paintings or manuscripts but who exhibit the artistic impulse nevertheless. Alice Walker speculates about these artists in her essay "In Search of Our Mothers' Gardens":

> What did it mean for a black woman to be an artist in our grand-mothers' time? In our great-grandmothers' day? It is a question cruel enough to stop the blood. Did you have a genius of a great-great grandmother who died under some ignorant and depraved white overseer's lash? Or was she required to bake biscuits for a lazy backwater tramp, when she cried out in her soul to paint watercolors of sunsets or the rain falling on the green and peaceful pasture lands? (233)

One might enlarge this category to include characters who could have been artists had they had the materials or leisure time. Sula is this kind of artist. Her stifled creativity is potentially dangerous: "Had she paints, or clay, or knew the discipline of the dance, or strings; had she anything to engage her tremendous curiosity and her gift for metaphor, she might have exchanged the restlessness and preoccupation with whim for an activity that provided her with all she yearned for. And like any artist with no art form, she became dangerous" (105).

The legacy of African American metafiction can also be identified as "mimesis of process." In *Narcissistic Narrative*, Hutcheon traces the history of Aristotelian theory to suggest:

> The mimetic concept . . . after Plato and Aristotle did become restricted, concentrating on product, on the relation of subject matter to empirical reality and truth. It is to *this* general critical tradition and *not* to the natural line of novelistic development

in particular that the concept of "traditional realism" as a genre (rather than a period) description would seem to belong. In demanding recognition of diegesis or narrative process as part of mimesis, metafiction is in a sense demanding a reworking of the Aristotelian theory. It is not that the emphasis has shifted *from* mimesis *to* the creating imagination, but rather that the critical terms in which we discuss that which is imitated in fiction must be opened again to make room for the new novels being written and read. (41)

Johnson's *Autobiography of an Ex-Coloured Man* and Hurston's *Their Eyes Were Watching God* exemplify mimesis of process. Both are about the process of creating a story. This theme becomes even more apparent in postmodern works such as Ishmael Reed's *Mumbo Jumbo*, which describes a litany in search of its text. PaPa LaBas searches for the text of the Black Aesthetic, only to discover that the aesthetic is always changing and that its evolving form is integral to it. William Demby's novel *The Catacombs* is about an ex-patriot living in Rome, writing a novel about an ex-patriot living in Rome, writing a novel about an ex-patriot living in Rome, ad infinitum. Clarence Major's *Reflex and Bone Structure* and Alice Walker's *The Temple of My Familiar* fit into this category as well. An interest in the psychology of writing makes these novels process as well as product.

Another manifestation of the legacy of black metafiction is audience involvement. Novels use call-and-response to encourage audience participation, or they use other strategies to suggest that the readers invent their own "reality" in the same way that writers invent fiction. These novels illuminate the readers' roles in constructing worlds both external and intrinsic to the work. Hutcheon says, "As the novelist actualizes the world of his imagination through words, so the reader—from those same words—manufactures in reverse a literary universe that is as much his creation as the novelist's. This near equation of the acts of reading and writing is one of the concerns that sets modern metafiction apart from previous novelistic self-consciousness" (27).

Hutcheon points out that epistolary novels, diaries, or journals help place the reader in the novel. Genres such as science fiction and detective fiction also involve the reader in the self-conscious construction of the fictive world. Instead of regarding such texts as foolish, solipsistic escapes from reality, one can read them as critiques of the reality that they reject. Octavia E. Butler invents other worlds to critique ours and suggest solutions.

Morrison's *Playing in the Dark* and Gates' *Loose Canons* are probably the best evidence of the legacy. The novelist has written theory; the theorist, a Sam Spade detective story. As representatives of the culmination of a tradition, these works suggest that the distinction between fiction and theory is arbitrary and that the most pleasurable, most significant, and most traditional work is done on the margin.

What follows is a survey of self-consciousness in contemporary African American fiction. There are two possible methods of proceeding with this task. The first of these is a book-by-book study of canonical texts. Each would be dissected to reveal the types of metafiction it employs. I have, however, rejected this method in favor of an approach that allows for the comparison of techniques employed by different writers. Instead of a chronological survey, I have drawn the perimeters of this study around recent fiction—post, postmodernism or new realism.[11] Historical studies have been done and evidence of self-consciousness as being part of the tradition has been collected, but insufficient attention has been paid to the fiction of the last decade, the fiction published after the watershed of African American literary theory. *Black Metafiction* is a response to PaPa LaBas' inquiry concerning the time and place of the next Jes Grew epidemic. These novels are symptoms of the resiliency of the Jes Grew virus. The form continues to mutate, but the virus never dies.

The next chapter, "Mimesis of Process: The Thematization of Art," builds on Hutcheon's distinction between Aristotle's mimesis of product and mimesis of process. Texts that fit into this category are those that imitate the creative process and the activities of the imagination rather than confine themselves to describing its products. Texts that demonstrate mimesis of process focus on their own production and often suggest that the production of this text is parallel to the creative process that we are involved in in the creation of the world. Charles Johnson's *Middle Passage* and Alice Walker's *The Temple of My Familiar* are extended discussions of artistic process.

The African American *künstlerroman* is the subject of the third chapter. This genre of novels about artists includes characters who demonstrate artistic inclinations that are stifled by their limited freedom, such as Toni Morrison's Sula and Alice Walker's Celie. It also includes characters who achieve satisfaction through their art, such as Virginia, the musician and puppeteer who stands center stage in Rita Dove's *Through the Ivory Gate*, and Lucas Bodeen, the traveling blues man in Arthur Flowers' *Another Good Loving Blues*.

The fourth chapter is about self-consciousness that makes itself manifest through the text's relationship to its literary predecessors. Parody constitutes one oft-cited subdivision of this category, but this chapter refers to two novels that are not parodies. Ernest J. Gaines' *A Lesson before Dying* acknowledges Richard Wright's *Native Son* as a literary forerunner. Toni Morrison's *Tar Baby* refers to several versions of the folktale. Examination of these works allows us to test several theories of revision and intertextuality.

Chapter 5 examines voice in Charlotte Watson Sherman's *One Dark Body* and Leon Forrest's *Divine Days*. As a transition between discussions of mimetic and diegetic metafiction, this study of voice illustrates how introducing African American literature into the discussion of metafiction shifts the perimeters of the discussion and recasts the classifications.

The sixth chapter is a study of genres of metafiction. A brief examination of detective fiction and science fiction demonstrates how African American writers are contributing to the evolution of these forms. As a family man who is involved in a variety of community activities, Walter Mosley's Easy Rawlins defies the stereotype of the hard-boiled detective as a loner. Similarly Lauren, the protagonist of Octavia E. Butler's *Parable of the Sower*, blends stories about the past and future in the diary that serves as the foundation for a new religion. Both writers extend the limits of their genres by introducing elements from the African American vernacular.

Mimesis of Process:
The Thematization of Art

El proceso es la revolución. El proceso es todo.
—Ntozake Shange, *Liliane*

The thematization of art in black fiction makes the redefinition of metafiction imperative. Until now, mimesis of process has been regarded as more or less synonymous with the self-referential fiction of postmodernism. When African American literature is considered, both our understanding of the technique and its genealogy are altered. Black metafictionists thematize art in several ways. They recognize artistic creation as an ongoing process. They see artistic process as a metaphor for identity and self-invention, and they focus on the experiences of the artist rather than just on the artwork and its effects on an audience. They trace mimesis of process to vernacular aesthetic traditions and stress the necessity of tapping into this resource. Storytellers, musicians, and painters benefit from a knowledge of the past that informs them of their roles and responsibilities

29

to others. Charles Johnson's *Middle Passage* and Alice Walker's *The Temple of My Familiar* illustrate these characteristics. Before commencing an analysis of these novels, it is necessary to examine mimesis of process in its postmodern context.

John Barth identified the postmodern dilemma as "the literature of exhaustion." In the essay so titled, Barth suggests that like "classical tragedy," "grand opera," and "the sonnet sequence," "the novel's time as a major art form is up" (28). According to Barth, the contemporary writer resembles Scheherazade, whose life depends on her ability to entertain the king with old stories made new. Like Scheherazade, contemporary writers assume the task of creating new stories through the retelling of the old. "The literature of exhaustion" is shorthand for the belief that every story has already been written, already been told, and that the only "new" thing a writer can do is to refashion the old stories. For many of the postmodern writers, parody fills this important function of making the old new again. This approach is adopted by Barth, as well as many of his contemporaries. For example, Donald Barthelme reinvents the fairy tale of Snow White in his experimental novel *Snow White*, and John Barth retells the stories of Sinbad and Scheherazade in his *The Last Voyage of Somebody the Sailor*.

This postmodern understanding of literature's "usedupedness" is central to Hutcheon's classifications of "mimesis of process." Although Hutcheon defines "mimesis of process" as "the thematizing within the story of its storytelling concerns," her classifications reflect a preoccupation with literature's usedupedness (53). This is reflected in her discussion of parody as the most popular type of "mimesis of process."[1]

Black metafictionists regard parody differently, and their engagement of it is not always a response to literature's "usedupedness." Rather than view it as a desperate effort to keep a dying art form alive, many black metafictionists view parody as a pause in the continual metamorphosis of a work. Reed's Law rests on this definition of parody.[2] It says, "When the parody is better than the original a mutation occurs which renders the original obsolete" ("Shrovetide," 285). While white metafictionists are preoccupied with the novel's obsolescence at "the end of the road," black metafictionists envision mutating forms and limitless possibility. Charles Johnson encourages student writers to tap this resource: "Except in the case of mathematical objects, or experiences known *a priori*, we find meaning in flux, on the side of Heraclitus (change) and not Parmenides (stasis); we find, I am saying, the black world *overflowing* with meaning, so rich and multisided that literally anything—and everything—can be found there, good and bad, and one of the first chores of the writer is to be immersed in this embarrassment of rich, contradictory material" (11).

Although Hutcheon and Waugh recognize a type of metafiction that makes the creation of art its theme, neither acknowledges the tradition of mimesis of process as Reed and Johnson describe it, as part of the ongoing evolution of the work. Acknowledgment of these ideas mandates a reassessment of Hutcheon's categories. In the same way that Hutcheon reintroduces "mimesis of process," fashioning it so as to address contemporary developments,[3] scholars of African American literature must assume the task of redefining such terms as "metafiction" and "mimesis of process," ensuring that terms that have been generated from an exclusionary body of literature are made inclusive. Going forward with this task necessitates a redefinition of the thematization of self-consciousness in literature or "mimesis of process," one that is distinct from parody because African American writers create thematically self-conscious fictions that are neither parody nor an acknowledgment of literature's "usedupedness."

Because of the emphasis on process, African American fiction has never succumbed to the exhaustion caused by "usedupedness" or the celebration of mimesis of product *at the expense* of mimesis of process. In the context of the black vernacular, process and even the words that signify process—verbs—are privileged. The language of the Allmuseri, the fictive African tribe in *Middle Passage*, emphasizes process and change through the elimination of nouns and the use of double descriptives. Baker's description of a blues singer's performance captures this quality:

At the junctures, the intersections of experience where roads cross and diverge, the blues singer and his performance serve as codifiers, absorbing and transforming discontinuous experience into formal expressive instances that bear only the trace of origins, refusing to be pinned down to any final, dualistic significance. Even as they speak of paralyzing absence and ineradicable desire, their instrumental rhythms suggest change, movement, action, continuance, unlimited and unending possibility. Like signification itself, blues are always nomadically wandering. Like the freight-hopping hobo, they are ever on the move, ceaselessly summing novel experience. (*Blues* 8)

Charles Johnson's *Middle Passage* foregrounds process, but unlike Vladimir Nabokov's *The Real Life of Sebastian Knight* or John Barth's *Floating Opera*, works in which the veneer of verisimilitude dissolves to reveal the underlying mechanics of fiction-making (Oz behind the curtain), Johnson's *Middle Passage* portrays the accumulation of ideas comingling in the imagination to produce fiction. Johnson's phenomenological foundation—or, as he calls it, his "aboriginal faith"—is the ability to transcend one's identity, assume another's, and move back and forth between them, "comparing evidence, collating profiles, criticizing the other's perspective for what it lacks, and, according to what we find, amending our own."[4] There is no Oz-like wizard, no omnipotent writer pulling levers to create the illusion of reality in fiction. Instead there is a crowd of real and imaginary, past and present identities interacting and exchanging parts of themselves like tidbits of gossip at a cocktail party. According to Ishmael Reed and Charles Johnson, what goes on behind the curtain of fiction-writing is mysterious and more difficult to explain than what goes on in front of it.[5] The process is more enigmatic than the product. Nevertheless, in *Middle Passage* Johnson raises the curtain to reveal the process of artistic creation.

Middle Passage is told by Rutherford Calhoun, a former Illinois slave who is granted freedom by a dying master and takes up the life of a thief in New Orleans. The threat of marriage to a schoolteacher prompts him to steal the papers of a sailor who is signed on with a slave ship, the *Republic*. With the stolen papers hidden in his boot, Calhoun stows away and commences upon a series of transformations, which begin with a symbolic death and rebirth:

Standing aft, looking back at the glittering lights ashore, I had the odd sensation, difficult to explain, that I'd boarded not a ship but a kind of fantastic, floating Black Maria, a wooden sepulcher whose timbers moaned with the memory of too many runs of black gold between the New World and the Old; moaned, I say again, because the ship—with its tiered compartments and galleys, like a crazy-quilt house built by a hundred different carpenters, each with a different plan—felt conscious and disapprovingly aware of my presence when I pulled back the canvas on a flat-bottom launch and laid myself down in its hull . . . with hands crossed on my chest. And then waves lapping below the ship gently swung me left then right as in a hammock, sinking me like a fish, or a stone, farther through leagues of darkness, and mercifully to sleep. (21)

Positioned as a corpse in a coffin, Calhoun experiences loss of consciousness as a symbolic death and begins his transformation by assuming the state of mind that Johnson recommends to his writing students: the ability to transcend one's identity, assume and relinquish others at will. Calhoun, the eager acolyte of a Zen master, takes to heart the lessons inherent in Johnson's observation that "fiction, in a funny Buddhist sense, might even be called a way" (45).

The first lesson is instruction in the importance of words and their relation to meaning. Although Johnson believes that "black writing" (with the exception of Clarence Major's) "must assume the traditionally held correspondence between word and world," he believes that "angling in on this problem through phenomenology" (37) will reveal that "language is not a neutral medium for expressing things but rather that intersubjectivity and cross-cultural experience are already embodied in the most microscopic datum of speech" (38). Although Johnson insists on referentiality—the correspondence between words and the things they represent—he acknowledges the flux of personal and cultural information with which each word is imbued.

This is the lesson Calhoun learns when he awakes on the *Republic*. The name of the slave ship is also a reference to its country of origin, and repeated references to the ship accentuate this multiplicity of meanings. Calhoun confronts this multiplicity every time the ship's name is cited. Words like "republic" are not disassociated from meaning or meaningless, as they are for many of the radical postmodernists; they are, instead, supersaturated with meaning. The course navigated by the *Republic* recounts the republic's involvement in the slave trade. The decimation caused by a cannon misfiring on board, ripping the *Republic* in half, recalls slavery's tearing the republic in half. The suggestion that the *Republic* will be replaced by a riverboat foreshadows the next episode in American history, one that would be documented by the riverboat driver, Samuel Clemens, who took these ambiguities and multiplicities of language and found in them an occasion for his own art.

Like the republic that shares its name, the ship is "perpetually flying apart and reforming" (35–36). "In a word," says Calhoun, "she was, from stem to stern, a process. And a seaman's first duty," he adds with subtle irony, "was to keep her afloat at any cost" (36). The perpetual reinvention of the ship symbolizes the reinvention of the republic during the Jacksonian era, and the ship's amorphous shape is analogous to the continually changing perimeters of the country. General Andrew Jackson made his own contribution to the changing perimeters of the republic when he defeated the British troops in New Orleans in 1815 and captured Pensacola from the Seminoles in 1818. Calhoun's commitment to "keeping her afloat" reflects the optimism with which many viewed "Jacksonian democracy" or government by popular rule. It also serves as a reminder of President Jackson's support and appreciation of the black troops who fought the War of 1812: "If this weird, upside-down caricature of a country called America, if this land of refugees and former indentured servants, religious heretics and half-breeds, whoresons and fugitives— this cauldron of mongrels from all points on the compass—was all I could rightly call *home*, then aye: I was of it. There, as I lay weakened from bleeding was where I wanted to be. Do I sound like a patriot? Brother, I put it to you: What Negro, in his heart (if he is not a hypocrite), is not?" (179).

This passage reveals that Calhoun has learned how words like "republic" are infused with multiple meanings, which invoke history and culture at every mention of the word. He has also learned that as former slave, thief, stowaway, and sailor, he himself has an identity that resembles that of the republic: it too is in flux and encoded with cross-cultural meanings. As a matter of fact, Calhoun represents an amalgam of experiences more multifarious than those of the *Republic*. These experiences include those of the kidnapped and enslaved Africans during the middle passage and after, for Calhoun recalls his life as a slave and a freeman. These experiences also include those of his namesake, John Caldwell Calhoun, the "great defender of the agrarian South," the politician who authored South Carolina's nullification, defended slavery and secession, and secured the admission of Texas to the Union as a slave state. This is the J. C. Calhoun who spills his wine when President Jackson calls for a toast to the Union and resigns from the vice presidency because Jackson would not approve nullification.[6] Johnson "collates" the profiles of the statesman and slave for instruction by example, but like all aspiring writers, Calhoun must tap his own "aboriginal faith" to fully appreciate the historical resonances that reverberate through him and all around him. Lesson two requires Calhoun to acknowledge his affinity to the slaver's captain, Ebenezer Falcon.

When Calhoun is escorted to Captain Falcon's private quarters, the stage is set for the re-creation of a pivotal scene in slave narratives. Like the newly arrived African making his first acquaintance with Anglo-American culture, Calhoun recalls his encounter with the objects on Falcon's desk: Bible, quadrant, chronometer, spyglass, and ship's log. As in *The Narrative*, these items represent the knowledge and beliefs on which the *Republic*—ship *and* country—remain afloat. Falcon and Calhoun engage in a repartee that makes the stasis of stereotypes and the fixed identities of assigned roles a site of humor and invention. Falcon, who believes Negroes "don't think too well, or too often" (30), assumes that Calhoun intended to stow away on a riverboat: "Poor creature, you probably thought we were a riverboat, didn't you?" (31). Calhoun, assuming the role of "the crafty Negro" (28), feigns a surprised response to Falcon's question: "This *isn't* a riverboat?" (31). Although the relationship commences with each playing his expected role, the men come to like each other. Calhoun, engaging in an initial trial with transcendence, claims to be able to "see something of himself in him" (Falcon) (33). Not long after their meeting, he uses the pronoun "we" to indicate his identification with the captain, and he acknowledges, even to his own embarrassment, attributes that they share. After hearing Falcon's tale of being lost at sea and barbecuing "that Negro boy" as an antidote to his hunger, Calhoun realizes that Falcon "*enjoyed* telling this tale— enjoyed as I did, any experience that disrupted the fragile, artificial pattern of life on land" (33). The taking of pleasure in the "disruption" of experience that explains Calhoun's identification with Falcon demonstrates mastery of lesson three: defamiliarization.

The disruptive experience that compels Calhoun to acknowledge his similarity to the man-eating Falcon is a form of "phenomenological variation," which is "performed on the phenomenon in order to exhibit its full range of meaning and profiles" (32). Citing Don Ihde's *Existential Technics*, Johnson notes several other techniques that serve to make the familiar strange, thereby giving the perceiver an opportunity to experience the phenomenon anew. Among these "phenomenological variations" are "figure-ground reversals, juxtapositions of content, the isolation of dominant and recessive characteristics, transformations of perspectives and even deconstruction" (32). According to Johnson, these are some of the devices that can be used to "shock and cause disjuncture, thereby freeing perception from the familiar" (32). However, Johnson adds another technique to Ihde's list. He calls it "phenomenological description" and defines it as "the manner in which we use words, particularly in prose that is charged or poetic or surrealistic, to fling the reader of fiction toward revelation and unsealed vision" (33). One of the aims of Johnson's writing is to dislocate the reader, disorient him or her so that the reader experiences the gestalt of an "unsealed vision." The Allmuseri god who is stowed below deck personifies this "unsealed vision," but before we can fully understand this aspect of "phenomenological description," we must conclude our discussion of identity. Although Falcon shares with Calhoun a limited mastery of transcendence, he is incapable of loosing himself as completely as is required either to author phenomenological description or to experience the gestalt of defamiliarization that is its aim. The captain is trapped in a narcissism that curbs his experiments in phenomenology. Unlike Calhoun, who writes to free himself from the voices in his head

(189), Falcon writes to immortalize himself and his own glorious deeds. Like Benjamin Franklin, with whom he is repeatedly compared, he believes future generations will benefit from the example he bequeaths in his autobiography.

From the journal on the captain's desk, Calhoun learns that the captain, "like the fledgling republic itself," was obsessed with the desire to take what he needed (50). Adopting a personal "Manifest Destiny," the captain was wanted for murder and treason, the latter for a proposition made to the British minister to "divide the western region of the continent into empires . . . one of which the skipper hoped to shape himself . . . into a true American utopia" (50). He was anti-British, anti-Jefferson, and agreed with Pierre-Joseph Proudhon "more than any sane man should" (50). He was driven by the twisted Puritan drive to achieve perfection. He saw himself as profoundly misunderstood, his deeds terribly underrated (52). Like Benjamin Franklin, the tinker, he invents what he needs, such as garters that run from his socks to his shirt hem to keep his shirt neatly in place during battle, and, like Franklin, the self-made man, he practices self-improvement through the study of foreign languages and oriental philosophy. Like Franklin, who could never claim to have succeeded in acquiring the virtue of humility, Falcon's "species of world conquerors thrive[s] upon the desire to be a fascinating object in the eyes of others" (33) . Though Falcon is a dwarf, he reminds Calhoun of an oversized sculpture such as the one that immortalizes Benjamin Franklin in Philadelphia's city hall: "He was famous. In point of fact, infamous. That special breed of empire builder, explorer and imperialist that sculptors loved to elongate, El Greco–like, in city park statues until they achieved Brobdingnagian proportions" (29).

This egocentrism is exactly what the Allmuseri god lacks. Falcon explains to Calhoun that the god has a thousand names, and that it is immaterial and material and full of innumerable other contradictions. Among them are that it knows everything in the universe but itself. Falcon, who is excessively self-centered, notices the absence of this characteristic as the god's most noteworthy attribute. Falcon says: "A god can't know its own nature. For itself, it can't be an object of knowledge. D'you see the logic here? The Allmuseri god is everything, so the very knowing situation we mortals rely on—a separation between knower and known—never rises in its experience. You might say empirical knowledge is on man's side not God's. Omnipresence means it forfeits our kind of knowledge. Omnipotence means, ironically, that it can create a stone so heavy it cannot lift that same stone from the floor" (102).

Falcon is an Icarus whose self-consciousness is the reason for seeing himself as superior to a god. Obsessed with himself, regarding himself as a model for mammoth sculptures that litter public parks, he cannot relinquish his identity. As such, he is the most extreme postmodernist, who regards language as self-referential and doubts the existence of everything but himself and language. The crucial difference between Calhoun and Falcon lies in their perceptions of others, an extension of their understanding of language. In the following exchange, Falcon resembles John Barth or John Cage, Walter Abish or Donald Barthelme, the extreme metafictionists who are suspicious of objective reality. Calhoun is the black metafictionist, appreciative of the postmodernist's extreme subjectivism, but not at the cost of suspending his belief in the "real world." Instead he regards it as evidence of the wealth of contradictions that are a writer's most valuable resource. Calhoun's position is that of the new realist who is aware of the subjective nature of all experience and the self-referentiality of language. He is simultaneously aware that reality can be defined by consensus and language can refer to shared experience. Calhoun acknowledges the others who contribute to this consensus reality; Falcon does not. In fact, Falcon's egocentrism signals a distrust of others that blossoms into paranoia. Fear of being poisoned makes him have Calhoun taste his food before he eats it. The following exchange reveals their views of this procedure and its motives. Falcon says,

> "D'you think I'm overly cautious?"
>
> "Well—a wee bit, yes."
>
> "I gather you trust, even *like* other people, don't you?"
>
> I was a little startled by his question. Was he joking? I laughed a second too late. "Yes, I do, sir. Don't you?"
>
> "Not a bit. Never have. I suppose they've never been real to me.

Only I'm real to me. Even you're not real to me, Mr. Calhoun, but I think you like me a little, so I like you too." (95)

This final sentence is a "jab in the ribs" to the extreme post-modernists who, like Vladimir Nabokov, insist that reality wear quotation marks to indicate its tentative, hypothetical nature. Even though Falcon confesses to having doubts about the existence of others, he can't keep himself from liking them. These contradictory feelings are the best argument against solipsism. They also serve as an illustration of the plenitude of contradictions that Johnson encourages his writing students to explore.

A magnetic ring binds Calhoun and Falcon. It is a special ring, which allows Calhoun to make use of the weapon Falcon gives him, but in this world of multiple meanings, it is also the ring that marries the black man and the white in shaping the destiny of the republic. Calhoun's past, especially his education by a Thomist theologian and the influence of his older brother, reinforces the bond that unites the men. This bond is the subject of Falcon's final words. With a mutinous crew and rebellious cargo, Falcon uses his dying breath to explain that he and the members of the crew resemble the Africans stowed in the hold. Falcon's debt to wealthy speculators and investors makes him see himself as "no freer than the Africans" (147). He tells Calhoun that even powerful people such as ships' captains like himself serve those with wealth. His description of his financiers emphasizes the parallel:

He let *me* talk—get it—'cause even though the lubber could barely write his name he didn't have nothing to prove in this world. He could buy men such as myself with his pocket change. Buy beauty, if he couldn't produce it. Buy truth, if he was too busy to think. Buy goodness, even, for what blessed thing on God's earth don't have its price? Who ain't up for auction when it comes to it? Tell me that? All the while I gabbed, squirming in my seat beneath his family's coat of arms (the head of a Negro), sipping hot coffee from a cup that kept shaking in my hands, he was just smiling and studying me. Not as one man studies his equal—

and I was *more'n* his equal on water or in the wilderness—but the way I've seen Ahman-de-Bellah appraise blacks fresh from the bush.

. . . I felt closer . . . to the illiterate swabs and heathens I'd gone through hell with on ships in the heart of the stinking jungles. Thing is, he made this voyage possible. (149)

Falcon makes this confession before his suicide. Falcon, the writer Calhoun will replace, confesses that while he has identified with others, he has never relinquished his own ego to become unhinged, to experience revelation.

Previous to this confession, Falcon tells Calhoun to continue writing the ship's log. Like Benjamin Franklin, who is motivated to write his autobiography partly because of his fears of what biographers will say about him, Falcon tries to maintain control of the logbook. He tells Calhoun that he "wants others to know the truth of what happened on this voyage" (146). He tells Calhoun to include everything he can remember that Falcon told him when they met "alone in secret" and not just the "story the mutineers will spin" (146). Calhoun "reluctantly" agrees, but as he retrieves the logbook from the ruins of the captain's quarters, he promises himself that "even though I'd tell the story (I knew he wanted to be remembered), it would be first and foremost, as I saw it since my escape from New Orleans" (146).

The novel is the logbook that Calhoun authors. It fulfills his promise to serve as Falcon's biographer, and it fulfills Calhoun's promise to himself to tell his own story. The similarities in these stories, the biography and the autobiography, are as evident as the identical rings the men wear and the tales of their childhoods, including fathers who haunt their adult lives. Falcon's life and story are framed by Calhoun's. Calhoun's story contains Falcon's story, the story of the crew and the story of the Allmuseri, thus revealing his skill at transcendence and his success with phenomenological description.

The men differ in their relationships to the world around them. Falcon is at odds with the world around him, always antagonistically engaged, while Calhoun is a part of the world around him, submitting to fate and the process of living. His friendship with the Allmuseri reinforces this part of his identity, but it is one to which his brother introduces him when he refutes the concept of ownership and tells Reverend Peleg Chandler, their dying master, that the Calhouns want nothing for themselves. According to Jackson Calhoun, everyone would benefit from the equal distribution of the wealth bequeathed to Calhouns. Like the Allmuseri, he views himself as a participant in a cosmic order. Like Saint Francis, with whom he is compared, he has "an uncanny way with livestock" (112). For Rutherford Calhoun, this older brother is a "negative of myself . . . the possible-me that lived my life's alternate options, the me I fled. Me. Yet not me" (112). The individualism that Falcon represents is counterbalanced by the part of Calhoun, which replicates his brother and the Allmuseri. As a manumitted slave aboard a slaver with human cargo, Calhoun—patriotism notwithstanding—can distance himself from the Benjamin Franklin individualism that Falcon epitomizes. Evidence of this and of his mastery of Allmuseri values occurs when Calhoun almost cuts off his hand while throwing a corpse overboard. He has no sense of where the dead man's body ends and his own begins. This alternate definition of self goes into Calhoun's writing, and the log becomes evidence of a transcendental self and the conflicts between Anglo-American and Allmuseri definitions of self. Rather than seek to resolve these conflicts, Calhoun does as his writing teacher instructs and relies on them as a source for artistic invention. Living with internal and external contradictions leads Calhoun to conclude that "the black self was the greatest of all fictions" (170). One self cannot represent the multitude of selves that live within Calhoun.

The mythical tribe of the Allmuseri, the "Ur-tribe of civilization" whose palms bear no lines and whose historians recall life's beginnings, gives Calhoun the language he needs to discover his history and to navigate the middle passage. Their language reflects the fluidity that Baker observes in the blues. Its use of verbs, metaphor, and double descriptives makes it an ideal example of the characteristics that Hurston regarded as the "Negro's greatest contribution to the language" (51). Calhoun's description of Ngomyama's language illustrates language breaking out of stasis. It also exemplifies phenomenological description, an additional defamiliarizing technique:

When Ngonyama's tribe spoke it was not so much like talking
as the tones the savannah made at night, siffilating through the
plains of coarse grass, soughing as dry wind from tree to tree. Not
really a language at all, by my guess, as a melic way of breathing
deep from the diaphragm that dovetailed articles and nouns,
nouns and verbs. . . . The predication "is," which granted existence to anything, had over the ages eroded into an article of faith
for them. Nouns or static substances hardly existed in their vocabulary at all. A "bed" was called a "resting," a "robe" a "warm-
ing." Furthermore, each verb was different depending on the nature of the object acted upon, whether it was vegetable, mineral,
mammal, oblong or rotund. When Ngonyama talked to his tribes-
man it was as if objects and others he referred to flowed together
like water, taking different forms, as the sea could now be fluid,
now solid ice, now steam swirling around the mizzenpole. (77)

Calhoun describes Ngonyama's speech with an alliteration of s's
and invented words like "siffilating," which derive their meaning
from the sounds they create. The amelioration of parts of speech is
suggestive of the flux of experience, and the emphasis on verbs and
gerunds underscores process and change. This is reiterated in the final sentence and the comparison of objects to water as liquid, solid,
and gas. The alternative to the "fictional black self" is posited by the
Allmuseri as a fluid self capable of transcending its own form in order
to participate in the flux of experience. This is the source of phenomenological description. Invented words, figurative language, and
onomatopoeia defamiliarize readers with language at the same time
that they explain and demystify the Allmuseri language and its process of mystification.

Ashraf Rushdy describes this quality as "intersubjectivity" and argues that it "represents a philosophical solution Johnson has developed for an aesthetic problem he encountered when he first began
his career as a writer" (373). He argues that it is from this position of
"intersubjectivity" that Calhoun authors the log and the novel, but
this is to suggest that he favors his identification with the Allmuseri
above his identification with Falcon, that his logbook is a record of a
search for himself, one that is completed when he embraces the All-

museri "world view." Are we to understand him as having got in touch with his roots to retreat into a mythic past, like Son galloping to join the chevaliers in Toni Morrison's *Tar Baby*? The final scenes suggest an alternative reading, one more consistent with the theory of phenomenology and its emphasis on contradiction and change. The scenes aboard the riverboat suggest that Calhoun is equal parts Allmuseri and American. His identity is situated on the hyphen of the African-American experience. It incorporates Allmuseri transcendence and American individualism as it is personified by Falcon. The former is evident in Calhoun's attitude toward marriage. He is not "Allmuseri enough" to regard himself and Phillipe Zeringue as one and the same thereby making it inconsequential which of them Isadora marries. He maintains an ego as great as Odysseus', whose story is invoked in his return. Isadora, an anxiously awaiting Penelope, knits and unravels booties for her pets to stall her impending marriage to Papa Zeringue. Placing himself in the tradition of Scheherazade, Calhoun says: "Telling her all I'd endured since I'd seen her last would take a thousand more nights than Scheherazade needed to beguile King Shahryar" (205). Nevertheless, change is evident in his feeling that he wants "our futures blended, not our limbs, our histories perfectly twined for all time, not our flesh" (209). Moreover, the closing sentence of the novel suggests an Allmuseri sense of time and history: "Isadora drifted toward rest . . . where she would remain all night while we, forgetful of ourselves, gently crossed the Flood, and countless seas of suffering" (209).

On the other hand, Calhoun writes the novel that recounts the events that befall the *Republic*. Evidence of his own narcissism is the novel itself, which is very much in the tradition of the book Falcon was writing. Both depict themselves as protagonists, heroes of "Brobdingnagian proportions." Although the black self is the greatest of fictions, there would be no book at all without it. Calhoun tells the story as he saw it. Ego provides the fabric that holds the logbook together, keeping it and the ship from flying apart in a hundred different directions. Although he has been transformed by the experience of being someone else, that experience has been a part of a continuous process, a moment in his own evolution. Following Johnson's prescription, he criticized the other perspectives for what they lack and, "according to what he has found, amended his own" (43). This is an ongoing process, one never completed. Identity is never fixed except as it is reflected in the eyes of others. When Calhoun sees his reflection in Ngonyama's eyes, he sees a two-dimensional fixed image, which he contrasts with a three-dimensional one that changes as rapidly as a corpse thrown overboard:

> In Ngonyama's eyes I saw a displacement, an emptiness like maybe all of his brethren as he once knew them were dead. To wit, I saw myself. A man remade by virtue of his contact with the crew. My reflection in his eyes, when I looked up, gave back my flat image as phantasmic, the flapping sails and sea behind me drained of their density like figures in a dream. Stupidly, I had seen their lives and culture as timeless product, as a finished thing, pure essence or Parmenidean meaning I envied and wanted to embrace, when the truth was they were process and Heraclitean change, like any men, not fixed but evolving and as vulnerable to metamorphosis as the body of the boy we'd thrown overboard. (124)

Just as self-consciousness is necessary to the Allmuseri god in order for it to be cognizant of its power, self-consciousness is necessary to the writer who wishes to depict Allmuseri transcendence and intersubjectivity. Phenomenological description and defamiliarization can occur only when identity is at least momentarily fixed. Walker's *The Temple of My Familiar* provides another view of mimesis of process. Like Johnson, Walker illuminates the African influence on the artistic production of African Americans. She creates an internal dialogue between Anglo-American and African artistic traditions within several characters. Like Johnson, she also envisions artistic creation as participation in an intergenerational conversation that demands an acknowledgment of the importance of the historical collective past on the personal present. Like Johnson, Walker thematizes mimesis of process in the description of artistic production and its implications and effects on character development. Johnson believes that character is the single most important element of fiction.[7]

Walker's fiction, and her portraiture of artist-characters, suggest that she shares this belief.

Johnson's paradigm for artistic production includes African and Anglo-American definitions of art. The Allmuseri represent the former. Falcon represents the latter, and Calhoun vacillates between them. Walker summons the tensions of competing definitions of art within each character. She complicates this balancing act by introducing personal associations, dream memories, and myths. Nevertheless, the resulting message resembles Johnson's: African creative processes rejuvenate artists who stagnate on a diet of Western prescriptions for artistic production and Western aesthetic judgments. Suwelo is the best example of this. When the novel begins, he is a professor of history absorbed in researching and writing books that will gain him recognition in his field. His writing and research rest on assumptions he never questions. Among these is the belief that the past can be recovered through the analysis of documents housed in the university library, an assumption that represents Suwelo's submission to racism. The library excludes all versions of history that are not literary, and it excludes all histories authored by those who are not among a circumscribed group of academics. Suwelo fails to question these principles of exclusion. Raised on a diet of Western academic history, he cannot comprehend Fanny, whose knowledge of the past is unmediated and immediate. She has firsthand experience of the events that he reads about in books: "Fanny Nzingha found the spirit that possessed her first in herself. Then she found the historical personage who exemplified it. It gave her the strange aspect of a trinity—she, the spirit, the historical personage, all sitting across the table from you at once" (186). Fanny and Suwelo are historians whose methods for retrieving information are diametrically opposed. Though husband and wife, they must pursue separate paths in their metamorphoses as artists.

In response to her troubled marriage, Fanny travels to Africa, where she meets her father, Ola, a revolutionary playwright and former minister of culture. He introduces her to her half sister, Nzingha Fanny. Meanwhile Suwelo travels to Baltimore to settle the estate of his deceased uncle Rafe. Their respective journeys lead them to understand that the success of their work as artists and historians necessitates embracing their ancestors and their stories of the past. They must acknowledge these traditions as influences on their own work. Suwelo's friendship with Lissie and Hal escorts him from scholarly writing to storytelling. Instead of doing his research in the library, he does it by walking the streets looking for old people who are willing to tell their stories of the past. He has left the orthodoxy of the academic community behind. This change is largely the result of Suwelo's listening to Lissie's stories of her previous lives. The tapes and letters that record her stories provide Suwelo with a history and a new role as a historian. He has forsaken Western history and embraced an understanding of history that does not rest on consensus, objectivity, chronological time, the white man's understanding, or the need to resolve contradiction. He exchanges everything that is represented by his role as a history professor to transcribe the extraordinary stories of old black people, a role reminiscent of that of the narrator's in Ernest Gaines' *The Autobiography of Miss Jane Pittman*. Because Lissie's tapes self-destruct and the ink she uses to pen her letters disappears, he learns that the historian is participant as well as observer and that the storytelling process is as important as the story told. He learns about this process from Lissie and Hal, who ceremoniously tug a scarf down over the television set to block its interference with their storytelling. He is an apprentice griot who learns from listening to Lissie and Hal tell stories and from practicing storytelling with this audience of friends. When Hal and Lissie listen to Suwelo tell the story of his relationship with Fanny, he is a master storyteller who teaches *and* learns through the telling of his own stories. Now he is worthy of his name, "a rune for wholeness," and ready to be a historian and storyteller, transformed by the stories he hears and tells, by process as much as product. When he holds Lissie's last painting before Hal's sightless eyes, he is enacting the dual roles of storyteller and healer, giving vision and insight.

Because Fanny has always heard the voices of her ancestors and listened attentively to their stories, her journey is different. She must overcome the hatred for white people that is a consequence of her knowledge of the past. Her introduction to her father's second wife helps her to accomplish this. First she learns of Ola's first wife, the mother of her sister. This first wife was a soldier in her nation's war of independence, but her husband and daughter deserted her when the fighting ceased. Fanny must mourn the woman who would never be recognized as a wartime hero before she is ready to meet Ola's second wife. She is Mary Jane Bidden, a white woman whom Ola married in defiance of the postrevolution mandate that required all whites to depart from the country. Mary Jane owns and runs an art school and orphanage for children who have lost their homes as a result of the civil war. Her marriage to Ola allows her to stay and continue her work. Fanny's encounter with Mary Jane is a landmark in her journey. Just as her father atones for his sins against her sister's mother by eulogizing her in a play, Fanny's play about her father and his second wife atones for her feelings about white people. As a manifestation of her newfound goodwill, Fanny accepts Mary Jane's invitation to stage rehearsals of her play in the school gym. At the conclusion of their respective journeys, Fanny and Suwelo are writers, and as such Walker describes them as "a special kind of people with a curlicue in the brain. They come into the world with a certain perspective and drive to share it" (259).

Fanny and Suwelo are writers who are process- rather than product-oriented. They are more interested in the process of artistic creation than in the artifact produced. Other artists in the novel make their own contributions to Walker's portrait of creativity. Carlotta and her husband, Arveyda, a rock musician reminiscent of Jimi Hendrix, also contribute. The novel opens with Carlotta delivering a cape of feathers to Arveyda. A talented and sensitive artist, he is able to appreciate the art of capemaking. He learns that Zedé, Carlotta's mother, learned the art of capemaking from her mother, Carlotta's grandmother, who fashioned feathered garments for the priests of their South American Indian village. Arveyda's appreciation of the cape extends to its maker, his mother-in-law, Zedé, and inspires their running away together. Although Carlotta is devastated by their elopement, when he returns, she begs Arveyda to share the stories her mother told him. She understands that Arveyda (named after a bar of soap meaning "health") is the perfect "ear" for her mother's tales, tales that she would not be ready to hear for many years. Arveyda's music is inspired by the joy and pain of his relationships with

Zedé and Carlotta. His music tells Zedé's story and the story of his own growing appreciation of women.

During Arveyda's absence, Carlotta becomes a teacher of women's literature, but this pursuit does not resolve her anger. Although she is familiar with feminist theory, it fails to affect her personal life, and she continues to direct the anger she feels toward her husband and her mother at herself. Like Suwelo, she becomes increasingly dissatisfied with academe: "I grew frustrated, *and so fat,*" she complains (378). At the end of her journey, she is a musician, like her husband, mother, and grandmother. This intergenerational foundation for her art is more helpful than all the reading and writing she accomplished as a professor of women's studies. Carlotta's art connects her to generations of women artists. It makes her feel comfortable with her "womanliness" in a way that no objective, scientific research can. The following exchange reveals this new confidence:

> "You don't look like a woman, anymore," he says, impulsively. Surprised to be saying such a thing. Fearful, after he's said it.
> Carlotta only laughs. "Obviously," this is how a woman looks.
> "Anyway," she says. "There was one part of the story that"— she laughs—"rang a bell in me. It was the story about my grandmother, Zedé the Elder, who created the capes made of feathers for the priests; the woman who taught my own mother how to make beautiful feathered things. She had been a great artist, and she had a little chime outside the door of her hut. She would strike it, and listen closely to it, and if the sound corresponded with the vibration of her soul at the time, she would nod, once— Arveyda told me Zedé told him—and begin to create." (398)

This remembrance is in response to Suwelo's criticism of her slender, "flat-breasted body" and "short spiked hair" (398). His questioning of her womanliness is rebuffed with the confidence gained from her knowledge of her female ancestors. Arvedya has shared her mother's stories of her grandmother with Carlotta. The surrounding dashes emphasize the importance of this. Even more important than the story is the fact that it has been passed from one storyteller to the next. Carlotta becomes the fourth teller of this story and the fourth artist to shape it. Her connection to these generations of women and her continuation of this lineage of artists give her the confidence to respond as she does to Suwelo's remark. Her art and its connection to her maternal ancestors make her confident of her sexuality. She is a woman secure in her knowledge of her "womanliness" because she has these ancestral connections.

Although all the characters are artists who practice "mimesis of process," characters who are shaped by the telling of the story and characters who tell stories about artists engaged in the production of art, the female characters create art that is self-exploratory. Deborah McDowell's distinction between public art and private art is appropriate to account for the differences between the art produced by female and male characters.[8] Arveyda's music and Suwelo's "histories" take others as their subject or focus (both tell the stories of women who have told their stories to them), but Carlotta's chimes and Fanny's massages are the means of self-exploration. Even the play that Fanny writes about her father is written with her sister, and as a joint venture it is as much about herself and her African half sister as it is about their father. We can also understand this gender-based "difference" in the context of Barbara Christian's work. In the chapter "Trajectories of Self-Definition," Christian observes how contemporary black women's fiction pursues the tradition of self-definition by allowing women's definition to come from within rather than without.[9] This is an accurate assessment of the female characters in *The Temple of My Familiar*, who learn to define themselves from within. The importance of this lesson is apparent in the episode for which the book is named. Eager to impress the white man, Lissie traps and silences her familiar. After it escapes, she realizes that the favorable impression she has made on the white man is meager recompense for the loss.

Male storytellers tell tales about others; female storytellers tell tales about themselves or tales that they discover within themselves. While Fanny's stories reveal a self inhabited by many different spirits, Lissie's stories and paintings reveal that she is many different people. When a white female history professor, "one of those Afrophiles who was so protective of Africa that she claimed Idi Amin was framed," asks Lissie to refrain from using the phrase "I remember thus and so" about her experiences on a slave ship, Lissie explains that she "knew the professional way to present my experiences was as if they had merely been told to me" but adds "some people don't understand that it is the nature of the eye to have seen forever, and the nature of the mind to recall anything that was ever known. Or that was the nature, I should say, until man started to put things on paper" (65). The professor resumes the discussion by saying that "she couldn't even imagine what it must have been like on the slave ship," and Lissie proceeds to recall the experience (65). This contrast between student and teacher illustrates the important contribution that imagination makes to the understanding of others.

Lissie, whose name means "the one who remembers everything," has memories in addition to those that recall events from her previous lives (52). These are dream memories, which she explains as follows: "I do not remember with my brain itself anyway," she says, "but with my memory which is separate, somehow, yet contained within it. Charged with memory . . . like a battery" (52). Within this memory is dream memory, a second, more remote level of the unconscious. If memory houses the collective unconscious, dream memory represents our collective dreams and aspirations, and is the site of mythmaking. Lissie explains: "In the dream world of my memory, however, there is something. I do not remember this exactly, as I remember the other things of which I have told you. But the memory, like the mind, has the capacity to dream, and just as the memory exists at a deeper level of consciousness than thinking, so the dream world of the memory is at a deeper level still. I will tell you of the dream on which my memory, as well as my mind, rests" (83).

The story that Lissie tells is a myth. It explains human society evolving from gender-based compounds to gender-integrated nuclear families. Lissie and her mate defy tradition by living among the "cousins" and cohabiting as they do. Lissie wonders how "we, so little, so naked, so easily contentious, had splintered off" from this other species (87). She also remembers the violence of the fathers and uncles who "carried sticks with sharp points on them," who "sometimes cooked and ate our cousins' bodies" (87). The result of this carnage was that "the little people, as we now recognized ourselves—pygmies, perhaps—developed their own weapons—poisoned arrows, blowguns and slingshots—and sought to control and dominate others, including the cousins" (87). Like most myths, this one links the past with the present and future:

> It was our way of living (like the cousins who mate for life) that gradually took hold in all the groups of people living in the forest, at least for a very long time, until the idea of ownership—which grew out of the way the forest now began to be viewed as something cut into pieces that belonged to this tribe or that—came into human arrangements. Then it was that men, because they were stronger at least during those periods when women were weak from childbearing, began to think of owning women and children. This very thing had happened before, and our own parents had forgotten it, but their system of separating men and women was a consequence of an earlier period when men and women had tried to live together—and it is interesting to see today that mothers and fathers are returning to the old way of only visiting each other and not wanting to live together. This is the pattern of freedom until man no longer wishes to dominate women and children or always have to prove his control. (87–88)

In *Mythmaking and Metaphor in Black Women's Fiction*, Jacqueline de Weever describes how black women writers revise and invert existing myths. She says that such techniques "correct the myth . . . by turning the myth and, therefore, the society to which it relates, inside out" (29). The result is a paradox: "while the inversion undermines, without destroying, the meaning of the myth when it is applied universally, it validates its essential message within the particular context of black life" (29). Alice Walker uses myth in this way in *The Temple of My Familiar*. Her "inversion" of the Judeo-Christian creation myth, the biblical myth of the fall and expulsion from paradise, and the scientific myth of human evolution illustrates the fictional status of these myths. Walker's myths point to their own status as fiction at the same time that they point to the fictional status of existing myths. Cognizance of the implications of this "inversion" is possible for readers who are aware of how existing myths are accepted as fact and often serve as the foundation for racist and sexist ideologies. Walker's inversion of accepted myths draws attention to the process of mythmaking rather than to the product, the myth. It makes readers acknowledge the imaginative component of accepted myths while inspiring them to invent myths (and corresponding realities) that are relevant and meaningful to them. Walker's novel illustrates the process of mythmaking, showing by its own example how we can create the myths we need and reject the ones we don't need.

One of the most interesting dream memories is recalled on the opening pages of the novel, where Lissie describes the unfortunate consequences of man's jealousy of woman's reproductive capabilities: men cut off their genitals to resemble women and usurp the power of procreation. Another dream memory explains the origins of white people. In an inversion of the Yacub myth, Lissie recalls life as the first white man. She remembers her mother and mate covering her body with tinted oil to camouflage her whiteness. The sight of her own naked phallus causes an explosion of anger during which she kills Ba, the prelapsarian snake that is her lover's pet familiar. She seeks shelter in a cave outside the tribal compound, killing animals for skins to hide her nakedness and fathering a race of white people.

Both myths demonstrate the unfortunate consequences of excessive self-consciousness. While black characters use self-consciousness as a lever to transcend the boundaries of self and connect with ancestors, white self-consciousness is the result of comparing oneself to others, and it produces self-imposed alienation and violence. The women inspire jealousy because they wear jewelry and colorful garments. Like Narcissus, they take pleasure in gazing at their own reflections. Men are jealous of this pleasure, and this is how they become conscious of their difference and convinced of their inferiority. Self-consciousness is also illustrated in the myth of the first white man, who is happy until he becomes, through his initiation into sex, aware of his white skin. Recognition of this difference propels him to a life of self-hate and solitude. Like Falcon's self-preoccupation, the self-consciousness of these characters is a wall that separates them from others and halts their own growth.

The most important dream memories serve as the source of inspiration for paintings as well as stories. In one of the final scenes in the novel, Lissie and Hal are working at easels set up in the backyard of their home. On this occasion, they paint Suwelo sleeping on the porch. Other paintings capture more remote realities. Lissie paints herself and the cousins residing in trees. She paints herself in one of her former lives as a lion. Hal's painting is discouraged by his father, and it is Lissie's lifelong job to provide him with the space and the security to paint. When they are young, she steals supplies; when they are older, she works so that Hal's time is unencumbered.

In order to appreciate the significance of mimesis of process in Walker's fiction, we need to understand how the artistic process functions as a metaphor for the creative process of making one's self. It is not just that art is central to character development but rather that art provides the ideal metaphor for depicting the growth and evolution of the human personality. Self-exploration and creativity are apparent in the "composing" of one's self as one composes a painting, a musical score, or a poem. It is not coincidental that each of the characters in Walker's novel is an artist—Walker sees all people as artists busy at work on the canvases that are ourselves. Art is a metaphor and measure of self-development. Like artistic invention, painting, or throwing a pot, the invention of self requires a momentary loss of self-consciousness. While Calhoun's authoring of the logbook requires self-consciousness, the writers and artists in *The Temple of My Familiar* relinquish self-consciousness and authorial privilege.

Calhoun must author the logbook. His success depends on a consistent, identifiable point of view, but there is neither central protagonist nor point of view in Walker's novel. All four artist-characters contribute to the "central consciousness" of the novel. The result is an egalitarian narrative in which no character or point of view is privileged. The reader is introduced to a community of characters who are equal. No voice is subordinate to others. In this polyphony, each character contributes her voice to the score, which is the novel. Like the characters, the reader pursues her own artistic development, and the invention and exploration of her own character becomes another contribution to narrative pluralism.

Writers such as Alice Walker and Charles Johnson understand mimesis of process as a part of the Black Aesthetic. In this context, textual self-consciousness is not a by-product of a writer's belief in literature's "usedupedness" but is, instead, an affirmation of boundless creativity. Whereas John Barth's floating opera is the site of negation and nihilism, the *Republic* and the temple are sites of discovery and rebirth.

The solipsism of Barth and other "unhappy metafictionists" is balanced by the metafiction of writers such as Johnson and Walker who are fascinated with the image reflected in the mirror but know they must break with the gaze it reflects if they are ever to learn who they are.[10] These writers seem to advise that it is better to find out who you are by looking into the eyes of others than into the eyes in the mirror. Better yet, find out who you are by looking at the people you came from and listening to their stories.

The black metafictionist refuses to be trapped by the gaze. The narcissism that serves as a cornerstone in Linda Hutcheon's theory fails to explain self-consciousness in black texts. It explains the narcissism of Ebenezer Falcon and the tribe of men who dominate others. Black metafiction constructs its own reading of self-consciousness.

In both novels, the fiction that is the black self shatters. The shards of glass reflect the images of ancestors and past lives. Transcendence of the self and recognition of the interconnection of all life redefines self-consciousness as an awareness of the others who reside in us.[11] This awareness suggests a new definition of "character." It is one that encompasses a chorus of voices remarkable for its harmonious and dissonant blending of sounds, its embodiment of democratic ideals, and its subtle, demure invitation to the audience to sing along. The central protagonist is replaced by a collective of characters, and Kierkegaard's couch-potato reader becomes the baton-wielding choirmaster.

CHAPTER 3   ➤ ➤ ➤ ➤ ➤ ➤ ➤ ➤ ➤ ➤

The *Künstlerroman* and the Blues Hero

Today. My simple passion is to write our names in
history and walk in the light that is woman.
                                        —Sonia Sanchez, *Poem*

Linda Hutcheon's discussion of mimesis of process situates metafiction in its classical context by explaining how mimesis of product superseded mimesis of process and became the sole criterion for evaluating and interpreting fiction. Her examination of classical rhetoric is a persuasive argument for the reintroduction of mimesis of process into the discussion of literature. As a point of entry into black metafiction, mimesis of process yields important findings. The first is that black fiction has always celebrated mimesis of process. The process of artistic production has always been portrayed as equal or greater in value than the product. Such novels as *The Color Purple* remind us of that history and speak out on behalf of the continuation of this tradition.

The second thing we learn is that mimesis of process functions metaphorically in black texts. Art is bigger than life. Novels such as *The Temple of My Familiar* advise readers to regard life as a painter regards a canvas: creativity is essential to success. An examination of mimesis of process culminates in a discussion of artist-characters who benefit from the reciprocity of artistic and personal lives. Rutherford Calhoun, Suwelo, and Ola overstep the boundaries that separate the worlds of artistic creation and those of everyday life. Unlike the protagonist of John Barth's "Life-Story," who is catapulted from the real world to the imaginary and disoriented by the shift, characters in black metafiction move gracefully from one world to the other, taking advantage of the juxtaposition of the imaginary and the real worlds.

Discussion of the artist-character culminates in an analysis of the African American *künstlerroman*. Recent studies of women's bildungsromans and Canadian *künstlerromans* make the examination of the African American *künstlerroman* timely.[1] Like the study of bildungsromans by women, difficulties are evident in locating a working definition of the term. Glossaries and dictionaries identify the *künstlerroman* as a subclassification of the bildungsroman.[2] The *künstlerroman*—from the German *Künstler* (artist) and the French *roman* (novel)—is a narrative that "traces the development of the author (or that of an imagined character like the author) from childhood to maturity" (Shaw 215). Such works usually "depict the struggles of a sensitive, artistic child to escape the misunderstandings and bourgeois attitudes of his family and youthful acquaintances" (Shaw 215). The term is synonymous with "apprenticeship novel," a term derived from Goethe's *The Apprenticeship of Wilhelm Meister* (Holman 55). Scholars cite James Joyce's *Portrait of the Artist as a Young Man* as the best example of a *künstlerroman* in English.

The first problem is evident in an attempt to locate the definition in an African American context. The definition calls for a plot that revolves around an artist-protagonist in conflict with society, but the plot of African American *künstlerromans* cannot be reduced to this conflict. Artists in black novels are often strongly connected to their communities, and art often serves to strengthen this connection. Eighteenth-century African American autobiographical narratives are evidence of the beginning of a tradition of *künstlerromans* that portray the artist as a representative or spokesperson of the community. James Weldon Johnson's *The Autobiography of an Ex-Coloured Man* describes an artist whose work languishes as his distance from the black community increases. His talents are nurtured, not threatened, by the community. Altering the definition to allow for distinctions between black and white communities does not make it more relevant. White society is not cast in the role of the antagonist in the *künstlerromans* reviewed here, although internal conflicts founded on the distinction between classical or "high" art and vernacular or "low" art are central in the novels by Johnson and Dove.

A second difficulty with the definition is the meaning of the word "artist." The meaning of the word changes as we move from nineteenth-century Germany to twentieth-century America, but the definition of *künstlerroman* does not allow for these changes. In her collection of essays, *In Search of Our Mothers' Gardens*, Alice Walker speaks of the importance of literary ancestors and the community to her work. She also discusses artists who might never be acknowledged as artists according to standard definitions, but who nevertheless play a paramount role in keeping artistic traditions alive and viable. In the title essay Walker imagines artists who were never free to practice their craft. In the short story "Everyday Use," she suggests that crafts such as quilting be recognized as art. The everyday use of the quilt—its functionality—is important to its aesthetics and links African American quilting with African weaving and cloth-making. Walker's story juxtaposes the functional art of the black vernacular with the nonfunctionality that distinguishes Western art as a luxury reserved for the economically privileged. The history of Western art—as cultural artifacts produced and consumed by the leisure class—is imbued in this definition of the *künstlerroman*, which privileges fine art over craft, classical music over ballads and folk music, and theater for passive spectators rather than a responsive audience.

Black metafiction requires redefining the *künstlerroman* to encompass diverse artist-protagonists and alternative central conflicts. Black metafiction also affects preexisting controversies among theorists of the *künstlerroman*. One such controversy concerns whether or not narratives about artists are metafiction. In *Private Lives in the*

Public Sphere, Todd Kontje argues that the bildungsroman is metafiction because it theorizes about itself and its status as fiction at the same time that it portrays the life of an artist (9–15). Kontje maintains that the bildungsroman is a "self-critical genre" (16). Inger Christensen takes the opposite stance in *The Meaning of Metafiction*, contrasting John Barth's *The Floating Opera* with Nathaniel Hawthorne's *The Blithedale Romance* to distinguish between "metafiction and the nineteenth century *künstler-roman*" (12). Christensen says that although the themes are similar—both "deal with the artist-writer's existential situation"—important structural differences warrant recognition of the distinct genres represented by these works: "While Hawthorne stops after having described his narrator-protagonist's existential dilemma, Barth goes on to disclose Todd Andrews' difficulties in writing the very book in which he figures as the narrator. By revealing the technique of *The Floating Opera* in the novel, Barth stresses the parallelism between the narrator's difficulties as an artist and as a man" (12).

Christensen concludes that Hawthorne's novel is not metafiction because it "does not in any way explore the process of its own making" (12). Although critics might disagree with his reading of *The Blithedale Romance*, the distinction that Christensen observes is legitimate. His argument that Hawthorne's novel is not metafiction severs nineteenth-century realism from the history and evolution of metafiction. Unlike Hutcheon and Waugh, who regard metafiction as being as old as fiction itself and see literary realism as a moment in its evolution, Christensen regards it as a by-product of postmodernism. This argument is similar to Donald Gibson's attempt to distinguish between African American novelists who privilege content and those who privilege form. Linda Hutcheon's historicizing of metafiction provides an alternative that allows us to envision realism as a part of the evolution of metafiction. Rather than argue that Hawthorne's text is not metafictional, she would classify it as an example of fiction that is thematically self-conscious. She argues that texts that simply thematize or allegorize the role of the storyteller compose one type of metafiction, but a second type draws attention to its fictionality by linguistic play, such as invented words. Hutcheon says that such novels *actualize* their preoccupation with themselves.

Robert Scholes makes a similar distinction,[3] one that allows critics to envision realistic novels about artists—*künstlerromans*—as metafiction without obscuring the importance of innovations characteristic of postmodern literature.

The distinction between thematic and actualizing techniques and the controversy concerning the scope of metafiction explain why black novels are often excluded from discussions of postmodernism, especially the solipsistic, "unhappy metafictionists." Critics, like Christensen, who regard metafiction as synonymous with postmodernism omit discussion of thematically metafictional black texts. Others believe that there is no such thing as African American postmodernism, that the term itself is an oxymoron.[4] The resolution of these dilemmas warrants an investigation of the African American *künstlerroman*. Rita Dove's *Through the Ivory Gate* and Arthur Flowers' *Another Good Loving Blues* exemplify the contemporary African American *künstlerroman*. Both are about artists, hence they are thematically self-conscious, and both demonstrate *actualizing* techniques indigenous to the black vernacular.

Robert Stepto's distinction between "articulate survivor" and "articulate kinsman" assists in characterizing the differences between the novels' protagonists (167). Dove's novel examines the interplay of classical European and African American vernacular musical traditions. Like the "ex-coloured man," Virginia juggles European and African American artistic traditions and learns that mastery of the cello and her own destiny requires a balance of Duke Ellington and J. S. Bach. Her story follows the plot of the ascent narrative: she leaves her family to enter the least oppressive environment, at the price of loneliness. *Another Good Loving Blues* is a self-proclaimed blues novel that traces the history of the blues from the lone traveling blues man to the big bands and race recordings. Bodeen's story is the prototype of the immersion narrative: he "forsakes mobility in the least oppressive society for a posture of relative stasis in the most oppressive environment" (167). Both *künstlerromans* are meditations on art and culture. Dove's extensive travel (especially time spent living in Germany) and Flowers' experiences as a jazz musician provide their autobiographical foundations.

The protagonist of *Through the Ivory Gate* is Virginia King, a cellist, mime, and puppeteer. After receiving a degree in theater arts from the University of Wisconsin, Virginia joins Puppets and People, a performing arts troupe that combines the art of Japanese theater with the pageantry of the three-ring circus. When the troupe disbands, Virginia accepts employment with the National Arts Council to visit public schools introducing students and their communities to puppetry. When the novel opens, she is beginning a six-week residency at Booker T. Washington Elementary School in Akron.

Although her stay in Akron is brief, it is long enough for Virginia to be reintroduced to the family she lost when her parents moved to Arizona. Visits with her father's mother and sister, Grandmother Evans and Aunt Carrie, acquaint her with a disturbing event from the past: she learns that the abrupt move to Arizona was prompted by her mother's discovery of her husband's incestuous relationship with his sister. Although this occurred before their courtship, Belle could not forgive Ernie or Carrie, and she insisted that the family relocate immediately.

Unlike her mother, Virginia can "let go of the anguish" (256). Virginia lets go of this anguish in her family's past, as well as the more recent anguish resulting from her frustrated longing for a gay man. She also lets go of the anguish inspired by the limited opportunities available for black actresses. This ability is consistent with the blues hero's acceptance of misfortune. Virginia is able to accept anguish, whether it is the result of social inequities or her own poor judgment, as an inescapable part of life. In "The Hero and the Blues," Albert Murray describes the blues statement as "an experience-confrontation device" that enables people to accept "the difficult, disappointing, chaotic, absurd . . . facts of life" (104). Virginia excels at this experience-confrontation strategy. While her mother's anguish causes her to retreat to the deserts of Arizona, Virginia's anguish is abated by a process that empowers her to accept misfortune. Unlike Belle, who will not listen to anyone's explanations, Virginia accepts the variety of explanations and homespun truths that her grandmother shares from her "talking seat" in the living room (56). Although she acknowledges the family's riddled past, her grandmother does not warn her of impending doom—the sins of the fathers will be visited upon the heads of their children. Instead, she urges Virginia to forget past sins and get on with her own life: "old bones, dead and buried" (248). Virginia acts on this advice by arranging a visit to her long estranged aunt and listening to her account of the event. Listening to the stories and advice of her women relatives provides Virginia with a sense of her own past and the confidence to determine her own future.

The novel is organized according to Virginia's progression through the *Six Suites for Unaccompanied Violoncello*. Although Virginia decides to be an actress rather than a musician, music is the scaffold on which her narrative is arranged. It provides a means of assessing her growth. Each of J. S. Bach's six suites serves as a signpost of Virginia's increasing autonomy and self-definition.[5] Her initial frustration with the score sends her to the library, where she reads that Bach's *Suites* fulfill "the established rule that every union of parts must make a whole and exhaust all the notes necessary to the most complete expression of the contents, so that no deficiency should anywhere be sensible by which another part might be rendered possible" (91). Her friend Clayton puts it more simply: "If a cellist were stranded on a desert island all he would need are his instrument and the Suites—no piano, no trio, no orchestra backup. The Suites are entirely self-sufficient. They can sustain you for a lifetime" (180).

Although Virginia's response is "Give it a rest, Clayton," Clayton has predicted her future (180). The *Suites* sustain her through a painful episode of unrequited love, through college, Puppets and People, and the start of an acting career. The *Suites* provide a metaphor for Virginia's growing independence. Mastering the *Suites* means imagining herself as a symphony instrument playing solo: each suite is a higher plateau of independence. Her mastery of the *Fifth Suite*—"the music of a human being probing the darker corridors of the unachieved"—occurs when she hears the truth about her family's past (210). Her mastery of the *Sixth Suite* reflects the blues hero's triumph over pain and her ability to move on: "It was less indulgently sorrowful than the Fifth, more self-possessed and bittersweet and—adult, a chin lifted to the chill wind. It was the suite of departure, the conscious leave-taking of one who knows when it's time to move on" (258).

Because the *Suites* are central to the protagonist's development, knowing something about their composition provides additional insights into Virginia's position as a blues hero and the novel as a *künstlerroman*. J. S. Bach, their composer, is credited with the popularity of counterpoint in classical music, a technique of combining two or more independent melodies to make a harmonious melody. This technique, also known as polyphony, is present in much African American music. Therefore it is not surprising that Virginia's familiarity with jazz assists her in mastering the *Suites*—not only because jazz and they are both polyphonic—but because jazz involves improvisation, the musician's adaptation of the written score. Virginia can play the *Suites* when she applies the techniques of a jazz musician: "She had been so concerned with the score's harmonic structure . . . that she had failed to hear the musical line. It was like jazz, what Ellington meant by *It don't mean a thing if it ain't got that swing.* Playing Bach, she had to put inaccuracy into every note, that supreme inaccuracy—call it mistreatment, call it love—that makes the notes 'blend' and become music" (98–99).

What Virginia refers to as "inaccuracy" is the jazz musician's ability to improvise. She discovers that the musician who plays classical music must "swing" just like Duke Ellington. The musician must find a balance between personal expression, the summation of his or her own musical expertise, and the composer's directions as they are indicated by the score. At first, Bach's score appears to be crowded with notes, allowing no room for improvisation or the musician's personal interpretation, but after repeated attempts to play the music as written, Virginia discovers room for personal expression. The successful musician of classical music *or* jazz combines her own interpretation with what has been written by the composer: "eight notes to a measure, regular as clockwork; but that didn't mean the phrase ended at the bar, or for that matter, that each eighth note had the same value. The music lurked in this intricate grid of notes; but she had to take a little from her guts and the air and then shape it, make it live" (98).

Both counterpoint and improvisation are central to Virginia's development. Counterpoint suggests appreciating the beauty of each individual, each melody, while at the same time appreciating the community, the collective of sounds and individuals. This describes

Virginia's simultaneous movement toward independence and immersion into her family's past and the community where she is teaching. Her mastery of improvisation gives her the confidence needed to act according to her own feelings. There are several climactic moments when Virginia must choose between two courses of action—one reflecting her own idiosyncrasies and personal inclinations and another reflecting a generally approved or accepted route. By applying improvisation to life and trusting her own intuition, she makes the right choices. She violates the score her mother wants her to play by refusing to take the safe road of an acceptable career and marriage into the middle-class world of mediocrity. Instead, she trusts the unknown and chooses a profession without guarantees. She continues to follow her own instincts, to live improvisationally, when she rejects Terry's marriage proposal in favor of the unpredictable life of a teacher and actress. Accepting uncertainty, developing confidence in her ability to improvise, and trusting her own abilities to handle whatever the future may hold make Virginia a blues hero. Unlike the protagonist of the *künstlerroman*, whose art signifies withdrawal from the world, the blues hero's art is a means of confrontation and immersion.

Like the ex-coloured man practicing Schubert, Virginia marries black and white musical traditions when she plays her cello. Both musicians recognize that improvisation and other elements of black style enrich their performance of classical compositions, yet both remain committed to careers as classical musicians. The ex-coloured man's familiarity with ragtime and Virginia's knowledge of jazz help them to excel as classical musicians.

Dove's explanations of her views on race and writing provide insight into Virginia's character. Like her protagonist who seeks to master classical music, Dove says she will not be restricted to writing about "black concerns" (Taleb-Khyar 364). Efforts to "transcend" race cause Virginia and Dove to dismiss "black art" and black artists and to overlook vernacular aesthetic traditions. Virginia reveals this lack of understanding when she speaks of black musicians: "Most black musicians she had met before were either horn men—saxophonists of every stripe—or the ubiquitous percussionists who were always clicking out rhythms with their tongues and drumming on tabletops. She hated to fall into stereotyping, but it was true" (24–25). Virginia's criticism of the tabletop percussionist suggests that she is not cognizant of the historical forces that give rise to this impromptu drum solo. She fails to connect this drumming to the talking drum, one of the few African instruments that survived slavery. The drumming does more than just allude to a method of communication. It signifies the longevity of African American artists and art forms. Finally, as an illustration of synchrony, the drum suggests an important difference between African and Western music and thought. Dove stereotypes black writers in a similar way, criticizing those who write about "the Black cause" or "the female cause" and those whose writing is influenced by black music:

> What I find distressing, for example, is the notion that if you're Black you're going to write in the Blues mode. Half the people who are writing these Bluesy-Jazzy poems really have no appreciation for the Blues as an art form. They think, in a very superficial way, that if you're Black, then you're Blue, so let's get down to it. That's fine, if the writing is good. What I don't like is the kind of poetry praised in certain cliques and journals for its "Blackness" or cultural verisimilitude when so much of it is just badly written. It's extremely frustrating to read a poem that has wonderful ideas and a few interesting images, but on the whole doesn't cohere because the writer is caught up with being hip and clever. (364)

Through the Ivory Gate makes use of a musical trope but avoids being "hip and clever" by choosing a trope that is relevant to music in the eleventh, thirteenth, eighteenth, and twentieth centuries. By selecting this trope, Dove aims to transcend the issue of race. Although Virginia's behaviors are occasionally determined by race, they are more frequently determined by her personal idiosyncrasies. Paradoxically, this rugged individualism—in Virginia and Dove—is one of the defining characteristics of the blues hero. Although Dove may not want to write a what-did-I-do-to-be-so-black-and-blue novel, she responds to this type by creating a blues hero, a protagonist who represents a repertoire of black aesthetic traditions. Virginia's staunch individualism—a refusal to do anything to be in style or to fulfill the expectations of others—is a central characteristic of the blues hero. Although Albert Murray sees this "emphasis on rugged individual endurance" in the blues tradition as an extension of the American frontier tradition (106), Dove explains it as a part of her politics:

> I think my "role" is or what it is that I'm trying to do in a so-cial sense is to constantly remind myself, my students, and my readers of our individuality. To me, one of the greatest dangers for people in this country is the temptation to think in terms of groups rather than extol each person's uniqueness . . . . I try very hard to create characters who are seen as individuals—not only as Blacks or as women but . . . as persons who have their very individual lives, and whose histories make them react to the world in different ways. One could argue that insisting upon that individuality is ultimately a political act, and to my mind, this is one of the fundamental principles a writer has to uphold. (361)

Virginia's insistence on her own individuality is political. This is apparent when she joins Puppets and People and devotes her time to writing and performing satirical plays to be performed on the streets of Madison, Wisconsin. The political dimension of her independence is made plain when she disregards her mother's plea to choose a career that would "advance the race" (94). She is attracted to Clayton for his adamant individualism. She compares this black gay cellist to the bumblebee whose flight defies the laws of aerodynamics (29). Virginia chooses to master the cello because she also seeks to defy the laws that discourage girls from preferring ungainly, unmanageable instruments. She defies the law of custom when she becomes the first black girl to join the majorettes. She insists she doesn't do it to be the first but because she enjoys the power and control of twirling. The baton, like the cello, is an instrument to conquer and to love. It tests her self-confidence and reflects her success at self-definition, but it also reveals the important role the vernacular plays in this, a role that goes unnoticed by Virginia:

And so she became one of the girls, the only black face and legs
on a line of spanking white-and-blue uniforms. In that shimmer-
ing outfit she felt the membrane of illusion rise between her and
the audience. Her baton spun easily, as though the twirling itself
were a breathless silvery web slipping effortlessly from her magic
wrists. In the majorette uniform she was a Titan, a fifty-foot
woman whose legs stretched high and away joining together
somewhere above a cloud. The princess lines of the bodice, its
frog fastenings and brass-buttoned epaulets! The perfect circle of
the skirt, cobalt-blue cotton lined with white silk! Tall with blue-
and-white pompons (they used one skein of yarn for each boot),
the shiny-hard white hats with those outrageous plumes! For the
first time in her life Virginia felt not only attractive, but effective—like she knew how to handle what she had and, as they said
in the lavatories, "deal that stuff." (121–122)

Virginia's is the black face in the orchestra and the black face in
the majorette squad, but whether she is learning to play Bach with
some "swing" or twirl a baton "dealing that stuff," she resorts to the
language of the vernacular to make sense of her experience.

Music is a barometer of her inner life. Acting is a barometer of her
growth in relation to others. This explains her decision to major in
drama and minor in music. She perceives the life of a musician as
one of "solitary struggle" with "all the joys and grief of private experience transplanted into wordless ecstasy" (148). If she understood
the history reverberating with every fall of the drummer's hand, she
would know a music that reflects "collective struggle" and the experience of a community told in a complex, intricate language. However, Virginia's understanding of music is monopolized by symbols
from the Western world; therefore she imagines the musician as a
solitary figure, and she imagines his music as wordless.

Ekaterini Georgoudaki notes that Dove believes that language
shapes perception (421). This explains why Virginia thinks in the vernacular, but it raises the question of why she chooses to major in
mime. She arrives at this choice after viewing *Children of Paradise*,
a film featuring a mime "who takes off his white paint and becomes
merely ordinary" (94). Thereafter "pantomime was Virginia's pas-

sion" (94). The paint that masks the face dramatizes the "double-consciousness" that Dove perceives as an integral and unalterable aspect of black consciousness.[6] It also serves as an allusion to minstrelsy. If Virginia had enrolled in courses on black music and theater, she would know the history of vaudeville and the black minstrel shows—the black actors who painted their faces to parody the white actors who blackened their faces.[7] What originated as a white racist entertainment was recast as a black parody. Black minstrels were engaged in what Ishmael Reed calls "loa-making," "an ancient survival form" that involved "adopting the oppressor's parody" of one's self and "evolving, from this, an art form with its own laws" ("Shrovetide," 33). "Loa-making" is a part of the black vernacular, a way of signifyin(g), but it also serves to disarm double-consciousness. Virginia is ignorant of this heritage, so while her mime achieves the political, it falls short of filling Reed's prescription for parody. Like the artist-protagonist of the nineteenth-century *künstlerroman*, Virginia wrestles with contradictions.

When Dove veers from a strictly chronological account of the proceedings, her novel diverges from the path taken by conventional *künstlerromans*. Frequent lengthy flashbacks to Virginia's childhood and adolescence are interjected into a narrative about her experiences as artist in residence. Dove disrupts chronology to demonstrate the importance of internal mental clocks. In this respect, the artist resembles her nineteenth-century precursor, who is also governed from within. For the contemporary African American writer this is both a celebration of the creative self and a political act because it subordinates Western time to C(olored). P(eople's). T(ime). or personal time. In an interview with Mohamed B. Taleb-Khyar and Maryse Condé, Dove discusses the representation of time in *Thomas and Beulah*. She says that the chronology is "a parody on history because private dates are put on equal footing with the dates of publicly important happenings" (357). Although she later satirizes black nationalism and writing inspired by political reform, Dove's subordination of objective time is political and nationalistic.[8] Equally important to the foregrounding of an Afrocentric definition of time is the juxtaposition of past and present enacting the principle of counterpoint, the musical term that functions as a central trope in the novel.

Through the Ivory Gate is both thematically self-conscious and structurally self-conscious. It exemplifies the actualizing techniques that Hutcheon describes by interweaving song lyrics with the narrative. Changes in typography remind the reader that she is engaged in reading a text. The novel is a collage of such diverse materials as scripts for puppet plays, surrealistic dream sequences, excerpts from reference books on music and Javanese theater, letters and notes written by characters, folk songs, and the antics of an imaginary Sambo. This collage fulfills the definition for actualized metafiction, but it is a pastiche of actualizing technique from the vernacular.

Virginia's appreciation for music is grounded in its escapism. She speaks of music as making her feel complete and autonomous, transporting her to the "upper ether" where there is "no memory or hurt" (30). "Real music," she says, "makes you forget where you were, made you forget where your arms and legs ended and luscious sound began" (22). This contrasts with the experience of the musicians who inhabit Flowers' novel. His characters hear the voices of their ancestors in the music they play. Their music is a means of immersion into the folk culture rather than a means of ascending beyond it.

Examining Dove's novel for endemic definitions of art produces the idea that loss of consciousness plays a prominent role in artistic creation. This "loss of consciousness" resembles the artistic process portrayed in the Romantic *künstlerromans*. The novel, however, doesn't stop here in its investigation of art but pursues it to uncover the relationship between art and reality. As part of her final exam in mime, Virginia mimics a cellist. After her performance, her teacher explains that the successful mimicry of a cellist does not depend on the ability to play the cello and that on this occasion Virginia's ability to play interferes with her skill at mime. This advice makes Virginia a better mime *and* a better cellist.

Virginia's instruction in mime has taught her the difference between art and reality. As an artist and teacher, she takes pleasure in substituting one for the other and celebrating the purely imaginative. She collaborates with her students to write a love story about a talking football. At the Javanese play, she assures her students' parents they need not worry about the plot. She compares her own experiences to their rendering on stage and finds humor in the fact that there are few happy endings in real life. Art serves as the middle term in a scene that juxtaposes Virginia's imaginings with reality. Listening to music performed by Clayton and his lover, she notes: "In the theater, the curtain would have fallen just then, with the two musicians upstage right, encapsulated in a silver-blue spot, and the woman downstage left, drenched in the warmth of a yellow gel. But in the real world she had to listen on to the end, struggling to keep her composure among the lumps of the red couch, which made her feel mortal and messy" (200).

She knows that art does not mimic reality, and like most blues heroes, she knows that reality is often more dismal. This fosters her appreciation of nonrepresentational art. It also keeps her from trying to make life resemble artistic production. She refers to the story of Narcissus to explain this to Terry, an attractive divorcé whose pursuit of her persists in spite of her disinterest. She tells him about a story she read in German class. It is about a handsome young man who wants to be a dancer. "No one knew if he had talent, but he had natural grace and was totally unaware of his own beauty" (169). His demise occurs when a dancer tells the young man that he looks "like a Greek sculpture." Thereafter, the narcissistic young man spends hours in front of the mirror trying to re-create the pose: "The more he looked, the more self-conscious he became—his smile grew forced, he would pinch his eyes into a squint he thought provocative, and his lilting walk became a calculated jaunt" (169). When the dancer sees him again, he doesn't recognize him: "The boy waving from the other side of the street was no different from the swarm of other teenagers heading downtown" (169). Although this anecdote is meant to warn Terry about the evils of excessive pride, it reveals the complexity of Virginia's thoughts on art and artistic creation. Virginia's retelling of the myth of Narcissus, the myth that Hutcheon cites as an allegory of metafiction, defines and exemplifies metafiction.

Dove's novel celebrates art that breaks the rules, including the rule that art mimic reality. This may explain why Virginia's puppets have "magical properties inversely proportional to the probability that they could exist: an apple tree with a hundred red eyes, a talking bush, a blue-eyed dragon, a ballerina bewitched in the hide of a hippopotamus, a cross-eyed peacock" (34). The theory that issues from the novel is one that celebrates the process of artistic creation as personal and improvisational but also stresses the importance of artists' interacting with their communities. The African American *künstlerroman* as exemplified by Dove's novel is a celebration of self and a celebration of community. It is this duality, this demonstration of counterpoint, that makes it unique yet vital to the definition of the term.

While novels such as Rita Dove's *Through the Ivory Gate* allow for some initial observations about the African American *künstlerroman*, discussion of this genre would be incomplete without an examination of the portraiture of the artist whose goal is mastery of African American aesthetic traditions. Like the ex-coloured man, Virginia is more concerned with "high" art than "low," and her knowledge of jazz becomes a means of achieving her goals as a cellist and classical musician. Arthur Flowers' second novel, *Another Good Loving Blues*, portrays a musician whose exploration of his African American musical heritage is an end. Like most protagonists of bildungsromans, Luke "Bodacious" Bodeen, a Memphis City blues man, is an autobiographical character who shares both his place of residence and his vocation with his author. Unlike Dove's novel, which veers from a chronologizing of the events in the artist's life, Flowers' novel obeys the rigorous chronology characteristic of the *künstlerroman*. Instead of flashbacks of the key episodes in the protagonist's life, it provides a close scrutiny of the five years during which Luke metamorphoses from novice to master musician.

It is no coincidence that the five years documented in the musician's development are five of the most eventful years in the history of jazz. Bodeen's story is a detailed account of the evolution of African American music from the traveling solitary blues musicians of the teens to the big jazz bands of the twenties. It documents the increasing professionalism of the blues musicians, from the solitary blues musician who felt called on to do the blues, felt he had received his talents by luck or by God, to the professional jazz band member who had been trained to read music and schooled in the European musical traditions:

> He had played a little of that Jazz himself during one of his early
> New Orleans sojourns. Played with boys like mad Buddy Bolden
> and smooth Jelly Roll Morton and wasn't half as contemptuous
> as he sounded. Those New Orleans boys did some good work.
> Trained musicians a lot of them. He had been there when it
> started it. Had sneered cause it wasn't the blues; he liked the
> power of the word with his music. Bodeen remembered back
> when there wasn't no such thing as the blues, or jazz. He was a
> young boy then, about 15, maybe 16, new to Memphis, living off
> his wits and fascinated with the piano. They were playing ragtime
> back then. He'd haunt the places they were playing it and watch
> the old guys' fingering. (56–57)

Instead of riding the tide of history on the wave of the Great Migration, which would transplant the Arkansas-Tennessee blues man in Harlem, Chicago, or Detroit at the height of the "renaissance," Bodeen follows the lead of a blues-inspiring conjure woman, Melvira Dupree (a possible relation to blues musician Jack Champion Dupree) to Taproot, Mississippi. This physical journey south is a spiritual journey as well, during which Bodeen discovers the precursors and prerequisites of the blues. While other musicians are heading north, this blues man is going south to learn about the roots of the music he is playing: the gospels and spirituals, the plantation music and the work songs. Declining a scout's offer to record "race records" in Detroit, blues man Luke Bodeen and conjure woman Melvira Dupree choose to travel against traffic and head south.

The journey that begins in Sweetwater and ends in Taproot makes a short stop on Beale Street. During this stop in Memphis the solitary blues man rehearses with other musicians, and the conjure woman becomes apprentice to the great hoodoo, Hootowl. Both artists gain expertise as a result of their interaction with other artists. Hootowl instructs Melvira to visit Jackson's Drug Store, "the premier gathering hole of Beale Street resident intellectuals," where she becomes acquainted with the opinions of "Doc Marcus Mosiah Garvey," "Dr. Du Bois," "the Lincoln League" and "the NAACP" (113). Debuting as a fictional character, Zora Neale Hurston hoists herself onto the stool next to Melvira's and engages in this conversation:

> "How come you be a hoodoo?" asked Zora.
> "How come you be a writer?" asked Melvira.
> They were too much alike not to try each other. They had every-body's attention now, two strong women, each determined to be the question and not the answer. Zora, worldly and already jaded, Melvira, a provincial country hoodoo with a lot to learn. Yet they recognized in each other sisters of the cloth. (118)

Although Melvira "hadn't really thought about coloredfolk as writers" and the "thought of writing books on hoodoo was totally new to her," she comes to understand, with the guidance of Miss Rush and Hootowl, that both "literature and hoodoo" are "tools for shaping the soul" (119). The more experienced Hootowl regards writing and conjure as the "rootwork" that shapes the tribal soul and its destiny: "If you would provide tribal guidance, you must work with the tribal soul. Strategies now, they change with time and circumstance. Each makes its contribution in its proper time and place. But if you want to have fundamental influence on the colored race's destiny, you shape its soul and the soul shapes everything else. Rootwork" (120).

This conversation helps Melvira to understand her work. Although she is a powerful and respected hoodoo who is said to hold the town and its inhabitants in a spider web, her power multiplies during her apprenticeship to Hootowl because he instructs her on how her work resembles the anthropologist's and, more important, how both acknowledge the "African way" (122). Melvira's reading and writing will transform conjure in the same way that the recurring epidemic transforms the Jes Grew virus in Ishmael Reed's *Mumbo Jumbo*. These transformations make conjure and the virus responsive to the needs of the community they serve.

While Melvira is learning how knowledge of the personal and collective past can increase her powers and clarify her objectives, Luke is also gaining insight into his work. He realizes that he must relinquish his Stetson and ruffled shirts, the clothes he wore when he played the riverboats, and don the epaulets and brass-buttoned uniform that band musicians wear. This change of clothes is indicative of other changes as well. The success of the blues man who played by ear is past, and proud Luke Bodeen is forced to admit that he needs to learn how to read music if he plans on keeping up. When W. C. Handy asks Bodeen to join his band, Bodeen makes instruction in musicology a condition of the contract. Melvira's development as a conjure woman also depends on her ability to read. When Hootowl sees her reading her Bible, he realizes that this ability is what will enable her to transform hoodoo into its next phase, just as the influence of classical instruments, large orchestras, and written scores transformed blues to jazz. Hootowl notes:

Over the years his thriving hoodoo business fell off. The race was getting far too sophisticated for his kind of hoodoo. They took their bodies to the doctor and their souls to the preacher. Considered becoming a Baptist preacher himself once. But he felt with all his heart that the colored race deserved a spiritual tradition of its own. Needed one desperately. He knew that if the hoodoo way was to remain valid, it would have to find new life and purpose.

It didn't come together for him until the day he saw Melvira Dupree reading her Bible after leaving church. Standing there watching her read her Bible was like a revelation. Like many coloredfolks of his day and time he had never learned how to read, a power he had never mastered. Now that he understood the power of being able to read when other folks couldn't, he was just too old to try. But this Dupree, possibly this was the new study of hoodoo that would save the hoodoo way. In her he saw the future and the future was good. He saw in Melvira Dupree his last chance to serve the colored race. (125–126)

Reading and writing are central to the future of music and conjure. This novel thus pays tribute to literacy and its history in the quest for freedom and civil rights. This is an allusion to the narratives of writers such as Frederick Douglass and Booker T. Washington, whose ambitions depend on the mastery of the written word. Located in a narrative of immersion, this tribute to literacy should not be misread as the rhetoric of assimilationism, for it is an affirmation of the survival of vernacular traditions. The futures of hoodoo and jazz run parallel; they will employ an increasing number of Western artifacts but will retain what is essentially and exclusively African American.

The events depicted in *Another Good Loving Blues* introduce Luke to the technical innovation and expressive content of the blues. He learns from experience what members of the Sacred Blues Band know: "If you want to sing about life, you got to know what you talking about. Everybody know you got to get all down in there if you wanna do the blues. But you can't get lost" (99). Luke gets "all down in there" with Melvira Dupree. Her romance keeps the traveling man in Sweetwater for a year, longer than he has ever stayed anywhere. When the sound of the train whistle is an irresistible siren's song and life on Beale Street is an overwhelming distraction, Luke and Melvira go their separate ways. The duration of their separation is indicated by chapter subtitles announcing the length of time they have been parted. As in Dove's writing, time in Flowers' novel is gauged according to personally significant events rather than consensually agreed-upon minutes, hours, and years. Over the course of time, Luke becomes an alcoholic and a cocaine addict who is forced to trade his fancy shirts and shiny guitar for a washboard and a tin cup. A broken heart humbles the cocky piano man, who "gets lost" in a blues that has him sleeping on Melvira's doorstep. He learns the blues by living the blues, but he also learns living isn't the only ingredient in good music. Like Virginia, he learns that the raw experiences of life must be "rendered" to produce good art. For Virginia this means learning to forget playing the cello to convincingly mimic cello playing. For Luke, it means learning to recast the experience in the telling of the story. Luke, the blues man, is a storyteller as well as a musician (he dreads the wordlessness of the new jazz). Unlike Virginia, who recalls Duke Ellington's words and discovers the importance of improvisation in rendering classical music, Bodeen learns to listen to the loas who speak through him and to be attentive to the religious and spiritual components of his music. Although he initially shuns religion, eventually he is as comfortable playing in church as he is playing in the familiar environs of the jook joint. He learns that in the vernacular tradition secular and religious practices are located on the same continuum.

Craig Hansen Werner describes both blues and gospel as a three-stage process of brutal experience, lyric expression, and affirmation. In the idiom of the church, the brutal experience is the burden, the lyric process is possession by the spirit, and the affirmation is salvation. Werner observes that this "blues/gospel process provides a foundation for the African American artists' explorations of new possibilities for self and community" (xxii). This interpretation explains Bodeen's religious conversion. In order to be a master musician, he must acknowledge the similarities among blues and religious conversion experiences. Not surprisingly, the loss of Melvira and his religious conversion are simultaneous occurrences that pave the way for the third and final step in the process: an affirmation that will foster the creation of art.

Love and death are popular subjects of the blues. Often these themes are intertwined, as they are in *Another Good Loving Blues*, where death shuffles in to take Jake, Luke's buddy, his father, and Melvira's mother. Jake's death, which occurs in the first few pages of the novel, makes Luke think about his own mortality: "Up to now the blues had took every kind of hammer life ever threw at him and defeated em. Tribulations that crushed other folk and sent em crying to God wasn't nothing but material for another blues for Luke Bodeen. But even the blues cant take on death and win. Or can they?" (40).

Melvira teaches Luke that death can be overcome by identifying with the community and heritage. When he accompanies her to visit her dying mother in Taproot, Mississippi, he learns the history of the community and the power of its spiritual and folk traditions. He learns that hoodoo summons hoodoos like a telepathic underground railroad; he learns that shooting the tree from which a lynched man hangs only hurts the tree; and he learns that he has a responsibility to the ancestors and to the community.

Encoded in this is a recognition of the power of the spirit world and belief in God: "*Oluddumare mojuba*" (123). These words, which translate to "God's blessing on us all," serve as the refrain that is repeated periodically in the novel as a chorus in Bodeen's song. After experiencing the humbling effects of "a-good-woman-done-left-me" and the spiritual effects of God, Luke is ready to make music in church as well as jazz band.

Like country blues, *Another Good Loving Blues* is a solo performance, and like the older blues and their forerunners, the spirituals and work songs, this blues is performed by a single voice whose importance cannot be overemphasized. It is evident in the toast with which the novel begins: "I am Flowers of the delta clan Flower and the line of O Killens—I am hoodoo, I am griot, I am a man of power. My story is a true story, my words are true words, my lie is a true lie—a fine old delta tale about a mad blues piano player and a Arkansas conjure woman on a hoodoo mission" (1).

The voice of the storyteller is as important to the story as the characters and plot are. Both storyteller and characters issue from the vernacular tradition. Because the story is one with which the audience is already familiar (a blues man hoodooed by a conjure woman), the storyteller is obliged to make the old new by contributing his own comments, interpretations, and style:

> Course what folks saw from the vantage points of their big wraparound porches wasn't the whole story. Never is. Any good story is always at least 4 or 5 stories deep. And since this is a good story, I expect you to pay close attention to the weave of it. Even they couldn't tell the whole story. But what they did come to understand deep down in once starved and lonely souls, is that when you do find yourself some of that real good loving, if you got any sense at all, you hold on to it.
>
> Truth. I swear by all thats holy. (7)

This is thematic and actualizing metafiction that issues from the African American vernacular tradition. The marriage of the secular and the religious is one of its hallmarks. The voice of the storyteller is foregrounded to draw attention to the skills of the speaker/author. Readers find themselves members of a back porch audience, a com-

munity of listeners. The written text mimics the rhythm and into-
nations of the voice. Repetition creates the cadences of speech. Punctuation indicates time and rhythm. Finally, the didacticism and the
"universality" of the story's message situates this writing in the tradition of the African American vernacular.

Also noteworthy is the switch to the second-person point of view.
Because of this shift in point of view, Gates describes Zora Neale
Hurston's *Their Eyes Were Watching God* as a "speakerly text" and
a momentous contribution to the evolution of African American
literature. Houston Baker also observes this shift in his discussion
of Hurston's poetics.[9] Both theorists refer to a narrative voice that
"slips" from first person to second and third, singular and plural, like
the blurred notes played by a jazz guitarist. This is an important characteristic of point of view in *Another Good Loving Blues*. Throughout the first four chapters, the narrator's voice "slides" among various points of view. The result is a narrative that re-creates the oral
tradition of storytelling. It emphasizes the importance of storyteller-
audience interaction while positing a definition of identity as transient and amorphous rather than fixed. It is as if narrator, audience,
and characters participate in a game of musical chairs. In the following examples, italics are introduced to emphasize the shifts:

> It was nice being back on Beale. *He* could feel himself get-
> ting better every day, picking up new licks, stretching out, Beale
> did that to *you*, *you* either kept up or fell behind. Music was all
> around *you* and it was as important to other folks as it was to *you*.
> *You* constantly being exposed to new licks and *you* constantly
> growing. On Beale Street in those days *you* could live music. Mel-
> vira complained about the time *he* spent out. (67)

> *He* didn't hardly ever remember his daddy being sick, couldn't
> afford to be sick. Life sure was hard. *His* folks had worked hard all
> their lives and they were still struggling. Look like it don't ever
> let up on *you*, *you* just struggle on up to the day *you* die. When do
> *you* get to rest? *He* thought about how *he* had been out here hav-
> ing a good time and using up *his* life in the fast lane. (137)

The narrator's voice refers to the reader and the character as "he" and "you" to suggest that these identities are interchangeable. This shift from third person to second person also creates a community of reader, character, and narrator that has sympathetic understanding as its foundation. The narrator's repeated addresses to the reader, "you," facilitate the reader's identification with the character and the situation. Additional shifts occur at the conclusion of the novel, where the third-person point of view is interrupted by a shift to first person singular and plural. The latter, "us" refers to a present audience, a visible gathering of friends on the back porch, for example, and an untraceable audience of departed ancestors:

> Melvira scraped a shallow hole into Effie's grave with her fingers and put Hoodoo Maggie's mojohand in it. She savored Effie's approval. Yes, *I* know momma.
>
> The ancestors approve. She does well doesn't she? She does *us* proud. (209)

This passage extends the storyteller's community to include actors, audience, and ancestors—all of whom are transformed and regrouped. It also proffers a solution to mortality that is accessible via hoodoo and the blues. Whereas hoodoo provides transcendence by accessing the spirit world, the music achieves immortality through repetition. If Jake's death is the call that sets the novel in motion, Luke's response is its conclusion: "One day I'm gon do me a immortal blues Melvira. A blues that will still be here touching folk long after I'm dead and gone. A Luke Bodeen was here and he played a helluva blues blues. You can put that on my stone" (43).

Martin Swales concludes *The German Bildungsroman from Wieland to Hesse* by suggesting that his study provides a "model which can prove helpful in understanding certain kinds of contemporary fiction" (165). According to Swales, the study of the bildungsroman is especially helpful to understanding fiction authored by women because such writing focuses on identity-related subjects; however, "identity" and "self-knowledge"—the salient themes of the bildungsromans examined by Swales—are central to African American literature as well.[10]

This examination of two bildungsromans adds to the storehouse of information concerning literary self-consciousness in African American literature and the vernacular. Consistent with the findings produced in the previous chapter through the analysis of *The Temple of My Familiar* and *Middle Passage*, they make a persuasive argument on behalf of the eagerness among contemporary writers to use fiction as an opportunity to explore ideas about art: the process of artistic composition, its history and cultural contexts, and its influence on aesthetic traditions. They also draw attention to the fascination among writers with the craft of writing and with their lives and work, for artist-characters reveal their autobiographical underpinnings undisguised. Like Narcissus, these artists enjoy gazing at the reflections mirrored in their fiction.

African American writers such as Rita Dove and Arthur Flowers may view race and vernacular traditions differently. Their novels may urge rediscovery of aesthetic traditions or the assimilation of them with other aesthetic systems, but regardless of the context, their novels enact the African American tradition of literary self-consciousness.

Robert Scholes notes that "fantasy and irony" are "the two principal resources of metafiction" (109). While this may be an appropriate conclusion to his study of "four young American writers," four white male writers, it is an inaccurate description of metafiction by "others" (107). African American metafiction demonstrates that his categories fail to represent the variety of metafiction. "Fantasy," "irony," and "parody" are but a few of the many categories of metafiction. Instead of parody or irony, Dove and Flowers create metafiction that achieves self-consciousness through the ruminations of artist-protagonist blues heroes and their art.

Revision, Dialogism, and Intertextuality

Writing is a conversation with reading; a dialogue with thinking.

—Nikki Giovanni, *Racism 101*

Any study of metafiction must include a discussion of influence, for in the acknowledgment of literary predecessors, fiction demonstrates an awareness of its own status. Parody is perhaps the most frequently cited example of this type of literary self-consciousness, for repeated allusions to the work parodied serve as acknowledgments of a work's artifice. Whether motivated by a writer's desire to outdo his or her literary predecessors (as postulated by Harold Bloom) or by a writer's desire to connect and collaborate with literary ancestors (as assumed by Deborah McDowell and Mae Henderson), influence provides a porthole through which fiction can be viewed talking candidly about itself.

If "writing is a conversation with reading," as Giovanni suggests,

Ernest Gaines' *A Lesson before Dying* is conversant with the genre of African American crime fiction, particularly Richard Wright's *Native Son*.[1] Toni Morrison's *Tar Baby* is engaged in a different dialogue, which addresses Zora Neale Hurston's novel *Their Eyes Were Watching God* and the tar baby folktale. Because the tale has a history that includes numerous versions and transcriptions, Morrison establishes her own authority as storyteller by incorporating several of these versions into her own. Like the musician performing a live rendition of a recorded hit, Morrison's story pays tribute to earlier versions. Before examining these examples of influence, it will be helpful to review several theories of influence and the responses they have evoked from scholars of African American literature.

Harold Bloom's *The Anxiety of Influence* is the cornerstone of contemporary theories of influence. Borrowing from psychoanalysis, Bloom argues that poets have an oedipal relationship with their literary predecessors, and he identifies six strategies employed by writers in the symbolic slaying of those predecessors. Bloom's theory of revision has been criticized by feminists and multiculturalists whose interests exist beyond the periphery of Bloom's theory, and their revisions of Bloom's theory have produced additional theories.[2]

Henry Louis Gates' theory of literary ancestry is one revision, which incorporates Bloom's oedipal model into a theory of influence among African American male writers. Gates surveys the African American canon to identify three elements "which tend to be involved in the relationship of ancestry": "texts that provide models of form, texts that provide models of substance, and the text at hand" (*Signifying* 122). In an effort to be more accurate, Gates notes that many of the "canonical texts in the Afro-American tradition" wear a "two-toned Harlequin mask of influence": "they are related to other black texts primarily in terms of substance or content, whereas they seem to be related to Western texts in terms of form" (122). The ensuing discussion tests the fit of this harlequin mask.[3]

Deborah McDowell is more skeptical of Bloom's theory. She shares the difficulties experienced by many feminists who attempt to impose Bloom's theory of influence on women writers. While she acknowledges that some studies of relationships among black male writers seem to support Bloom's theory,[4] her analysis of Frances

Harper's influence on Alice Walker leads her to conclude that women's writing is not a manifestation of neurosis but a means of establishing community and "female bonding" among generations of writers ("'The Changing Same'" 105). She describes the limitations of Bloom's theory of revision and suggests an alternative:

> Bloom's linear theory of the oedipal war between literary fathers and sons does not obtain among black women writers, many of whom reverently acknowledge their debts to their literary foremothers. Unlike Bloom, I see literary influence, to borrow from Julia Kristeva, in the intertextual sense, each text in dialogue with all previous texts, transforming and retaining narrative patterns and strategies in endless possibility. ("'The Changing Same'" 107)

McDowell's preference for "intertextuality" typifies responses of scholars who are revising theories of influence to include relationships among women writers and their literary foremothers.[5] Scholars of African American literature and scholars of women's literature find it necessary to test the relevance of androcentric and Eurocentric theories of influence and posit alternative theories. They prefer dialogism and intertextuality because these acknowledge the ongoing interaction among works. Moreover, unlike revisionism, they are not "author-centered": they do not emphasize biographical studies of unresolved childhood complexes. Finally, they do not culminate in the production of a "severely limited canon in which strong poets compete with other similarly strong figures" (Clayton and Rothstein 9).

Unlike Bloom's theory of revision, Bakhtin's dialogism was not conceived as an explanation of literary influence. Its origins are neither psychology nor literary studies, and its application and relevance to the study of literature is an unanticipated benefit of an investigation of philosophy and rhetoric. Michael Holquist describes dialogism as "a version of relativity," which overturns the Hegelian dialectic by "insisting on differences that cannot be overcome" (20). Bakhtin adopts metaphors from literature to describe the epistemology of the self. He parallels self-invention with novel-writing:

I am always answerable *for* the response that is generated *from* the unique place I occupy in existence. My response begins to have a pattern; the dialogue I have with existence begins to assume the form of a text, a kind of book. A book, moreover, that belongs to a genre. In antiquity, too, the world was often conceived as a book, the text of *libri naturae*. Bakhtin conceives existence as the kind of book we call a novel, or more accurately as many novels (the radically manifold world proposed by Bakhtin looks much more like Borges' Library of Babel), for all of us write our own such text, a text that is then called our life. (Holquist 30)

Bakhtin's metaphors have been read as an open invitation to literary theorists who have long hypothesized the relationship between self and text. Bakhtin's literary metaphors make dialogism especially relevant to the study of metafiction; however, such analogies do not lead to a study of the *künstlerroman*, autobiography, or literary ancestry. Instead they direct attention to the plurality of languages and the multiplicity of voices present in the smallest unit of discourse:

The word, directed toward its object, enters a dialogically agitated and tension-filled environment of alien words, value judgments and accents, weaves in and out of complex interrelationships, merges with some, recoils from others, intersects with yet a third group: and all this may crucially shape discourse, may leave a trace in all its semantic layers, may complicate its expression and influence its entire stylistic profile. (Bakhtin 276)

Bakhtin's insistence on the importance of the social and historical dimensions of language further complicates this matrix:

The living utterance, having taken meaning and shape at a particular historical moment in a socially specific environment, cannot fail to brush up against thousands of living dialogic threads, woven by socio-ideological consciousness around the given object of an utterance; it cannot fail to become an active participant in social dialogue. After all, the utterance arises out of this dialogue as a continuation of it and as a rejoinder to it—it does not approach the object from the sidelines. (276–277)

Baker and Gates emphasize the social and historical dimensions of language in their discussions of double-voiced discourse and hybrid construction. Baker uses the latter to refer to "an utterance that belongs, by its grammatical (syntactic) and compositional markers, to a single speaker, but that actually contains mixed within it two utterances, two speech manners, two styles, two 'languages,' two semantic and axiological belief systems" (304). Gates employs the former, double-voiced discourse or "double-voicedness" in his definition of signifyin(g). Like the hybrid construction, double-voiced discourse refers to the multiple meanings.[6] Because it allows for "arbitrary substitution," Gates prefers this to Saussure's schema of "shifts in the relationship between the signified and the signifier":

> The masses, especially in a multiethnic society, draw on "arbitrary substitution" freely to disrupt the signifier by displacing its signified in an intentional act of will. Signifyin(g) is black double-voicedness; because it always entails formal revision and an intertextual relation . . . I find it an ideal metaphor for black literary criticism, for the formal manner in which texts seem concerned to address their antecedents. Repetition, with a signal difference, is fundamental to the nature of Signifyin(g). (*Signifying* 51)

Mae Henderson has also adapted Bakhtin's theories to the study of African American literature. Her essay "Speaking in Tongues" combines Mikhail Bakhtin's theory of dialogics with Hans-Georg Gadamer's theory of dialectics. She introduces Bakhtin's definition of consciousness to argue that "black women's speech/writing becomes . . . a dialogue between self and society and between self and psyche" (119). She uses Gadamer's dialectical model of conversation to argue that black women writers use language to develop community and consensus. She insists that black women writers speak in a "plurality of voices as well as a multiplicity of discourses" (122): "black women writers enter into testimonial discourse with black men as with white women as women, and with black women as black women. At the same time, they enter into a competitive discourse with black men as women, with white women as blacks, and with white men as black women" (121).

Responses to Bloom's theory of revision point to the importance of gender. Gates employs Bloom's theory of revision in his analysis of literary ancestry, but feminists dismiss it in favor of intertextuality and dialogism. McDowell and Henderson argue that Bloom's paradigm is not applicable to black women's writing. Gates, Henderson, and McDowell borrow from dialogism to describe relationships between contemporary writers and their predecessors. All seize the opportunity to discuss voice as polyphonic and dialogic. Finally, McDowell and Henderson incorporate the dialogic definition of identity as indeterminate and ever-changing. This chapter will test these theories on Ernest J. Gaines' *A Lesson before Dying* and Toni Morrison's *Tar Baby*. Each analysis will commence with a discussion of the text's relationship to its predecessors and will advance to an analysis of the polyphonic voice and dialogic utterance.

Ernest Gaines has repeatedly denied Wright's influence on his work. But this denial suggests his affinities with Wright, for, like Wright, who describes his "association with white writers" as the "life preserver of my hope to depict Negro life in fiction" in the essay "How Bigger Was Born" (Wright xvi), Gaines has repeatedly spoken of the importance of white writers in shaping his own style. In a 1969 interview for the *New Orleans Review*, he cites Ernest Hemingway, Ivan Turgenev, F. Scott Fitzgerald, William Faulkner, James Joyce, and Leo Tolstoy for teaching him to "get what was in me onto the paper" (Simpson 113). As if looking in the mirror to describe his own harlequin mask, Gaines compares the influence and abilities of white writers with those of black writers: "They [white writers] showed me how to get it much better than the black writers had done because so many of them really dealt with style, whereas the black writers are much more interested in content—you know, putting it down like it is—and the style is sort of secondary" (Simpson 113–114). Nineteen years later, Gaines repeated this in an interview with Marcia Gaudet and Carl Wooton. He spoke definitively: "No black writer had influence on me" (*Callaloo* 229). He said that although

Invisible Man and *Native Son* were the subject of much discussion and imitation by writers of his generation, "*Native Son* would not have had an influence on me had I read it" (*Callaloo* 231). Gaines explained that the urban experience central to Wright's work was alien to his own experiences and that though he tried for a short time to claim New Orleans as his place of birth, he could not do so convincingly because his experiences in rural Louisiana were all he knew and all he wanted to write about (*Callaloo* 231). Valerie Babb summarizes these experiences as commencing with Gaines' birth into the fifth generation of a family on River Lake Plantation in Pointe Coupeé Parish, Louisiana. He was christened Baptist, attended Catholic school, and was raised by his aunt, Augustine Jefferson, who shares her surname with the protagonist of *A Lesson before Dying*. According to Babb, Aunt Jefferson traveled all over southern Louisiana selling cosmetics and speaking Creole (*Ernest Gaines* 1). These are the experiences that serve as the source of Gaines' fiction. They may also provide insight into the writer's confession that *Bloodline* was influenced by his favorite black writer, another Southerner, Jean Toomer (Gaudet and Wooton, *Porch Talk* 34).

In spite of his denial of Wright's influence, scholars have noted Gaines' affinities to Wright. Jeffrey J. Folks observes that Gaines resembles Wright in his "bitterly ironic response to the 'New' South" (33). Babb compares Gaines' sixth novel, *A Gathering of Old Men*, to *Native Son*, observing how Bigger and the old men must act "to achieve the self-affirmation society has denied them" (*Ernest Gaines* 112). Gaines' seventh novel, *A Lesson before Dying*, continues this investigation of identity, wrestling self-affirmation from an innocent protagonist wrongly accused and sentenced to die. Like Detective Roger Garrison in the Chester Himes crime novel *A Case of Rape*, Gaines demonstrates how race affects the criminal-justice system. In "How Bigger Was Born," Wright refers to the case of "some Negro boy being picked up off the streets as a plot which occurred over and over again" (*Native Son* xxvii). This is the plot that inspires *Native Son* and *A Lesson before Dying*. Both novels mingle fact and fiction in developing this story line into a novel. While Wright makes use of the trial of Earl Hick and Robert Nixon, Gaines plays investigative reporter by visiting rural prisons, examining cells, and talking to inmates.[7]

Folks and Babb lay the groundwork for an investigation of Wright's influence. In "Old Fashioned Modernism: 'The Changing Same' in *A Lesson before Dying*," Babb suggests that the "major attributes of modernism, a break from accepted history and an experiment with artistic forms, characterized all the fiction of Gaines" (251). Her examination of narrative technique—orality, literacy, and communal narration—provides evidence of Wright's influence, as does her suggestion that Gaines is an "old-fashioned" modernist.[8]

Gaines' assertion that he has not been influenced by black writers or by *Native Son* seems suspect when one examines his *A Lesson before Dying*, for the novel reads as a detailed response to the suppositions set forth by Richard Wright. There are three explanations for this. First, there is the 1993 publication date of *A Lesson before Dying*, which suggests that it was being written when the Modern Library unabridged edition of Wright's novel was being publicized. Discussion of the novel was a part of the environment in which Gaines labored. Second, Wright's novel is a mainstay in the canons of American and African American literatures. Although Gaines says he did not read Wright's novel because it wasn't part of the 1950s college curriculum, as a teacher and student of African American literature, he was surely familiar with it forty years later. Finally, Kristeva and Bakhtin provide convincing arguments that influence exists irrespective of the writer's intentions.[9]

Like Wright, Gaines choose the Jim Crow era as the setting for his novel. Other similarities are evident in the novels' plots. The catalyst that prompts the story's action is the robbing of a liquor store. Although this crime *does not* occur in *Native Son*, it is contemplated by Bigger and his friends, who plan to rob Blum's liquor store. On his way to the White Rabbit Bar, Jefferson is intercepted by Brother and Bear en route to the store. The proprietor, Brother, and Bear are killed during the attempted robbery. When the police arrive, they find Jefferson dazed and dumbfounded and take him into custody. Hence Gaines' novel investigates what *would have happened* if Bigger and his friends had proceeded with their plans. Moreover, the outcome of the robbery in Gaines' novel validates Bigger's reticence. In this way, the latter text enters into dialogue with the former. Gaines' revision of Wright's story is an example of signifyin(g). Like Count Basie's version of Oscar Peterson's "Signifying," Gaines "stretches the form" of Wright's text. His signifyin(g) creates a dialogue between what the listener or reader expects and what the artist plays or writes (*Signifying* 123). Readers familiar with Wright's novel expect the plans to fall through, but Gaines defies their expectations by having the robbery occur. In this way, he signifies on Wright's text.

Gates' idea of "stretching the form" is compatible with Bloom's theory, and Gaines' novel provides evidence of both. One of Bloom's six techniques of revision is "clinamen." It refers to instances in which a writer revises the work of his predecessor for the purpose of correction. Bloom identifies clinamen as "poetic misreading or misprision proper": A poet swerves away from his precursor by reading his precursor's poems so as to execute a clinamen in relation to them. This appears as a corrective movement in his own poem, which implies that the precursor's poem went accurately up to a certain point, but then should have swerved, precisely in the direction that the new poem moves (14).

Revision for purposes of "correction" may provide an explanation for the next difference as well. Whereas Bigger commits several crimes—the murders of Bessie and Mary, forgery, and ransom—Jefferson commits only petty crimes. This clinamen has two consequences: it eliminates the most frequently cited defect in *Native Son*: the long-winded attorney, Boris Max, who lectures on Bigger as a victim of centuries of oppression and on racism as the formidable foe of society; and it reveals the injustices of the law in the sentencing of an indisputably innocent man. Unlike what occurs in *Native Son*, in *A Lesson before Dying*, the protagonist's criminal activities do not obscure recognition of the injustices of verdict and sentence.

The death sentence propels Bigger and Jefferson on the journey of self-discovery. Houston Baker characterizes journeys such as theirs as "the theory underlying Afro-American experience": "to figure out who the *me* is 'let me go on living today,' who the *I* is who's doing the speaking" (Bérubé 556). Incarceration precipitates a relentless self-study, during which Bigger and Jefferson become aware of how racism has defined them. Bigger takes a huge step toward self-definition when he acknowledges Max's concern for him and another when he recognizes murder as a means of self-definition: "I didn't want to kill!" Bigger shouted. "But what I killed for, I *am*! It must've been pretty deep in me to make me kill! I must have felt it awfully hard to murder" (501).

Jefferson's incarceration leads him down a different path. Like Max's visits to Bigger, visits from the schoolchildren, neighbors, and friends precipitate the change. While Bigger's self-affirmation results from the crime, Jefferson's realization of who he is circumvents the events of the crime and fixes on the events of the trial when the prosecutor questions his humanity. Jefferson invents an identity in answer to these rhetorical questions asked by the prosecutor:

> Do you see a man sitting here? Do you see a modicum of intelligence? Do you see anyone that could plan a murder, a robbery, can plan—can plan anything? Ask him does Christmas come before or after the Fourth of July? Ask him to describe a rose, to quote one passage from the Constitution or the Bill of Rights. . . . I surely did not mean to insult your intelligence by saying "man"; —would you please forgive me for committing such an error? What justice would there be to take his life? Justice, gentleman? Why, I would just as soon put a hog in the electric chair as this. (8)

Jefferson's godmother becomes obsessed with the attorney's closing remarks: "I don't want them to kill no hog . . . I want a man to go to that chair, on his own two feet" (13). Her determination that Jefferson become a man initiates a transformation that concludes on the closing pages of Jefferson's prison journal (255). His self-affirmation occurs in the writing of this journal.

Reminiscent of the writing that Gaines admires in Toomer's *Cane*, this diary excerpt locates self-creation in its vernacular context by making it a part of the creation of the cosmos and natural world:

> day breakin
> sun comin up
> the bird in the tre soun like a blu bird
> sky blu blu mr wigin
> good by mr wigin tell them im strong tell them im a man (234)

These jailhouse blues illustrate Jefferson's mastery of the "me" and the "I" that Baker refers to in his theorizing of African American experience, for the "I" or subject who describes the day becomes the "me" or object that Mr. Wiggins will describe. Bigger's inability to correlate subjective and objective experiences leads Craig Werner to describe him as a thwarted blues musician whose "inability to sound a call *is* his call" ("Bigger's Blues" 147). Jefferson's call is sounded on God's trombone, the instrument that James Weldon Johnson selects to describe the voice of the black preacher. Figurative language, rhythm, alliteration, repetition, an address to a specific audience, and an invocation for a response locate Jefferson's prose poem in the folk tradition. While Jefferson finds the voice and the words he needs to invent himself, Bigger's disassociation from vernacular expressive traditions renders him silent. In "How Bigger Was Born," Wright describes Bigger's disassociation as "the quirk of circumstance that estranged him from the religion and folk culture of his race" (Wright xiii). In her effort to illustrate the presence of the oral tradition in Jefferson's diary, Babb overlooks the issue of literacy and writing. As if apologizing for a weakness in the novel, she says: "This portion of the novel might seem to place an inordinate importance on the written word, one particularly uncharacteristic of an author so heavily steeped in the oral tradition, yet it is in actuality a segment that strikes a balance between the written and the oral. It is the power of the written word that assists in transforming Jefferson but this is a written word strongly overlaid by the oral cadence of Jefferson's speech" ("Modernism" 262).

By giving Jefferson a pencil and a tablet, Gaines signifies on the trope of the talking book and the role of literacy in the crusade for civil rights.[10] Writing is evidence that the black man is not a hog, but—as Jefferson writes—a "youman" (230). Jefferson's phonetic spelling inverts the attorney's argument by evoking the role of literacy in the history of civil rights. Moreover, as a book-within-a-book, the diary figures as a metafictional exploration of writing process. Jefferson's text is prefaced by the words of Grant Wiggins, whose schoolteacher English provides the same role of authentication as that of the amanuensis-editor introducing a slave narrative. Finally, it is Jefferson's vernacular text that Paul delivers to the bereaved com-

munity waiting on bended knee for word of Jefferson's death. It becomes a sacred text, a holy book housed in the tabernacle of a one-
room schoolhouse.

Jefferson discovers a vernacular voice with which he writes himself into being, transforming himself from hog to "youman." Unlike Bigger, whose identity is defined and described by others, Jefferson controls the meaning of his life and death through transcription of his experiences into the vernacular. The prison guards who
previously rough-handled Jefferson fear and respect him when they
learn of his writing. Hence Jefferson's writing extends beyond self-
definition to the defining of others. Barbara Johnson, in her analysis
of reading and writing in *Native Son*, notes that in their search for a
suspect, the police overlook the clues revealed in the ransom note:
Bigger's black English. Unlike the authorities in *A Lesson before
Dying*, the authorities in *Native Son* are deaf as well as blind to the
voice of the vernacular. While Wright's novel casts the vernacular as
invisible, Gaines invests it with the power to define the self and
others.

A second category of revision appropriate to this discussion is the
tessera, which Bloom defines as "the completion and antithesis" of
a predecessor's work (14). Bloom explains: "I take the word not from
mosaic-making, where it is still used, but from the ancient mystery
cults, where it meant a token of recognition, the fragment say of a
small pot which with the other fragments would re-constitute the
vessel. A poet antithetically 'completes' his precursor, by so reading
the parent-poem as to retain its terms but to mean them in another
sense as though the precursor had failed to go far enough" (14).

Gaines reassembles the events in *Native Son*, giving them different meanings. Both novels have tripartite organization. *Native Son*
contains three books—"Fear," "Flight," and "Fate"—narrated by a
third person. Gaines' novel is composed of three sections, narrated
by Wiggins, Jefferson, and the community-at-large. While both begin
with a description of the crime and the "fear" that follows, their
paths diverge thereafter. While Wright's "Flight" section depicts Bigger's escape and the police chase, the middle section of *A Lesson Before Dying* focuses on the many visitors to Jefferson's cell. Bigger's
physical "flight" is answered by Jefferson's metaphoric or spiritual
flight. There is no flight for the incarcerated Jefferson except as it is

described by Wiggins. This passage begins with an invocation of Bigger's ghost and directs Jefferson on a path of self-invention:

> You—you can be bigger than anyone you have ever met. Please listen to me, because I would not lie to you now. I speak from my heart. You have the chance of being bigger than anyone who has ever lived on that plantation or come from this little town. You can do it if you try. You have seen how Mr. Farrell makes a slingshot handle. He starts with just a little piece of rough wood—any little piece of scrap wood—then he starts cutting. Cutting and cutting and cutting, then shaving. Shaves it down clean and smooth till it's not what it was before, but something new and pretty. You know what I'm talking about, because you've seen him do it. You had one that he made from a piece of scrap wood. Yes, yes—I saw you with it. And it came from a piece of old wood that he found in the yard somewhere. And that's all we are, Jefferson, all of us on this earth, a piece of drifting wood, until we— each one of us, individually—decide to become something else. I am still that piece of drifting wood, and those out there are no better. But you can be better. Because we need you to be and want you to be. Me, your godmother, the children, and all the rest of them in the quarter. Do you understand what I'm saying to you, Jefferson? Do you? (193)

Like Jimmy in Gaines' previous novel, *The Autobiography of Miss Jane Pittman*, Jefferson finds himself the center of the community's hopes and aspirations. His final days are used to debunk the myth of the black man's inferiority, and he is willingly exploited to accomplish these ends. This contrasts with the middle section of *Native Son*, which describes a physical rather than spiritual flight. The closings of the novels coincide in their descriptions of the final days before the execution. Gaines has refashioned the events of *Native Son*, expanding on a minor event in the opening of the novel, portraying a metaphoric rather than a literal flight in the middle, and concluding, like *Native Son*, with a description of the final events of the protagonist's life. Gaines rearranges and reassembles fragments from Wright's work.

Studies of narrative and discourse have led scholars of both novels to describe them as modernist texts. Recent criticism of *Native Son* has provided a reappraisal of what has long been casually dismissed as its objective point of view. John M. Reilly cites examples of indirect discourse to demonstrate the narrator's partiality.[11] Probing "the hermeneutical complexities generated by the act of narration," Laura E. Tanner shows how the narrator uses a master language to undercut the experiential, nonlinguistic world that Bigger inhabits.[12] Werner describes these contrasting discourses as modernist and folk (147). These discussions of narrative voice validate the presence of heteroglossia. Although critics recognize competing discourses among the words spoken by the Daltons, the journalists, the narrator, and Bigger, by centering their discussions on the narrator and sharing his discourse or master language, they privilege unitary language and the centralization of the verbal-ideological world. Bakhtin's understanding of unitary language and ideological centralization as dialogic provide an alternate reading of *Native Son*. Bakhtin observes that "alongside the centripetal force, the centrifugal forces of language carry on their uninterrupted work; alongside verbal-ideological centralization and unification, the uninterrupted process of decentralization and disunification go forward" (272). Regardless of the critic's sympathies, the critic's discourse opposes heteroglossia and disunification. The alternative is present in Bigger's carnivalesque laughter, which horrifies Max because it puts Bigger beyond the realm of humanity. Like the wailing saxophone, it articulates a nonlinguistic blues response. It is a wail, a howl, a riff—a blues response inimitable in the critic's language.

Gaines has spoken about the obsolescence of the third-person point of view and the increasing importance of the first person in American fiction.[13] Babb has studied the oral tradition in Gaines' fiction and observed the three-part structure of the narrative that composes *A Lesson before Dying*: the first section is narrated by Grant; the second is the diary authored by Jefferson; and the third is the communal narrative of the townspeople on the day of Jefferson's execution. All these narratives are told from the first-person point of view even though Jefferson is their subject. This collection of first-person voices constitutes a heteroglossia that cannot be centrifuged by a master language. As subject of his own narrative as well as those of others, Jefferson fulfills the requisite "I" and "me" categories that Baker identifies as central to the African American experience.

The narrator of the first part is the schoolteacher, Grant Wiggins, who becomes involved at the request of his grandmother, a friend of Jefferson's godmother. His voice dominates the first part of the novel. It is a literary and vernacular voice. Although Wiggins' education distinguishes his writing from Bigger's and Jefferson's, his writing recreates the cadence of the speaking voice. Vocabulary and sentence structure suggest the ease and spontaneity of speech. It casts the "I" and "me" of Baker's theory as a Du Boisian double-consciousness. Balanced in symmetrical sentences, they accumulate to resemble Jefferson's prose poetry. In the following passage, Wiggins weighs what he thinks against what others think of him. The result is two voices joined to create hybrid discourse: "Inez left the kitchen as soon as the white men came in. I tried to decide just how I should respond to them. Whether I should act like the teacher that I was, or the nigger that I was supposed to be. I decided to wait and see how the conversation went. To show too much intelligence would have been an insult to them. To show a lack of intelligence would have been a greater insult to them. I decided to wait and see how the conversation would go" (47).

When his aunt asks him to visit Jefferson and help make him a "man," Grant says, "Now his godmother wants me to visit him and make him know—prove to these white men—that he's not a hog, that he's a man. I'm supposed to make him a man. Who am I? God?" (31). Skeptical of religion, critical of its role to pacify, he nevertheless acquiesces to play God and assist Jefferson in his transformation into a hero whose death will fortify the community. Distrustful of God and religion, he imagines his omnipotence in the world of writers and books. Like most writers, he is inspired by his reading rather than by a vision of reality.[14] A short story by James Joyce inspires his re-creation of Jefferson:

> I read the story and reread the story, but I still could not find the universality that the little Irishman had spoken of. All I saw in the story was some Irishmen meeting in a room and talking politics. What had that to do with America, especially with my

people? It was not until years later that I saw what he meant. I
had gone to bars, to barbershops; I had stood on street corners and
I had gone to many suppers there in the quarter. But I had never
really listened to what was being said. Then I began to listen, to
listen closely to how they talked about their heroes, how they
talked about the dead and about how great the dead had once
been. I heard it everywhere.

The old men down at the end of the bar were still talking about
Jackie Robinson. But I was not thinking about Jackie now, or Joe
Louis, or the little Irishman; I was thinking about that cold, de-
pressing cell uptown. (90)

Wiggins acknowledges Joyce's influence as candidly as Gaines
does. However, this epiphany suggests that Joyce's influence extends
beyond characterization. Wiggins confirms Gaines' assertion that
writers like Joyce provided him with the technique, the "how to say
it," while his own experiences provided the content. This seems to
confirm Gates' theory of the harlequin mask of influence, but on
closer observation it appears that Gaines' mask sits askew. His allusions to folktales, his investigation of the "me" and the "I" and
double-consciousness, his experimentation with multiple narrators,
hybrid discourse, and heteroglossia, which resists the centripetal
forces of unification, references to literacy and its role in African
American history suggest that Gaines' mask is a checkerboard of influences, reflecting those of white writers as well as those of Richard
Wright and the genre of African American crime fiction. Influence in
A Lesson before Dying is best described by McDowell and Henderson, who argue that it is a signpost of community. Retelling stories
is not a means of slaying the father but is instead a tribute to the
community and homage to the ancestors.

Influence extends beyond the circumference of literary ancestors
to include the extra-literary influences of folklore and oral literature.
Studies of these influences are complicated by the continual reworking of the material by anthropologists, folklorists, linguists, writers,
and storytellers who account for a complicated lineage of predecessors. Like Gaines' revision of *Native Son*, Morrison's revision of
the tar baby tale undermines a central consciousness and a single

authoritative voice. It subordinates unitary discourse with the discourse of heteroglossia. Use of multiple points of view, a Greek chorus of anthropomorphic vegetation, and metaphor fracture discourse.

Like l'Arbe de la Croix, the house designed by the Mexican architect and built by Haitian laborers, *Tar Baby* combines influences from different aesthetic traditions, but most theories of influence do not encompass this diversity. Although Bloom and McDowell differ in their understandings of the causes and effects of influence among writers, their theories study influence among writers from similar artistic traditions. Bloom's theory of revision is a study of influence among Western writers. Deborah McDowell develops a theory of influence founded on readings by black women writers. Influenced by Western, African, and African American literatures, the novel *Tar Baby* exists beyond the domain of either of these theories. Just as l'Arbe de la Croix is filled with intricately carved window sashes and ill-fitting panes, the novel is a synthesis of the "craft and art" of diverse artistic traditions (3).

Tar Baby has its foundations in folk mythology, as does *Song of Solomon*, but it proposes a different interpretation of history and its significance. While *Song of Solomon* describes Milkman's acceptance of and entry into the myth of the flying African as a process of de-Westernization, *Tar Baby* has its origins in a myth that asserts the impossibility of disengaging African American culture from Western culture.

Morrison's choice of the tar baby story as the subject of this novel reveals changes in her thinking. Whereas her choice of the myth of the flying African as the subject of *Song of Solomon* suggests the nationalistic objectives of transmitting cultural history and demonstrating its relevance to a contemporary black audience, her choice of the tar baby story, a story shaped by and familiar to both blacks and whites, suggests the altered objective of examining the interplay of cultures. This interplay is articulated in the interracial origins of the myth—generations of black and white Americans. It is voiced in the allegorical significance of the myth: Brer Rabbit is held fast by Brer Fox's tar baby. It is reinforced in the relationship between the Streets and Ondine and Sydney, their servants, and between Son and Jadine. Finally, it reverberates in the novel's synthesis of "craft and

art," the functional folk art of the Caribbean natives and the nonrepresentational postmodern aesthetics of self-exiled Americans.

If we acknowledge Morrison's use of the tar baby story as inher-
ently descriptive of the inextricability of African American culture
from its Western context, it must also be understood as a response to
the ethnological perspective embodied in Joel Chandler Harris' approach to it. The following passage from the introduction of *Nights
with Uncle Remus* reveals this perspective. Here, in a strategic effort
to assume authorial control over his material and establish its cre-
dence and reliability as a primary source of African American folklore, Harris attempts to raise suspicions about the accuracy of the
myths transcribed by those "educated natives" who share a greater
degree of intimacy with them:

> Theal, in the preface to his collection of Kaffir Tales, lays great
> stress upon the fact that the tales he gives "have all undergone a
> thorough revision by a circle of natives." It is more likely that his
> carefulness in this respect has led him to overlook a body of folk-
> lore among the Kaffirs precisely similar to that which exists
> among the negroes of the Southern States. If comparative evi-
> dence is worth anything,—and it may be worthless in this in-
> stance,—the educated natives have cooked the stories to suit
> themselves. (xvii)

Although there are many versions of the tale, Harris establishes
the criteria of objectivity to argue that the reliability of his research
is significantly greater than that which issues from scholarship based
on direct personal experience, the experience of the natives. It is,
however, paradoxical that the very values embodied in the subject
of his research, African American folklore, contradict his preference
for objective knowledge over direct personal experience. Moreover,
many of the stories that Harris transcribes allegorize this distinction
in the personalities of Brer Rabbit and Brer Fox.

Morrison makes use of this in establishing Valerian's relationship
to Son. Although Valerian confines his reading to the subject of botany and maintains correspondence with nurseries only, he needs Son
to tell him that mirrors, not thalomide-soaked muslin, will keep the

ants away from the greenhouse, and "shaking up" is what the stubbornly uncooperative cyclamen need to bloom (127). The catalogs on botany, like Harris' catalog of African American folklore, are rooted in the tradition of scientific objectivism, which is here criticized for omitting information retrievable by other systems of knowledge, particularly those that place a greater value on personal experience. "Black magic!" cries Valerian upon seeing his cyclamen in full bloom, and it is this "black magic" that Harris' ethnological position paradoxically excludes.

Morrison's "cooked" version of the story incorporates the personal. It is, to paraphrase Harris, "cooked to suit herself" and "cooked" according to Reed's recipe for "The Neo-HooDoo Aesthetic" in which the proportions of ingredients used "depend upon the cook."[15] Son's reflections on his possible discovery aboard *Seabird II* show the cook at work. Familiar with folktales and the oral tradition, he relies on improvisation to help him talk his way out of an unpleasant situation. Awaiting discovery aboard *Sea Bird II*, he realizes, "it was better not to plan, not to have a ready-made story because, however tight, prepared stories sounded most like a lie" (3). Son's explanation of his storytelling provides insights into Morrison's "cooking." Whereas Harris attempts to achieve authorial control by impressing his readers with the accuracy of his transcriptions, an accuracy that cannot be matched by the educated natives who are more concerned with cooking the stories to suit themselves, Morrison asserts her power as storyteller in the very fact that she cooks. For her, improvisation on the mythic theme is quintessential to its telling.

While Harris' insistence that his version preempt all others is executed in attacking the accuracy resulting from methods employed by rival storytellers, Morrison makes a place for her story by displacing accuracy as the primary criterion of evaluation. She argues this by pointing to its negligible value within the African American storytelling tradition. Creative improvisation, not accuracy and repeatability, is the tradition's mandate to storytellers.

In an interview with Nellie McKay, Morrison describes this improvisational quality of black storytelling and her efforts to capture it in her writings:

The fact is that the stories look as though they come from people who are not even authors. No author tells these stories. They are just told—meanderingly—as though they are going in several directions at the same time. The open-ended quality that is sometimes a problematic in the novel form reminds me of the uses to which stories are put in the black community. The stories are constantly being imagined within a framework. And I hook in to this like a life-support system, which for me, is the thing out of which I come. (427)

The framework that serves as Morrison's "life-support system" is the African American tradition of storytelling. Central to that tradition is the improvisational quality suggested by "meandering" about ready-made stories. Understanding these as assertions of the need for an aesthetic rooted in black culture suggests, though, only a partial understanding of their significance, one that omits consideration of the tar baby story's interracial content and historical context. These define a more complex aesthetic, which acknowledges the incorporation of Western traditions in black culture. More important, however, it suggests the political ideology that generates self-consciousness in African American literature.

In Harris' version of the tar baby story, Brer Fox makes a figure of tar and places it in a field visited by the rabbits. The fox then hides in the woods and observes the rabbit's anger when the tar baby does not respond to his greeting. Unable to control his anger, the rabbit strikes and sticks to the tar. The fox then comes out of hiding and taunts the rabbit. Harris' version of the tale ends here:

> "Did the Fox eat the Rabbit?" asked the little boy to whom the story had been told.
> "Dat's all de fur de tale goes," replied the old man. "He mount, en den again he moutent. Some say Jedge B'ar come 'long en lossed 'im—some say he didn't." [16]

Other versions end more happily for Brer Rabbit. In another popular version of the tale, the Rabbit uses "reverse psychology" to outsmart the Fox. [17] This version is interesting for its allegorical significance, which is readily apparent in the fox's strategy for killing the rabbit. First he plans to roast him over a "big hot fire." Then the fox plans to hang him, drown him, and skin him. Finally the fox does what the rabbit begs him not to do: he throws the rabbit in the briar patch. Brer Fox thinks he has succeeded in killing Brer Rabbit, but the rabbit scrambles out of the bushes crying, "Whup-pee, my God, you couldn't throw me in a better place! There where my mammy born me, in the briar patch" (Hughes 2).

Morrison incorporates both versions in the conclusion of her own. The first version, the one that concludes with the rabbit held fast, produces the understanding that Son has returned to the island to find Jadine and that he will search until he finds her. The second version of the story, the one in which the rabbit escapes, suggests that Son joins the horsemen, merging with the myth of the chevaliers and escaping the snares of tar baby Jadine. The inconclusive ending of this novel is reminiscent of the ending of *Song of Solomon*. Interpretation depends on what the reader believes takes place after the novel ends, how strongly the reader believes the folktales on which the novel is based. Morrison insists on the active participation of her readers in the story's construction. She calls this reader involvement "co-conspiracy," but it is a variation of the antiphonal interaction that exists between preacher and congregation, musician and audience ("Unspeakable Things" 23).

African and African American storytelling influences are also evident in the characterizations of Son and Alma. He is, of course, a trickster, a man "without human rites" and documentation (142), a man who can assume different forms and perform magic.[18] He moves easily from the realm of myth, the world of the chevaliers, to the "real" world. Like most of the gods in the African pantheon, he has a female counterpart: Alma, descendant of Thérèse. But even she, disguised in her red wig and school uniform, does not recognize her power. It remains hidden until she is denied the attentions of Son and the sisterhood of Jadine. She comes into her power when she tells Son a story about Jadine's departure: "She had seen the American girl getting on a plane bound for Paris with a huge bag on her shoulder and a black fur coat and that she had been met by a young man with yellow hair and blue eyes and white skin and they had laughed and kissed and laughed in the corridor outside the ladies' room and had held hands and walked to the plane and she had her head on his shoulder the whole time they walked to the plane" (258).

Alma's storytelling has the desired effect. Like the African storyteller, she invents the story for her audience. She knows that the description of Jadine and her boyfriend will cause Son pain. He hears Alma's story and realizes he is "stuck and revolted by the possibility of being freed" of his feelings for Jadine (259). He succumbs to despair and merges with the myths of the horsemen and the tar baby. This is adequate recompense for his negligence and hypocrisy. Like the Streets, who neglect to learn Thérèse's and Gidéon's names, Son does "not go to the trouble of knowing her [Alma's] name" (258). The pain her story causes him is also recompense for his hypocrisy: he espouses black culture and black heritage with nationalistic fervor but dismisses the woman who could give these to him in the pursuit of an unapologetic assimilationist. Alma is empowered as a storyteller and a prophet who orchestrates the final events in the novel.

Storytelling and authoring are central to the discussion of influence and artistic traditions in *Tar Baby*. Like Alma's storytelling, Son's storytelling incorporates features of oral tradition such as the didacticism apparent in Son's re-creation of the folktale of farmer and rabbit for Jadine. Jadine covers her ears, unwilling to confront her resemblance to the folk character. Acquiescing to the importance of the audience for successful improvisation, Son lets "the sex, weight," and "the demeanor of whomever he encountered inform and determine his tale" (3). Like Alma, he resembles the African griot who invents a story to suit his or her audience. Morrison also improvises on a well-known story to suit her audience.

Countering this is the aesthetic inheritance of the Streets: the postmodern world. Not only are the Streets incapable of telling stories, but their stories and myths are dysfunctional. Prodigal sons never return. Christmas loses its magic. The Streets are victims of the literature of exhaustion. Distrustful of language, they are unable to communicate. Margaret is mistaken for drunk because she forgets "the names and uses of things," stuffs a princess phone in her purse, wonders if lipstick is for "licking or writing your name" (46). Valerian reads only catalogs on botany, "having given up books because the

language in them had changed so much—stained with rivulets of dis-
order and meaninglessness" (11). Like John Marcher in Henry James'
The Beast in the Jungle, Valerian waits for a message worthy of deliv-
ery. At the close of the novel, he is silenced, unable to speak except
by making his "fingers dance in the air" (247). The master and king
is silenced; his signing is unintelligible.

One cannot discuss the conclusion of the novel without also con-
sidering Jadine's fate. She inspires Alma's storytelling and establishes
her connection to the animal world. She resembles the queen ant
who is haunted by the memory of "the man who fucked like a star"
(251). Poised in flight, she resembles Milkman and summons an image of the flying African. Though her flight can be read as a renunciation of her heritage and her ancient properties, it is also a subtle re-
enactment of a very powerful story about African American heritage
and the strength and vitality of African ancestry. Moreover, when Jadine chooses to return to Europe, she chooses a path that many black
American expatriates chose. She has chosen not to have Son's babies,
but she has chosen to have someone else's. Is this then a complete
renunciation of her "ancient properties" or is it an enactment of
them in a modern rather than an ancient world? Some critics are
quick to condemn Jadine and are unable to forgive her for her disregard of family and what she "owes," but others see her as a positive
character who represents the breakthroughs and triumphs of self-sufficient black women.[19] This understanding of Jadine provides yet another reading of the tar baby tale, one in which Son plays the role of
the tar baby. A final possibility is to see Jadine and Son as each other's
mutual "tar baby." Trudier Harris concludes her discussion of the
folkloric elements in *Tar Baby* with a similar observation:

> Morrison's use of the tar baby folktale in her novel allows for pro-
> vocative mixtures of tricksters, tar babies, and victims. As is true
> with all her works, she makes it impossible to delineate clearly
> agents of good and evil; qualification of some sort is always neces-
> sary. By assigning Son, Valerian, and Jadine overlapping parts of
> the tar baby trickster interactions, Morrison gives new dimen-
> sions to the racial and sexual dynamics inherent in that folktale.
> More important, she saturates her novel with a folkloristic base

designed to illustrate that the powerful and the powerless are as much victims of their own imaginations as they are of the trickster-generated actions in which they are sometimes caught. (126–127)

In her dialogic reading of *Beloved*, Deborah Ayer Sitter discusses the centripetal force of Morrison's narrative circumlocution (the retelling of the same story many different times), her "manipulation of narrative point of view," and her construction of metaphors that "accumulate an almost inexhaustible range of meaning" (20). These techniques are present in *Tar Baby* as well.

Narrative circumlocution occurs on several levels. Morrison's retelling of the tar baby story to include multiple versions has already been noted. Son's telling of the tar baby tale to Jadine is another example of narrative circumlocution. This *mise en abyme* provides an allegory of the story Son and Jadine are enacting at the moment it is told. Jadine's interjections—"Don't you touch me," "You better kill me," and "I am going to kill you"—interrupt his story, resulting in the entanglement of the two tar baby tales (232–33). Although Jadine objects to being a character in a fictional tale, both she and her objections are inscribed in the story. Though she may do everything she can to avoid and devalue folk culture, she cannot escape her role as a folk character. Regardless of who is the farmer, the fox, or the tar baby, Jadine's interjections foreshadow the tale's conclusion. In a desperate effort to avoid being trapped like a rabbit in tar, Jadine flees via the escape route, memory. Although she avoids hearing the conclusion of the tale, she is transported into an equally unpleasant story, this one a tar baby of her own invention. She recalls the mother-daughter days celebrated at college when she had no one with whom she could sing, sway, and hold hands around the beech bathed in moonlight (233). Bereft of the relationship that serves as a bridge in the intergenerational transmission of folk culture, Jadine learns to equate freedom with cultural exclusion. She is threatened by anyone—Son, Ondine, the swamp women—who attempts to inscribe her into the folk culture and its tales. Unfortunately, this limits her abilities to tell her own story as well. Her rejection of the vernacular makes her a cook unable to improvise and thus dependent on recipes like the ones she reads about in *Vogue* and *Elle*, "a rich and tacky menu of dishes Easterners thought up for Westerners in order to indispose them" (37).

Son "unorphans" Jadine, giving her both family and a legacy of stories that can be "cooked" any way *they* like (197). This romance inspires both artists. Sharing a life with Jadine in New York enables Son, the jazz pianist, to regard her as "a woman who is not only a woman but also a sound, all the music he ever wanted to play" (257). Jadine resumes the painting she had relinquished in favor of the study of art history. She looks at him and sees "orange, playing jacks and casks of green wine . . . still life, babies, cut glass, indigo, hand spears, dew, cadmium yellow, Hansa red, moss green . . ." (198). Their intimacy provides Son with a ready audience for his storytelling: "Regarding her whole self as an ear," he whispers "into every part of her," stories of icecaps and singing fish, the Fox and the Stork, the Monkey and the Lion, the Spider Goes to Market (194). Beyond the floodgates of intimacy, where "language diminishes to a code," comes an avalanche of words, all signposts of the vernacular (197). A tale of farmers, rabbits, and foxes summons images from the collective unconscious. This description exemplifies the "infusion of the Black cultural spirit" that Michael Awkward identifies as "denigration" (10). He astutely characterizes Morrison's improvisation of narrative forms when he notes that "Morrison denigrates the genre of the novel by infusing it with the spirit and specific elements of the African American cultural perspective" (9).

Awkward begins his study of influence with an analysis of Zora Neale Hurston's *Their Eyes Were Watching God*. His thesis rests on the assumption that this novel is an initiator of discursive practices that are revised and reissued in works by Morrison, Walker, and Naylor. He analyzes Morrison's *The Bluest Eye* as a response to Hurston's novel by focusing on the conflation of narrative voices made possible by Pecola's schizophrenia as a recasting of Hurston's call-and-response and free indirect discourse. He says Morrison's successful denigration of the [novel] form is accomplished not simply in her employment of dual narrative voices but especially in the ultimate merging of these voices (95). This insightful reading of influence in *The Bluest Eye* lays the groundwork for a discussion of Hurston's influence on *Tar Baby*. Before discursive strategies in Morrison and Hurston are compared, Jadine and Son's romance should be compared to Janie and Tea Cake's. Although it would distract from my objective to provide a lengthy examination of the two novels, I will briefly point to several similarities for the purpose of suggesting that Hurston's novel and the tar baby folktale have influenced the construction of Morrison's novel.

Both Janie and Jadine are orphans. Though diligently raised by their respective grandmother and aunt, these young women mourn the loss of their mothers. Both women embark on a series of relationships motivated in turn by economic, social, and sexual needs. Each falls in love with a transient, a musician whose connection to the natural world is evident in his name. Verifiable Woods and Son Green are "undocumented men distinguished by their refusal to equate work with life and to . . . stay anywhere for long" (132). Both are blues men. In an interview, Morrison could be describing Son or Tea Cake when she explains her interest in the type "who is fearless and who is comfortable with that fearlessness" and one who exhibits "a kind of self-flagellant resistance to certain kinds of control" (Tate 126). Although both relationships are short-lived, the women are profoundly altered by them.

Awkward argues that Morrison's narrative voice unifies discordant and competing voices in *The Bluest Eye*, but in *Tar Baby*, multiple points of view maintain autonomy. They define reality as a consensus or composite of competing views. Vacillation among the perspectives of six characters determines the novel's organization. Each time the plot moves forward, the narrator records the impression of the event on each character. Instead of moving from first to third person, blurring the boundaries between these points of view, as occurs in the use of free indirect discourse, Morrison interrupts a third-person narrative with questions addressed to the audience. The result is the blurring of distinctions among speaker, character, and reader. An example of multiple perspectives and shifting point of view occurs in chapter 2, which begins with a description of Sydney and Ondine sleeping "back to back" (36). Their well-earned sleep is contrasted with Valerian's insomnia. Down the hall, his wife, Margaret, lies awake hoping "she will dream the dream she ought to" (37). A door

connects her room to Jadine's. She has just awakened from a frightening dream of hats and the memory of the woman dressed in yellow.
These memories signal a switch in narration. Jadine, implied narra-
tee, addresses the reader in the second person. The narrative shifts
from third person to second for Jadine to defend her actions to what
she perceives as an unsympathetic audience:

> If *you* had just been chosen for the cover of *Elle*, and there were
> three count three gorgeous and raucous men to telephone you or
> screech up to your door in Yugoslavian touring cars with Bor-
> deaux Blanc and sandwiches and a little *C*, and when you have a
> letter from a charming old man saying your orals were satisfac-
> tory to the committee—well, then you go to the Supra Market for
> your dinner ingredients and plan a rich and tacky menu of dishes
> Easterners thought up for Westerners in order to indispose them,
> but which were printed in *Vogue* and *Elle* in a manner impressive
> to a twenty-five-year-old who could look so much younger when
> she chose that she didn't even have to lie to the agencies, and they
> gave what they believed was a nineteen-year-old face the eyes and
> mouth of a woman of three decades. (37)

This address to the audience is an example of co-conspiracy. In this
instance, it encourages the reader to identify with Jadine and view
her critically because of her naiveté concerning the art of ethnic
cooking. The narrative reverts to the third person to describe the
paradox of appearance nurtured by the fashion industry. Neither
the recipes nor the models are what they appear to be in fashion
magazines. The deceptive nature of appearances provides a thematic
continuity and coherence that the shifting point of view fails to
undermine.

These co-conspiratorial addresses can be regarded as a variation of
call-and-response and the "antiphonal interaction" that Awkward
perceives in Hurston's novel (50). This antiphonal interaction between Janie and Phoebe, storyteller and audience, is captured in
the interaction between Morrison's character and the reader. Abrupt
shifts to second person establish a community that includes narrator,
characters, and reader. One such address occurs in the description of

Margaret's confusion [italics added for emphasis here and in the examples that follow]: "After lunch with friends *you* could go to the powder room, twist the lipstick out of its tube and wonder suddenly if it was for licking or writing *your* name. And because *you* never knew when it would come back, a thin terror accompanied *you* always" (46). It is used to establish affinities between the reader and Son: "Now he was as near to crying as he'd been since he'd fled from home. *You* would have thought something was leaving him and all he could see was its back" (120). In another instance, women in New York "suffer from grief so stark *you* would have thought they'd been condemned to death by starvation" (186). Jadine's troublesome nightmares are shared by the reader, "the helpless victim of a dream that chose *you*" (225). This co-conspiratorial form of address can produce an uncanny effect when introduced in passages that feature anthropomorphism: "The soldier ants were not out in the night wind, neither were the bees. But heavy clouds grouped themselves behind the hills as though for a parade. *You* could almost see the herd assemble but the man swinging in the hammock was not aware of them" (142). This final example, an extended address, invites the reader to conspire with the narrator and implied author.[20] The resulting inquiry seems as if it has been excerpted from an intimate conversation between author and reader:

> At some point in life the world's beauty becomes enough. *You* don't need to photograph, paint or even remember it. It is enough. No record of it needs to be kept and *you* don't need someone to share it with or tell it to. When that happens—that letting go— *you* let go because *you* can. The world will always be there— while *you* sleep it will be there—when *you* wake it will be there as well. So *you* can sleep and there is reason to wake. A dead hydrangea is as intricate and lovely as one in bloom. Bleak sky is as seductive as sunshine, miniature orange trees without blossom or fruit are not defective; they are that. (208)

The implied audience of this passage is asked to view the world as an artist does. The existential renunciation of desire is depicted by visual images of the natural world—sky, sun, plant life. This metafictional digression asks the audience to look at the world and at life as an artist capable of appreciating beauty and the absence of beauty does. This illustrates the collapsing of Manichaean categories and the demise of binary oppositions that critics recognized in Morrison's work,[21] but this excursion into the metaphysics of artistic creation asks the reader to share responsibility and experience firsthand the controversies concerning representation and verisimilitude.

In "Life-Story," the narrator libels his readers, addressing them as "you dogged, uninsultable, print-oriented bastard[s]" (123). This insult issues from a different premise about the author, narrator, and audience. Morrison's address, informed by vernacular traditions of collaborative artistic production—call-and-response, co-conspiracy—encourages audience participation in the creative process. The above passage asks them to grapple with the difficult issues that artists confront in the construction of art. While Barth's readers remain readers, though they may think of themselves as fools for the effort, Morrison's readers are asked to answer the most disconcerting questions concerning the nature of art and reality.

All theories of influence aim to identify the sources that inspired an artist to create, but no theory accounts for what the reader brings to the construction of the work. No theory can fully account for influence in works that issue from traditions that require audience participation. No theory can identify the influence of a particular literary predecessor when the story is a communal legacy whose current renderings link the present to the future. Nevertheless, the theories assist our appreciation of a work's relationships to forerunners. Bloom's theory of revision identifies techniques. Gates' theory of literary ancestry sensitizes readers to the diverse traditions represented by the harlequin mask. McDowell, Henderson, and Awkward observe gender's effects on influence and note that influence can signal bonding among generations of writers. If Morrison's novel resembles l'Arbe de la Croix in its synthesis of craft and art, readers are to be counted among the "discriminating visitors" who acknowledge it as "the most handsomely articulated and blessedly unrhetorical house" (9).

Voice, Metanarrative, and the Oral Tradition

From the day you were born I've been speaking
to you in a language that I wanted you to master,
knowing that once you did, there was nothing that
could be done to make you feel less than what you
are, and I knew that they would stop at nothing to
break you—because you are *mine*. And I wanted
their words to be babble, whatever they printed,
whatever they sent over the radio. Babble—as you
learned your own language, set your own standards,
began to identify yourself as a man. You see, to
accept even a single image in their language as your
truth is to be led into accepting them all.

—Gloria Naylor, *Bailey's Cafe*

Most theories and classifications of metafiction distinguish between mimetic and diegetic types. This study reveals the shortcomings of this approach with examples that illustrate the spectrum of metafictional techniques and this discussion of voice. Although omitted from other theories of metafiction, voice blurs the platonic distinction between mimesis and diegesis by connecting the act of narration with the narrative (Hawthorn 127). It refers to thematic *and* structural elements.

Recent developments in theory have paved the way for the analysis of voice in fiction. Theories that resurrect the author and emphasize the reader's response have contributed to recent developments in African American literary theory. Unlike their predecessors who hoped to create a typography modeled on linguistics, the poststructuralists took their cue from specialists in communications. Although they would selectively pick and choose from the extensive vocabulary invented by the structuralists, these theorists remained committed to Roman Jakobson and an understanding of literature as operative according to the rules that govern communication. Rather than view literature as a hermetically sealed system, they perceive it as an act of communication that can be distilled to reveal a MESSAGE from ADDRESSER to ADDRESSEE (Lanser 66). This shift threw open the doors of narrative study to scholars whose readings were heavily predicated upon sociology.

Voice has been under continuous scrutiny by scholars of African American literature. In *From behind the Veil*, Robert Stepto shows that the history of African American literature has been a movement toward the invention of a self-authenticating voice. In *Self-Discovery and Authority in Afro-American Narrative*, Valerie Smith traces the development of voice from nineteenth-century autobiography, illustrating the resilience and adaptability of first-person narration. Gayl Jones makes "freeing the voice" the central trope of her study of the oral tradition in African American literature (178). Whether it is the voice of the first-person narrator in Harriet Wilson's *Our Nig*, the free indirect discourse of Zora Neale Hurston's *Their Eyes Were Watching God*, or the epistolary style of Alice Walker's *The Color Purple*, voice has been central to the exegesis of African American literature. Balanced between mimetic and diegetic, oral and written traditions, it functions as a Geiger counter for self-consciousness in black fiction.

In her second novel, *One Dark Body*, Charlotte Watson Sherman tests the range of voice, making the Geiger counter's needle fly. Like the narrator of J. California Cooper's "Evergreen Grass," who introduces herself as an "old, old lady" who knows "a lot of old, old sayins that [she] know to be true" (35), Sherman mines the vernacular tradition to uncover the voice of experience. This voice is an amalgam of the voices of the elder, the conjurer, and the prophet. It shares wisdom gained from personal experience and an intimate familiarity with folklife and its rituals. Unlike Cooper, who reserves this voice for the proprietary use of wise old grandmothers addressing the young and inexperienced, Sherman democratically distributes the voice of experience among her characters. Instead of being summoned by a particular speaker, it is evoked by a situation. Whereas Cooper's narrator interrupts the action with an enlightening author-ial side, Sherman's voice of experience is incorporated into the story as part of the action. The wanga-man, Blue, uses it to admonish his apprentice, Sin-Sin: "Ain't nuthin worse than a fool ain't got sense enough to hold on to they gods" (156). Nola Barnett uses the voice to speak to her daughter: "In church they always said the sins of the fathers would be visited upon the children, and I found out that say-ing was true" (91). Bess adopts the voice of experience to criticize her younger sister's way of dealing with romance. She tells Ouida, "You wanted to hang on to the memory of that man like it was a worry bead, rolling the same thoughts around in your hands till it made you sick" (39). She warns, "You can love them but you can't own them. Don't nobody own nobody else" (36). These words of advice are shared among sisters, mothers and daughters, fathers and sons, and teachers and their students. Fixed in dialogue, conversations that oc-cur in domestic or natural settings, at home or in forest clearings where the spirits of ancestors commune, the voice of experience re-veals a concern for others that is a part of the vernacular tradition. Blue's double negative, Nola's reference to the Bible, and Bess' meta-phors for theorizing about love (which echo Hurston's best witti-cisms),[1] illustrate the importance of the idiom of black expression to the voice of experience. The message conveyed by the voice of expe-rience is inseparable from the language by which it is conveyed. In this instance, mimesis and diegesis cannot be separated out like dif-ferent strands from a single skein of wool.

The following passage echoes the sentiments expressed by Naylor in the epigram that begins this chapter. Both passages, spoken by the voice of experience, self-consciously engage vernacular language to demonstrate its value and to warn the audience of the need to master this language or suffer the fate of being mastered by the language of others: "Watch out. White people don't know what they talking about. Don't want you to know nuthin about yourself. All you come out of is black, girl, pure dark. The beginning, the end, all black. Don't you forget it, neither. Them folks'll have your mind so turned around you'll be thinking crazy as them. But you look at this light in me. Look. You got the same in you" (166).

Blue's voice resembles that of the preacher in this rendition of the story of creation. It continues the tradition that James Weldon Johnson began in his transcription of the preacher's voice in *God's Trombones: Seven Negro Sermons in Verse*. It responds to his poem "The Creation" and to subsequent transcriptions and improvisations of the biblical story, such as the one that appears at the opening of Ralph Ellison's *Invisible Man*. Metaphors of light and darkness counter the conventional usage. The story is framed by staccato exclamatory remarks—"Watch out," "Look"—that suggest both the orality of this address and the necessity of heeding Blue's instructions. Phonetic spelling, contractions like "folks'll," unconventional grammar and punctuation, and a second-person address convey the "speakerly" quality of this passage. The voice of experience speaks in the vernacular to assert the value of blackness and black expressivity with incontestable authority. Blue's social status lends credibility and authority to the message. This affirmation of the power of blackness gains potency from pre-textual narratives of creation and spirituality: these narratives are, for many, the most compelling evidence that "white people don't know what they talking about."

This passage is Sherman's response to the call that begins the novel. It opens with this epigram from W. E. B. Du Bois' *The Souls of Black Folk*: "One ever feels his twoness—an American, a negro, two souls, two thoughts . . . two warring ideals in one dark body." Although this was written seventy years before Sherman's novel, its continues to evoke discussions of race and identity. Sherman's affirmation of black pride is a response to the enigma of double-consciousness. Her allusions to a literary ancestry are equally important to the solution. Blue's instructions to Raisin restate Sherman's response to Du Bois and establish an ideological affinity between author and character (Lanser 151).

In *Once upon a Time*, John Barth's fascination with tales of the Arabian Nights and the Ocean of Story result in a regressive search for an original story that consumes an entire tale. Instead of prompting this regression ad infinitum, black metafiction refers to literary antecedents to establish a continuum that reaches from the past into the future. Sherman's response is an acknowledgment of the oral tradition employed to instruct through the telling of stories that instill pride and encourage people to avail themselves of the wisdom of their ancestors. The adolescents, Raisin and Sin-Sin, master the lessons administered by the voice of experience and move into the future as conjurers responsible for shaping it. Unlike those who make up Du Bois' "talented tenth," they rely on continuous communications with their ancestors and an unwavering spirituality to assist in shaping the future. The epigram is an extra-literary, extra-textual act of signification that takes its authority from the antiphonal interaction characteristic of the vernacular. The novel paraphrases the original call and issues another, reproducing the congregation's response to the preacher's call.

Sherman's response to Du Bois is the story of Raisin, a fifteen-year-old girl whose mother, Nola, returns to claim her. Raisin was informally adopted by Miss Marius, the volunteer director of the unofficial orphanage, when her mother departed for Chicago after her birth. Nola learns that she must return to Pearl to confront the inescapable events that made her flee: her husband's suicide and her mother's jealousy. By burying her husband and confronting her mother's graveyard spirit, she frees herself from disabling pain, frees her daughter from the sins of her ancestors, and becomes empowered to inhabit the house of the wanga-man. While Raisin and her mother are learning to accept their family's past, Blue is indoctrinating Sin-Sin into the mysteries of the ancient past and the wisdom of his African ancestors. Both adolescents participate in rituals that introduce them to their communal African pasts. She celebrates menses and the advent of womanhood with a ritual immersion in the lake to dance with her sisters. He confers with the wise men who inhabit trees and undergoes a ritual circumcision. The "warring of two ideals" is replaced by the "oneness" achieved through the establishment of spiritual and physical connections to the past.

Both the mortal and the spiritual inhabitants of Pearl take turns narrating One Dark Body. The use of multiple narrators suggests that the voice of experience is accessible to those who desire to assist others. Sherman's multiple narrators fit Jean François Lyotard's definition of a "collectivity" in which "narration is the quintessential form of customary knowledge," and narrative is a key form of competence (19, 22). According to Lyotard, this community has no need of special procedures for remembering its past or authorizing its narratives because "it finds material for social bonding not only in the meaning of narratives but in the act of reciting them" (22). The community of Pearl, a community extended by the act of narration to include the narrator and the reader, is bound by its narratives and their rehearsals. The act of storytelling is of the utmost importance to storyteller and audience. A bond stronger than the familial joins storyteller and audience. Although he is a stranger, Blue's stories make him a central figure in the lives of Sin-Sin and Raisin. Nola's stories are the only link that withstands the discord between mother and daughter. Though a child, Sin-Sin is enabled through his stories to break out of his isolation and connect to the others. Storytelling provides the dispossessed, the orphaned, and the transient with a means of making connections with others. This is one of several episodes that depict storytelling as a means of social bonding. It suggests the importance of carrying on this tradition: "Blue looked deep inside Sin-Sin. He sighed and said, 'You gotta know other folks' stories to find your own. Here's mine, I'm passing it to you cause your daddy can't like my daddy didn't. It's yours now, too. If you take it, no soulcatcher can steal our story again' " (135).

To prevent the soulcatcher from stealing the story, it is passed from one character to the next. Like the Jes Grew virus, it must be passed along to be continually transformed and re-formed. Part of knowing the story is understanding the importance of keeping the story in circulation. Sherman creates a sense of the story's continual transformation through her introduction of sections and subsections. The novel is divided into eight chapters. Each of the eight chapters contains numbered subsections within it. The first subsection of each chapter takes a character's name as its title. The titles of the first sections of the eight chapters are Raisin, Nola, Sin-Sin, Raisin, Nola, Sin-Sin, Blue, and Raisin. The characters' names indicate the point of view from which the following events are described. But the only character to use the first person is Raisin. The other chapters introduce the voice of the character in dialogue and employ free indirect discourse to color the third-person narratives with the character's perspective. The narrator takes on the voice of the character being described. This third-person narration is coupled with Raisin's first-person narratives.

In the first section, "Floating," Raisin, like Tristram Shandy, remembers "when I was back in my mama's stomach floating like a pickle in a jar" (6). From her position in the womb, she overhears Miss Marius chastising Nola for attempting to induce an abortion with okra, cedar berries, and camphor. This marks the narrator in two ways. It marks her by scarring her skin with wrinkles. She says, "I come out so old and wrinkled everybody took to calling me Raisin" (7). It also marks her emotionally by granting her the prerogative to claim the voice of experience (usually reserved for elders) at birth: "I'm an old soul," she says (7). Like Sula's birthmark and Pilate's missing navel, Raisin's wrinkled skin is a sign of difference. The children at the orphanage compose derogatory songs about her, and the adults make prophecies about her future, but Raisin's storytelling assures her of respect and a place of prominence in a community that equates difference with superior abilities at least as often as with inferiority. More important, Raisin's masterful control of narrative is the life preserver that allows her to resurface after she sinks to the bottom of the lake with her own identity (and story) intact.

Three sections of the book are narrated by Raisin. The second, "The Space between Words Where People Live," begins with Raisin meeting Nola at the train depot and Nola narrating the story of her life in Chicago. It concludes with Raisin's angry outburst at the woman who imposes her story on Raisin in an effort to control her. In a voice that transcends the written word, insistent in its demand to be spoken, Raisin singsongs a childhood chant that expresses anger toward a mother who "appears out of nowhere" to take charge of her daughter's life: "All the time, it's what she want. She want to leave Pearl, she go. She want to come to Pearl, she come. She want to burn the letters, she do. She want to call me Septeema. She want to be my mama now. She want to give me answers, she want to ask questions. She want to walk home, she want to see the lake. Well, I don't want none of it. None of her smiles, her gifts, her stories. Don't want to walk nowhere and don't want to talk about nuthin" (94).

Nola attempts to control Raisin by giving her a new name. By becoming her mother's Septeema, the orphan, Raisin, becomes the obedient, conciliatory daughter, but Raisin is determined to keep the name assigned her because of her wrinkled skin. Her preference reveals her respect for herself and the community who named her. Her allegiance to this community is greater than her desire to accommodate the stranger who claims to be her mother. The repetitive "she" that Raisin uses to begin each sentence counters Nola's attempt to rename her. While her mother substitutes one proper noun for another, Septeema for Raisin, Raisin outdoes her mother by demoting "Nola" from proper noun to noun, "mama," and finally pronoun, "she." "She" is defined by the speaker's relationship to her rather than by any qualities or characteristics of her own. "She" can be easily contained and controlled in Raisin's narrative.

The final chapter, "One Dark Body," begins with a first-person account by Raisin, who narrates the story of the box she retrieves from Blue to give to Nola. The box is said to contain a remembrance from her father, El. An abrupt shift to third-person point of view signals the onset of menses: "Raisin looked at the dark brown stain on the white cotton drawers she held in her hands" (191). This voice proceeds to describe Raisin's initiation into the sisterhood of women who await her on the bottom of the lake. An old woman with hair like Medusa supervises the ritual smearing of her body with red ocher, instructs her to identify with the earth and moon and to pray to the Great Mother. With a vow of "divine blood, a vow more sacred than marriage," Raisin pledges herself to sisters who sing:

> We are women of the snake, the moon
> Our blood is the essence of all living things
> We are flowers, we are trees
> We shed our skins like snakes, the moon
> We heal our own wounds and make beautiful scars
> We spout from both mouths with our womanly flow. (199)

An epilogue demonstrates how initiation into this sisterhood alters Raisin's feelings for her mother. It begins: "Been three years since I come out of that lake and find my mama there, waiting for me with her arms open wide" (205). Though Raisin prefers to call her mother

Nola B. rather than "mama" and insists that her life is her own and not her mother's, she acts a daughter's part by choosing to live with her mother in "the wanga-man's shack" (205). She describes her mother anointing her with crushed comfrey leaves to remove the wrinkles. Using what the wanga-man has left, Nola eradicates the scars that marked her daughter as an unwanted child and inspired the town to name her in commemoration of this fact. Raisin comes to recognize her mother as a sister: "'I'm glad you come back mama,' I say, and start to hum like her mama hummed, and then she start, and we hum till we turn into one dark body inside the holy sounds" (209). This joining of voices illustrates what Karla Holloway identifies as the "recreative potential of voice" and the evocation of the ancestral past to address current concerns (198). This is also a final response to Du Bois: instead of two ideals warring in one black body, the prelinguistic hum joins Nola and Raisin into "one black body" that transcends identity, time, and place.

In the essay "The First-Person in Afro-American Fiction," Richard Yarborough suggests that the absence of the first-person point of view in African American fiction written before the twentieth century can be accounted for by the audience for which these books were written (Baker and Redmond 105–121). These writers were addressing a white-middle-class audience who was more familiar with fiction narrated from the third-person point of view. In addition, turn-of-the-century African American writers were not eager to establish the kind of intimacy and self-disclosure that the first-person point of view required. Yarborough sees this change with the publication of *The Souls of Black Folk*, "one of the single most important steps in the evolving conceptualization of the black self and the changing presentation of that self in narrative form" (Baker and Redmond 115). The result is an abundance of first-person narratives that dramatize "the tension between perception and reality, between the exposition of the self and the masking of the self" (Baker and Redmond 119). Yarborough brings his discussion of point of view up to date in the essay's conclusion when he notes that "the most important battleground of racial conflict is now seen to lie within the individual, and an understanding of that conflict entails a complex vivisection of identity itself" (Baker and Redmond 119).

One Dark Body suggests a remedy for this identity crisis in the blending of voices in song. The novel's experiments with first- and third-person narrators suggest that representation of the self and community hold center stage at the conclusion of the twentieth century. One can also read the novel as a condensed mini-history of the African American narrative as it is described by Yarborough. If Du Bois' book initiated an explosion of first-person narratives, Sherman's novel (and those by many other contemporary writers, including Walker, Morrison, and Naylor) signals an abating interest in internal conflicts and a growing interest in the community and individual relationships to it. This shift is apparent in fewer conventional first-person narratives and more experimentation with alternative points of view such as those that reset the perimeters of the self to enlarge investigations of autobiographical first-person narratives, those that include complementary first- and third-person narratives or multiple points of view, and those that insist that storytelling is a collaborative effort aided by readers and/or ancestral spirits. *One Dark Body* fuses first- and third-person points of view to simulate communal narration. This "one dark body" is a collective expanse and "these voices echo through generations of African and African American women and enact the memories that assure the continuity of their cultural traditions" (Holloway 198).

Robert Stepto and Eleanor Traylor comment on Yarborough's theory for omitting community. Stepto reasons that the use of third-person point of view by early African American writers can be understood as an effort to maintain cultural heritage: "Third-person narration was attractive to early Afro-American fictionists because it offered the opportunity to *resemble* the storyteller or balladeer in communal context, and to appear less, thereby, like a writing author expatriated to another culture" (Baker and Redmond 125). Traylor responds to Yarborough's description of contemporary first-person narratives by pointing to the "multiple narrators" present in many contemporary novels. She suggests that theorists need to acknowledge an additional point of view—that of the reader "who is encouraged to retell the story" (Baker and Redmond 132). She says the first-person narrator "cannot mine the lode which the third-person multiple narrator seeks" (Baker and Redmond 133), nor can the first-person narrator represent the community as do multiple narrators whose voices engage us in "acts" of "re-creation" and "liberation" (Baker and Redmond 134).

Raisin's first-person narrative is told from the perspective of a twelve-year-old. Complementary third-person narratives permit the reader to see the child in the context of the community she inhabits. An ancillary function of the third-person narrative in this instance is that it provides a means of verifying the stories narrated by a child and allows the reader to view the events outside the child's frame of reference. The child is the center of her world, and her narrative is affected by this vision. For example, when Sin-Sin appears in Raisin's story, he is engaged in clever dialogue that evokes the unpredictable, capricious behavior of flirtation. When he appears in the narrator's stories, he is a dedicated novice and apprentice wanga-man who has chosen to put worldly interests aside in order to master the alchemy of the wanga-man.

While the third-person point of view is reserved to describe Raisin's initiation, it is used consistently in the sections that describe Nola, Sin-Sin, and Blue. The voice of this narrator resembles the voices of the characters it describes. It is a vernacular voice, a rhythmic, spoken voice with a propensity for metaphor. This description of the pain evoked by Nola's memories of El exemplifies the voice of the extradiegetic or third-person narrator: "She was not immune. The long fingers of sorrow gently stroked her brow. She would not let the girl see her tears. She would not let that old dead thing crawl back into her body, into her opening soul. She was about to do what he had come to do, about to free herself, the girl. She would not let that thing in. She would not cry. She would not break. She would not bow down to that grasping emptiness. She would not" (106–107).

Elsewhere Nola recalls attending El's grave. Though her speech is bracketed by quotation marks to indicate her role as a intradiegetic first-person narrator, sentence structure, cadence, and the use of repetition suggest the shared discourse of intradiegetic and extradiegetic—first- and third-person—narrators:

"Can you hear me, El? Can you hear? I am bringing you this, bringing you all of me, all that is me, the swelling bowl of my life, like gold. I am bringing you the sun in my heart, a white slip of moon, in my grin, bringing you the dark petals of my life, my legs, my crooked yellow toes, I am bringing you my river of laughter, the sharp sea of my sweat when we love, bringing you my rambling tongue, my fat kisses, my one eye that never blinks, I am bringing you my hips that rock, shake, sing, bringing my fists and sharp elbows, my short fingernails, crazy eyebrows, the lashes that will bald when I'm old, the curious world inside my head, I am bringing you, bringing you me, all of me on this platter of earth, your earth, the place you call home." (173)

In Sherman's novel, first- and third-person points of view contribute to the narration of the story. The narrating is shared by a character who is a participant in the events she describes and an observer and nonparticipant, a disembodied voice that describes the action. This latter voice engages in free indirect discourse by borrowing attributes of voice that characterize the first-person narrator. Both voices are oral, "speakerly texts" that privilege the linguistic features of oral speech (Gates, *Signifying*, 181). Because of their shared speech patterns, first- and third-person points of view are indistinct, and the act of storytelling is affected by the story told. Categories of narrating and narrated, mimesis and diegesis collapse. The demise of the nonpartial third-person narrator is, in this instance, a triumph against the ideas of objectivity and narrative distance. *One Dark Body* insists on demonstrating the impact the story has on its teller. It is metanarrative that disrupts the foundations on which definitions of fiction rest: static, distinct identities, individuality, and difference.

Gates says free indirect discourse is mimesis passing itself off as diegesis and diegesis passing itself off as mimesis: narrative commentary with the immediacy of drama (*Signifying*, 208). Sherman takes free indirect discourse one step further. Whereas Hurston's free indirect discourse reflects the similarities in the speech of the character and narrator so that the narrator's speech resembles that of the character's, Janie's (Gates points out this is often called "colored narrative"), Sherman's use of free indirect discourse reflects the dismantling of these boundaries of identity. As Gayl Jones notes: "Not until James Baldwin, Ernest Gaines, Ellease Southerland, Toni Cade Bambara, Ntozake Shange, to name but a few contemporary writers, did the folk language become flexible enough to enter the fabric of the narrative to tell the whole story" (137). Sherman's name is to be added to this list of those who experiment with the interplay of first- and third-person narratives, allowing the inflections of the vernacular to color the language and meaning of narration.

Leon Forrest's novel is narrated from the first-person point of view. Many scholars identify this point of view as characteristic of the black vernacular and African American literary traditions. Gayl Jones expresses this opinion in *Liberating Voices*, explaining how a preference for third-person narration is inculcated in Anglo-European scholarship. The consequence of this bias has been the proliferation of a critical apparatus that is ill-equipped to analyze first-person narratives, as well as a negligent disregard for fiction that takes the first-person point of view and the theme of self-exploration as a premise. She says,

> In Western literature . . . most "great books" have been third-person narratives; in African American literature from the slave narrative on, the importance of telling one's own story has been the thrust. I think this is an important instance where the higher technique in one tradition is not recognized as the higher technique in another. Its influence on how most African American literature is read and received outside the tradition is probably greater than suspected. (All well and good, but what can you do in third person? says one standard. Yes, but I'm winning my—or my character's—voice and self, says another.) What this could imply for contemporary work could be something like judging English drama by Racine's dramatic method: oh what loose, illogical, flighty, chaotic dramatists the English are! (132)

Although *Divine Days* is narrated from the first-person point of view, it dramatizes the tensions that issue from competing perspectives. The voice of the fictive persona who narrates *Divine Days* struggles with issues of authority. Joubert's need to control the narrative, to make it *his* narrative by wrestling it away from other storytellers, mirrors his need to take control of his own life and destiny.

This is what inspires the protagonist to write the diary that constitutes the novel. Seven dated journal entries span the eleven-hundred-page novel. The first entry reveals that the writer's life has reached a hiatus. Just returned from Vietnam, he is troubled by "survivors' syndrome," questioning why he survived when others died. At times, the diary reads like the reflections of a religious novitiate about to take his or her vows. Extended investigations of metaphysical problems are lodged in monologues of intense self-reflection and spiritual assessment. Joubert's diary mixes lofty discussions of religion and philosophy with mundane descriptions of the customers who visit the bar where he works. In this way, the diary joins the communal and private, the spiritual and material, and the imaginative and real to reflect the "continuum of the religious and secular" that Leon Forrest and Geneva Smitherman observe in their study of African American culture.[2] In Joubert's diary, the secular and religious are not the antithetical categories that they are for the religious convert. Thus the narrative becomes the site of "a tensional resonance between homogeneity and heterogeneity," a characteristic that Houston Baker observes in rap music (Rap 95).

Recognition of "tensional resonance" and "hybridity of style" (Rap 15) permit scholars such as Baker and Mae Henderson to analyze the voice of the first-person narrator as a locus of empowerment, contest, and collaboration. Any discussion of "tensional resonance" in autodiegetic narratives, however, must also include discussion of the split subject: the distinction between the narrative voice and the character who appears in the narrative.[3] For memoir writers such as Saint Augustine and those schooled in Anglo-European autobiographical literary tradition, the split subject is a site of unresolvable conflict, but for Joubert it is the site of hybridity and the coexistence of competing discourses.

Before examining the presentation of voice in the novel, it will be helpful to review this excerpt from a recent essay by Leon Forrest. In "In the Light of Likeness—Transformed," an autobiographical essay about Forrest's development as a writer, he speaks of a day in the 1960s (the setting for *Divine Days*) when he receives a visit from Mahalia Jackson. Although he concludes the story with the assurance that it is fiction, it suggests the extent to which music and religion affect Forrest's work. It also introduces a representation of the split subject, which Forrest employs in *Divine Days*:

> She spoke to my running notes to God, in my profound lostness for words—addicted as I was to literature as my religion and as my soul's skullbone connection to a Divine Maker. My inflated afflatus. Mahalia seemed to move over mountains and reintroduce me to the motherlode and the mother tongue of the folk culture, transformed into a memorial art. She spoke not so much to affirm my talent, in its nakedness, body and soul; yet Mahalia's music seemed to evolve me out of my condition. *Mea culpa?* She would not stand for it. She seemed to underscore—in her proud peasant's soul in her powerfully forged art—what I had admired in the great literature that was my heritage (the Bible, Dostoevsky, the Greeks, Shakespeare)—that all great literature at its backbone was and is and ever shall be, world without end, amen, about man's spiritual agony and ascendancy. A spiritual agony that I seemed steeped in, like a child baptized in the chilly waters of Jordan. But I couldn't find a way out of no way, that was my labyrinth and my burden—and then she left me, all alone to wonder. (28–29)

In the following paragraph Forrest tells of Mahalia's return the next evening. She is singing "Didn't It Rain?" Forrest responds like one of the newly elect describing his conversion: "But how did she know that I wanted to be a singer of the language—in the tradition of her majestic self and the Negro Preacher?" (29). To which the imagined Mahalia cleverly responds: "I've knowed de Lawd to use cuiser tools dan dat" (29). This experience may be the culmination of Forrest's devout Roman Catholic upbringing. Writing is equated with preaching to reflect the continuum of secular and religious, high art and low. This passage also introduces Forrest's presentation of the split subject. There is the "I" who narrates (the storyteller) and the "I" who is the addressee of Mahalia's dialogue (a character in the story). The pluralism of discursive practices that characterizes "hybridity of style" is represented by the juxtaposition of the vernacular in the closing sentence (Mahalia's quip about God's tools) and the formal

English suggested by references to the Great Books of the Western canon. Finally, there is the tensional resonance of the historical and imaginative.

Phillip Brian Harper suggests that the fragmented self that is considered a fixture of postmodern fiction is a staple of African American literature. He argues that what appears to be new in American fiction is really the marginalizing of those in the center. In *Framing the Margins*, he discusses the "fragmented subject" as a self fragmented by the conflicting demands of its own psyche and society. Whereas this interpretation of the Lacanian split subject sheds light on the fragmented subject that appears in postmodern literature and assists in understanding Du Bois' double-consciousness, it fails to explain the splits that are not a result of individual/social and self/other dichotomies.

The narrator of *Divine Days* resembles the blues man described by Baker. He is situated at the crossroads of religious and secular, artistic and academic traditions. His inner self is the point of intersection. A matrix of forces resides within him as voices. Sometimes these voices are in harmony with each other; at other times they are in cacophonic discord. Sometimes they are unresponsive to Joubert's efforts to control them. Joubert has been hearing these voices all his life. Like Ishmael Reed, who is possessed by loas who dictate what he writes, Joubert is "being used as a folk instrument" and a "divining rod for God himself" (488). Incantations overtake him, speaking to him and through him (10). These loas seek active subjects to ride, voices to assume: "They throw their voices out there, as electrical charges, with the fond hope, or prayer, that some sonofabitch will pick up the vibrations, hook them up and run with their unharnessed spirits. For they are outlaw hitchhikers, with the spirit of hijackers, blessed with wings for stellar flight" (13). Joubert is the medium through which these voices speak as "flashes from consciousness and unconsciousness" (284).

Joubert considers three vocations that might allow him to tap his inner resources and control the voices that control him. He tries out a career in acting but discovers that "because [he] could never move from hearing voices to projecting a strong, singular interpretation," he gets into fights with directors over the identity of the characters he is to portray (11). Under his aunt's tutelage, he next moves to journalism but finds that he is too powerfully possessed by voices, real and imagined, to do the work of an objective reporter. The vocation he chooses by default is that of playwright. This job entails transcribing the voices he hears. Once he selects a career, he becomes an ambitious opportunist who hopes to debut the voices he hears in "the Great American Play" (88). This play will reveal a "heritage . . . hounded by the voices of oral tradition" (16). Joubert asks, "What must I do to produce a Black literary revival in order to be saved?" He answers: "First of all shut my mouth up! and listen to those voices wherever they take me" (16–17). The result of this experiment is *Divine Days*, a hybrid text that interpolates multiple speakerly texts. One of the many texts included is a "toast" to the folk hero Sugar-Groove. At times, other voices cause such a distraction that Joubert fears that incessant talk will overtake his literary ambitions: "So I enjoy the silence of writing out their world, most of the time. And to guarantee it all, I've recently taken to putting a gag in my mouth; or I'll place adhesive tape over my lips to seal my mouth and prevent these voices from getting out of hand. The danger is I'll become a talker, instead of a writer" (53).

The journal is a synthesis of the "real" voices heard from Joubert's position behind the bar and the "imaginary" voices that preoccupy him even when he is alone. Among the latter are the voices of W. A. D. Ford and Sugar-Groove. Joubert's spiritual quest is filled with an array of voices that resembles a gospel choir, capable of creating both harmony and dissonance, expressing the range of emotion from the joy of salvation to the despair of the forsaken. These voices are not positioned hierarchically, and there is no effort to establish "a position from which the text is most readily intelligible" (Belsey 67). Instead it presents us with a subject who is the site of contradiction, thrown into crisis by the alterations in language. Belsey identifies such a character as a "subject in process," one who "contains the possibility for change" (65). Forrest's novel is an interrogative text because it asks questions rather than supplies answers.

On the opening page, Joubert explains that keeping a journal will help him achieve his dream of becoming a major playwright. He hopes the journal will serve as a springboard for his dramatic ventures (9). His aunt, on the other hand, thinks this "exercise will exorcise the playwright out of his soul," and he will thereafter be content working as a feature-story writer for her newspaper (9). What this writing exercise actually does is enable him to see a multitude of discourses in contradistinction and to recognize himself as the subject encompassing them. Because this self is in constant flux and the voices recorded in the journal change abruptly and routinely, the journal presents a self in perpetual process. Voices are never silenced, nor are fictive voices subordinated to others that are more "real."

Joubert's transcription of these voices characterizes him as a writer of "historiographic metafiction." Hutcheon uses this term to describe "novels that are intensely self-reflective but that also both reintroduce historical context into metafiction and problematize the entire question of historical knowledge" (Pastime 54–55). Joubert says he is writing about "[his] history" and "history" (341). He will provide the story of "my people and my country. A story never heard nor read in school" (348). And with neither modesty nor apology, he declares himself to be "the snotty-nosed, uncircumcised unclean bard of my race" (437). Among his many identities, the voice-befuddled storytelling Joubert is a record keeper of black history.

Divine Days is a series of "nested fictions," or stories within stories (Harper 157). This is a popular structuring device in metafiction. It draws the reader's attention to the anti-representational nature of literature and to his or her status as reader of fiction. The reader who is looking for a resemblance between the real and fictive worlds recognizes that she resembles the writer who invents a world and characters to populate it. Hutcheon emphasizes this connection between the real and fictive worlds by suggesting that nested fictions "guarantee the autonomy of the inner world, and not as naturalistic proof of its direct link to any external life situation" (*Narcissistic*, 106). The nested fictions in *Divine Days* accomplish these objectives, as well as those that have been discussed in conjunction with nested fictions in African American literature. Gayl Jones says African American writers have modified the Western tradition by using the frame but not subordinating one language system to another (199). When Joubert recalls listening to Sugar-Groove tell his "saga of the South," he becomes cognizant of the dual purposes of nested fictions:

"Sugar-Grove had opened up the many hidden stories, like a pyramid of Chinese boxes, one on top of the other, but each volume tumbling out with more and more valuable, intimate intelligence, even as the actual size of the rectangular shapes diminishes in size, yet the volumes become more personal with innermost secrets, imprinted upon the walls of the formations" (363).

If writing is fighting for Ishmael Reed, writing is religion for Leon Forrest. This religion eases the tension between the voices of the journalist, the playwright, and the diarist. Forrest's religion is much more than a vehicle for introspection, a unifying force, or a way of making sense of experience. Religion is more than a metaphor. Life as a writer is a religious calling and a religious discipline. If one voice were privileged in the novel, it might have difficulty reconciling Forrest's views of religion and writing—but this refrain repeats throughout the novel and is emphasized, just as the particular passage the preacher has chosen to explicate and share with the congregation is. The text is Nat King Cole's *Nature Boy*, the narrative site where the vocations of writer, preacher, and blues man intersect:

> There was a boy . . . a very strange, enchanted boy . . . They say he wandered very far, very far over land and sea . . . A little shy and sad of eye, but very wise was he . . . And then one day, a magic day he passed my way. . . . And while we spoke of many things, fools and kings. . . . This he said to me: The greatest thing you'll ever learn . . . is just to love and be loved in return. . . . The greatest thing, you'll ever learn—is just to love and be loved in return. (311–312)

This is the message delivered in the sermon *Divine Days*.

Many theories that examine the relationship between author and audience characterize each as a coherent, unified entity, but scholars of African American literature often address the issues of multiple authors and diverse audiences. These scholars refer to sets of messages intended for different audiences. This sense of a dual audience is often alluded to in the writings of the black nationalists. Toni Cade (Bambara) and Nikki Giovanni prefaced their 1970s anthologies and autobiographical essays with instructions for black and white audiences. Werner Sollers calls this an address to a double audience (Butler-Evans 94). Joubert also addresses a double audience in *Divine Days*. The narrator usually addresses an audience familiar with black culture, but occasionally he interrupts his story to explain an attribute of black culture to an uninformed audience. The following passage is addressed to an informed audience familiar with the dozens:

> I started to call you about Gracie Rae, Red Black Velvet, and Daniel Conway having this big bang blowout last week when Gracie Rae befouled the pollution standards and cussed Daniel out of the Lion's Den. Put all of his ancestors back to cave dwellers, up and down the greasy pole of their origins, then shot them over and back and up a motherless tree of still-born life. Then she sped them down into a pock-faced cesspool of foam like sperm for starters . . . starting all over again, you see. Oh Joubert, I should receive a Pulitzer Prize for Clean Air, after that language cleansing effort. Gracie Rae would make Pig-Meat Markham blush, and Baby Bear—that ain't easy . . . ebony to eyeball, in nobody's mirror, you see? (173)

This story is told to Joubert while he is tending bar. The reader resembles the protagonist who is listening and interpreting this story, which assumes the reader's familiarity with the names and nicknames and the biblical story of Daniel and the Lion's Den. It assumes the reader knows how to play the dozens: the significance of libeling someone's family, especially someone's mother and family genealogy. The reader is also expected to understand the feigned neutrality of the storyteller, which releases him of any responsibility for what he says. In fact, he says, he deserves a Pulitzer Prize for his "language cleansing effort." The speaker engages in linguistic fabulation: alliteration, word invention. He subordinates mimesis to diegesis in what resembles the rap singer's skillful manipulation of language with an emphasis on sound. An implied audience who is unfamiliar with the black expressive tradition is addressed in this next passage:

> In addition to holidays, there were a few other times when I was allowed to speak up, but not to talk out or use talking as a way of

acting out. Let them know what was on my mind, and even in my soul without speaking my mind or, God forbid, giving them a piece of my mind, for then I would be guaranteed no peace of mind. (But you didn't talk back; signifying, and particularly the dozens, were games of verbal assault, where the tongue was used as a switchblade: I played these word games with venomous wit and most riotously with the fellows, often spinning up a salty palaver from the spew and split-tongued, flinging, stinging spit-fires I heard wrought initially in the kitchens of kith and kin.) (284–285)

What starts as a description of the etiquette that children are taught to observe when with adults (children should be seen and not heard) becomes an explanation of signifying. Forrest brings both reminiscence and explanation together at the conclusion of the passage where he explains signifying while demonstrating it. He defines the vernacular with the vernacular and addresses one message to a dual audience. Forrest chips away at the double audience by informing the uninformed and making it so entertaining that the already informed are neither bored nor offended.

The characters in *Divine Days* present their own theories about art. Joubert says he is glad to let his character experience the things he wonders about: he would rather be "Shakespeare than play Macbeth," would rather "conduct his characters through the coach of experience" than be a passenger in that coach (432). Galloway Wheeler, a Shakespearean, comments on the interpretive experiences of reader and critic: "Power of interpretation is similar to the power of redemption" (772). Theories are tested when characters talk candidly with their authors about how they wish to be portrayed. One such character tells Joubert, "I do hope you are correcting my syntax in the book you are doing" (248). Joubert converses with writers who are eager to discuss their craft. Milton Beefeater Raines has this to say about writing: "I also like to write things down too; because you get the order of it all screwed up when you try to tell things because you can't go straight forward, because you want to forgive the mystery of the flow. The flow fucks you all up. The flow sucks, as the Grey-boys say. Because memory tends to run horizontally, vertically, and ass-backwards, before it thrusts forward, rising in its coming" (403–404). The italicization of Joubert's response emphasizes his angry feelings of displacement: *"Ain't life the damnest . . . he's instructing me on the problems of art, as revealed to his wayward imagination. Go write your own fucking play, I almost said out loud "* (404). When Joubert considers writing about Latrina and her dog, Tulsca, regulars at the bar, his aunt reminds him that readers may believe Latrina is crazy, but they are as likely to believe that the writer is crazy.

Other artists are Marvella, a poetess, and Imani, a painter, "who can convey on canvas a perfect reproduction from a photograph of any famous person for whom she felt strong affection or patriotism" (41). This ability to paint realistic portraiture combines with her commitment to black nationalism to produce an artist who sits at the window of her luxury apartment reproducing "the faces of the ghetto in peace" (116). She is a caricature of enthusiasts of the Black Arts Movement and the "brotherhood" of black nationalists who are its founders. When Joubert asks why she "throws her talent up a pig's ass" by painting "Mafiosos in blackface," she quietly explains that she is "in the process of putting her family back together again" (121). Imani's apartment walls are crowded with examples of her work, super-realistic larger-than-life portraits painstakingly reproduced from photographs of "gang bangers, hucksters of mock African art or any parboiled nationalist looking for a hand-out" (125). Her most "memorable portraits" are those of Malcolm X and Martin Luther King, Jr. She veers from her commitment to verisimilitude when she does King's portrait because she adds "a teardrop trickling down to a frozen bead on the left cheek" (116). When Joubert asks about this instance of "poetic license," Imani says, "After Brother Malcolm . . . what is there to say, add or detract?" (116). Although Joubert makes fun of her commitment to the Lost-Found and her "developing cosmic consciousness" (139), he regards her as his closest "soulmate" because she also hears voices, but she hears the voices of her lost-found siblings (125). John G. Cawelti notes that Imani has fallen into the trap of believing that the only solution to her private chaos is to "escape into an idealized past" (443). This understanding of the past leads to Imani's tragic death. Her idealization of the past contrasts with how Sugar-Groove and Joubert visualize the past. For these storytellers, it is an opportunity for the imaginative improvisation necessary to the continuation of the tradition.

Reinvention is central to Forrest's aesthetic. One of the problems he recognizes in the Black Aesthetic is the absence of opportunity for reinvention. His sense of the Black Arts Movement includes artists, like Imani, who duplicate existing forms rather than re-create them. Forrest sees reinvention as central to the experience of African Americans. It is a premise for artistic creation and a survival technique. Like Reed's Law, Forrest's concept of reinvention acknowledges the importance of continually re-creating artistic forms. In a 1992 interview with Kenneth W. Warren, Forrest explains reinvention and its historical importance: "Reinvention seems to me so much a part of the black ethos of taking something that is available or maybe conversely, denied blacks and making it into something else for survival and then adding a kind of stamp and style and elegance. And it's all through African-American music and jazz and it's obviously all through sports of all kinds, and I think it's the link I have to Morrison and to Ellison" (Warren 397). Forrest notes that reinvention is characteristically African American, though it is antithetical to black nationalist ideology. This explains the frequent jokes about Imani's art and Forrest's critique of Afrocentric art: "It's [reinvention] something a lot of the Afrocentric people haven't seen . . . that we're not simply a repository nor a reflection of the African experience, but that we're constantly remaking everything that was left over from Africa, everything that we got from the europeans, into something completely new that both the Africans couldn't do and the europeans couldn't do. Europeans didn't create jazz and neither did the Africans. Black Americans did that" (Warren 397). The inability to "reinvent," to mix imaginary and real worlds, is what makes Imani's work incomplete, but she is not the only artist in *Divine Days* who lacks this talent. With the exception of Beefeater, most create mimetic reproductions of "reality." One result is the over-sentimental poetry of the lovelorn Marvella (391).

Reinvention is central not only to the African American aesthetic but also, of course, to the postmodern aesthetic, where it allows escape from the literature of exhaustion by providing a door to the re-creation of old forms. This perspective of reinvention appears in *Di*-

vine Days as the retelling of the stories of Oedipus and Tiresias. The reinvention of the Oedipus myth serves as the epic's centerpiece. It appears in the middle of the story that Joubert recalls Sugar-Groove telling him while a younger Joubert polished his shoes. The reciting of the story in the first person allows for the merging of the identities of older man and younger man as the story of Sugar-Groove's childhood unfolds. Like most heroes, including Joubert, Sugar-Groove is orphaned during infancy. His mother, Sarah Belle, is the mistress of the affluent Wilfred Bloodworth. Sugar-Groove, the "Negro son of Bloodworth and Sarah Belle," discovers his father in the library gazing at a nude photograph of his mother. The two men wrestle for the picture and are stopped from killing each other only by the intervention of Sarah Belle's ghost, who says: *"How can you destroy what we created?"* (352). This story is followed by a nightmare that Sugar-Groove recalls immediately after: "Now he swept up the father's genitals in his left hand, struck them off from the man's body with this butcher knife—without the slightest hesitation. He hurled the bloody instrument, then the instrument of his own creation into the river. Soon the bloody parts, the knife sprang up in the water, out of the foam, in the form of a magnolia tree—with drops of tears on some petals, drops of dark blood upon others" (359). Cawelti describes this episode as a "reinvention of Oedipus in terms of African-American history" (439). He says that it reflects a central theme in Forrest's fiction: "the archetypal experience of the loss of the mother and the father's lack of acknowledgment which creates the spiritual condition of the orphan, a state which Forrest views as fundamental to the experience of African-Americans" (439).

Although Sugar-Groove and Joubert are orphans, a family is established through the transmission of this story. Joubert's zealous efforts to understand Sugar-Groove's tale indicate its importance to him. The story is at least a partial explanation of his relationship with Tobias T., who bears a keen resemblance to Bloodworth in Sugar-Groove's story. The similarities of their pasts cement the father-son bond. Like Blue and Sin-Sin, Sugar-Groove and Joubert satisfy a mutual need when they enact a father-son relationship, which allows each to confront their private pasts and the absence of their own fathers. Joubert mourns Sugar-Groove's death like a bereaved inconsolable son.

Keith Byerman generalizes about the father-son relationships in Forrest's fiction by referring to Nathaniel, the protagonist of *There Is a Tree More Ancient Than Eden*, as a prototype. He says father-figures provide Nathaniel with "alternative Father-God figures, who seek not domination but the creative possibilities of the voice gained through suffering" (245). Like Cawelti, Byerman reads Forrest's father-son relationships as indicative of his understanding of African American culture: "Blacks have been made fatherless, motherless and pastless by a racist society . . . but . . . this, though devastating, also makes of all blacks a community, defined by outsiders in scandalizing terms, but from within by a determination to survive through the wisdom of a folk culture, by a belief in the power of their voices, and by an awareness brought by those voices of a life-affirming history of suffering and joy" (255). Although Byerman discusses synchrony in Forrest's fiction, neither he nor Cawelti analyzes the narrative to disclose how "life-affirming history" is presented through the use of voice. It is in the presentation of these voices and the interweaving of their histories that Forrest's ideas of reinvention are most evident.

This task begins with an examination of Sugar-Groove's tale. The other stories, nested fictions, are narrated by Joubert, and they often reflect his position as split subject: storyteller and character in the story. These stories often recall episodes that occur in the bar. Often they describe Joubert's interactions with one of the unusual characters who visit Aunt Eloise's lounge. Even though they may involve lengthy descriptions of the visitor's past—explanations of how he came to be among the people who visit the lounge—they are infused by Joubert's presence as listener, observer, and writer. His flair for extravagant language and his indulgent, forgiving satire distinguish his words from those that describe the conversation he had with Sugar-Groove while shining his shoes fifteen years before. Sugar-Groove usurps the role of storyteller but successfully distances himself from the subject of his narrative, the young, naive Sugar-Groove. He establishes this distancing by assuming the role of one who comments ironically on the white discourse and racism that is a subject of his story. The Sugar-Groove who tells the story tells it through the adaptation of a voice and vocabulary much like that of the imagined Bloodworth. From this third-person omniscient point of view, he achieves an extraordinary range, capable of truism without sounding trite: "But Joubert, this imperial theme is beyond all tongue of praise: filial recognition. It is as primal to human need as gestures—motion—grimaces are to speech, language to eloquence" (315). While this voice can make these observations and generalizations about humankind, it also comments on the events he recalls. For example, although he identifies himself in that story as "the Negro," "the Negro lad," or "the Negro son," the story he tells undermines this designation in its portrait of the conflict between a black son and his white father. The principal events in the narrative—the fistfight, the intervention of the ghost, and the dream of castration—are the results of that filial bond. Sugar-Groove's story establishes a hierarchy of discourses at the same time that it bestows the discretionary power that determines meaning and value to the audience. At the top of the hierarchy is the ironic discourse of distance of Sugar-Groove's self-proclaimed "Negro lad." This voice serves as the interlocutor for the voices of Uncle Ice and Aunt Gracie Mae, the family who raise Sugar-Groove, educate him with their version of the family's past, and assist him in interpreting and making use of the stories told to him by his father. These surrogate parents give him this advice on how to behave with his father:

Be lean and keen as a hound in there with him, 'cause old Mister Wilfred try to candy you up, streak-a-lean, streak-of-fat . . . into sweetness and too much ease. It's one thing to joke 'bout the lazy lad: his stomach don't never get tired if he can get through the sweat of saying grace. But you remember how it's the lean hound what leads the pack when the rabbit is in sight, don't you? Well all right. Go in there for seriousness. You don't know what parts of what will turn up to be most useful in your own will to be a man . . . maybe a leader . . . but never a boy . . . yea though you may have to turn them inside out and upside down to side-ways through to the light to find it; . . . Hell, you don't know what you might not use of his words and stories to make yourself a man even though words and tales was set down to set you up as a boy from here to eternity. Or, what we might use . . . or somebody else in the pass-a-long, hand-me-down. (327–328)

The above passage suggests that Forrest knows that language can liberate. He shares with Sherman and Naylor the belief that self-respect and pride are native to the vernacular in the same way that racism is inherent in alternative discourses. The same vernacular voice serves as the interlocutor of the folktale of "The Singing Bone," a story that prophesies the death of Roxanne, Sugar-Groove's white half sister. Here again Sugar-Groove skillfully chooses a stance in relation to his story that enables him to redistribute power in the narrative. This position also makes it possible for him to answer Joubert's questions about the meaning and significance of particular events. In this way, he is objective storyteller and interpreter who maintains the necessary distance to make his story credible. At the same time, he manipulates the audience's interpretation of the story. His interactions with Joubert provide this orphan with the story he needs to make sense of his own experiences and to forge the link between them that sends Joubert searching for him when the novel opens. They also provide Joubert with a contrast between these stories and the ones he hears in the bar, so that the novice writer recognizes that the early stories inspired by the barroom are without the "tragic sense of life" and the "wonderful cathartic balm" that quality stories demand (361). Once his apprenticeship to Sugar-Groove is completed, Joubert will reinvent those old barroom tales.

This section takes authority from the speaker to illustrate the authority of the listener. Aunt and Uncle, Roxanne's audience, Bloodworth's visitor—the listeners are empowered by the ability to interpret and construe meaning. Joubert will similarly provide the meaning for the text that Sugar-Groove narrates. The empowerment of the reader occurs again in the final scene, when the ailing journalist tells Joubert of Sugar-Groove's last days. This reinvention of the tale of Tiresias and Prometheus becomes the concluding refrain of Joubert's toast to Sugar-Groove.

The results of Sherman's and Forrest's experiments with point of view disrupt definitions of identity that rest on the distinction between self and other. *One Dark Body* and *Divine Days* engage the polyphonic voice of the vernacular to suggest an identity that is transient and a self that is composed of many. Storytellers empower readers to interpret existing stories and author their own: "In Forest County, you can always bounce back—if you have a series of contingency plans and plays and a rebounding style of grace and cunning" (*Divine Days* 160).

Metafiction as Genre

> Blanche looked around the lobby again. Despite the
> quiet and calm, there was an echo in the air of
> something not so serene. Something unpleasant had
> happened here, and not too long ago. She was sure
> she was right. She was good at sensing buildings,
> picking up the mood and personality of the place.
> She thought of this sixth sense as a skill she'd
> developed from years of cooking and cleaning
> houses, apartments and offices of all types.
>
> —Barbara Neely, *Blanche among the*
> *Talented Tenth*

Linda Hutcheon identifies detective fiction, fantasy, and erotic fiction as genres of metafiction. Although she omits science fiction from her list, it is included here, for it best exemplifies the self-reflexiveness resulting from the invention of an alternate reality. Furthermore, much of what Hutcheon says about fantasy literature is applicable to science fiction, a classification that is often considered a subgenre of fantasy. In these genres of covert diegetic self-reflexiveness, the "act of reading becomes one of actualizing textual structures" (Hutcheon 71). Because the reader is familiar with the "story-making rules" of these genres, his or her understanding of a work results from appreciation of it within the context of its class from its concurrence with and deviance from standard formulas best evident in the genres of popular romance and pulp fiction.

From her analysis of fiction by Jorge Luis Borges, Vladimir Nabokov, Alain Robbe-Grillet, and Dorothy Sayers, Hutcheon identifies three techniques characteristic of the genres of metafiction. The first is the presence of the detective or sleuth, who acts as a reader or interpreter of events. This character's role duplicates the reader's efforts to make sense of both fiction and "reality." The detective story thematizes the "hermeneutical paradigm" (72–73) and serves as an "allegory of reading."[1] A second strategy is the presence of a detective (or other character) who is also a writer and/or the presence or absence of manuscripts or other important written documents, as in Edgar Allan Poe's "Purloined Letter." Third is the belief—expressed by the detective or another character—that certain occurrences are part of real life, while others are present only in fiction. I expand this category to include all references to the imaginary and the real. Lauren, the protagonist of Octavia E. Butler's *Parable of the Sower*, explains this category when she says: "I've never felt I was making any of this up. . . . I've never felt it was anything other than real: discovery rather than invention: exploration rather than creation" (72). Before we commence this discussion of self-reflexiveness in science fiction, it will be helpful to examine Walter Mosley's detective novel *Black Betty*. A formulaic plot, stock characters, and insistence on closure in this and other detective novels lead scholars such as Roger Caillois to observe that the "pleasure one gets from a detective novel is not that of listening to a story, but rather that of watching a magic trick which the magician immediately explains" (Most and Stowe 5). Because this predictability is not always present in science fiction, the detective story is a good place to begin.

Walter Mosley is a master magician who juggles the conventions of the genre with issues of race. Tossing an array of items—history, politics, current events, and a detective in a dashiki—into the magician's hat assists Mosley in recasting the "whodunit" crime story. Although unique in its composition, *Black Betty* is the fourth novel in Mosley's Easy Rawlins Mystery Series, and like the others in the series, it contains everything that readers of hard-boiled detective fiction expect.

Although scholars may disagree about the origins and development of the detective novel,[2] they agree about its central characteristics. Hard-boiled detective fiction is most often identified by the character of the detective who is driven by a personal commitment to right wrongs. Speculating on the origins of the genre, Richard Slotkin suggests that James Fenimore Cooper's Hawkeye or Natty Bumppo is the prototype of the modern-day hard-boiled detective. Such characters are "out to rescue people—usually women—from some kind of threat" and "they achieve the rescue by following a path of clues to a hidden goal" (Slotkin 94). In addition to the characteristic detective, there is usually a "detective process." Stephano Tani explains this process as an "attempt to discover by rational means the solution to a mysterious occurrence—generally a crime— usually a murder" (41). Finally, there is the anticipated solution to the mystery, a principal ingredient in detective fiction: the women are rescued, the murderers are discovered, the mystery is solved. In addition to detective, process, and solution, the genre is renowned for action-packed plots, sensationalistic violence, and gratuitous sex.

Several features of *Black Betty* fit these descriptions. Like the Cooper prototype, Mosley's detective rescues a woman by pursuing a series of clues concerning Betty's whereabouts to a hidden goal. In this novel, the goal is a servant's secluded house surrounded by a maze of shrubbery, resembling the house in Charles Chesnutt's *The House behind the Cedars*. Consistent with the genre, it is a fast-paced adventure story, both violent and sexy. Easy's memories of Elizabeth are riddled with a desire that ignites his passion for Elizabeth's daughter, Gwen. Easy makes amorous advances to Gwen in the cab of his truck. Several pages later, he is driving home with a pickax in his back. Solutions are proffered to several murders and the usual motive—greed— is disclosed. Order and justice are restored at the close of the novel.

While detective process and solution fit the mandates of the genre, the black detective differs from the prototype in several important ways. Unlike most detectives, Easy—Ezekiel—Rawlins is not a member of the Los Angeles police force. Instead, Rawlins works for himself: writing, directing, and producing "little pieces of history" that have previously been "unrecorded" (147). The story that Easy tells is unrecorded because in 1961, "there wasn't a Negro in the world worthy of an article" (175). The events that made history—the inauguration of President John F. Kennedy, above- and below-ground nuclear testing in the United States and Russia, the building of the Berlin Wall, the Bay of Pigs, and the trial of Adolf Eichmann—reflect the prejudices of those who wrote the news that made history. This record of historical events excludes black people. Easy knows that what passes as the truth is a fiction that denies black reality. Easy's truth is nowhere in this account, so he assumes the responsibility of telling it himself. With Martin Luther King, Jr., as his hero and inspiration, Easy shares his story, believing that "the world was changing and a black man in America had the chance to be a man for the first time in a hundred years" (11). Being a man means telling the story that has been excluded and denied its reality. Like the Freedom Riders, Easy believes it is his responsibility to make the changes that might cost him his life and still not make the history books: "I didn't pay dues in the Southern Christian Leadership Conference or the NAACP. I didn't have any kind of god on my side. But even though the cameras weren't on me and JFK never heard my name, I had to make my little stand for what's right" (147).

What's right for Easy is not the peaceful resistance of Martin Luther King, Jr., nor the steadfast determination of those who conducted voter-registration drives or desegregated schools. Nevertheless, Easy is incarcerated in a jail cell "designed to take the overflow on those special days when there was some kind of protest or other civil unrest" (83). Although he may appear to have nothing in common with the heroes of the civil rights movement, upon closer scrutiny his actions reveal an affinity. He is jailed by the police for what he knows of their corrupt activities. He knows which ones of them are moonlighting from their jobs as police officers to work as hired gunmen. His brutal beating and illegal detainment are some of the routine scare tactics used by the police. Unable to uncover a warrant for his arrest, Faye Rabinowitz, an attorney who feels that "the people who run this world" are "the ones who should die," and state supreme court judge Mellon, "outspoken critic of racism and champion of the rights of the poor," secure his release (85). Police records show no evidence of his arrest, but when Rabinowitz urges Easy to press charges, he says, "Maybe later. . . . Right now I got too much already to do" (86). When she accuses him of shirking responsibility, he explains: "That man up there is a stone killer. You can't stop him with a writ and a lawsuit" (86). Like the attorney, he knows of the corrupt activities of those who represent the law, but while Rabinowitz believes in legal recourse, Easy knows what every black man in 1961 knew, what Huey Newton, Eldridge Cleaver, and the Black Panthers tried to defend the community against: the law could not protect a black man who had been wrongfully beaten by the police. This reality affects the conclusion of the novel. Although the formulaic detective novel ends with justice restored, justice cannot be restored in the unjust society depicted in Mosley's novel.

Saul Lynx, a private investigator employed by a wealthy client, gets Easy involved in the case, but Easy refuses the generous and much-needed financial reward offered at its conclusion. A monetary reward would compromise his role of savior and guardian of the underprivileged. Such moral scruples are typical of detectives, but one of the things that distinguishes Easy from most detectives is the skillful way he synthesizes his private and public lives. Unlike the Chandlerian heroes, "detached" loners who seek and find "individual integrity," African American detectives like Easy Rawlins discover that "Chandlerian heroism is not an option" (Rabinowitz 21). Like Grave Digger Jones and Coffin Ed Johnson, the heroes in Chester Himes' Harlem Detective Series, Easy is personally involved in his work. He has known Elizabeth since childhood, and he sees himself as a part of the community rather than as a loner.

Beside this "personal involvement," he is unique in his approach to the crime. It is a part of his busy day, which involves him in the multiple roles of detective, entrepreneur, father, and friend. Each day is orchestrated to take care of his personal business as well as the business of others. His own business includes several real estate ventures. As the story unfolds, we learn of his investment in Freedom's Plaza, a mall of shops "owned and patronized by black people" (57). The building permit has been granted, but the city has issued an injunction to build a sewage treatment plant in its place. The city forecloses on the development and pays the "Negro investment group," Freedom's Trust, only "what the land is worth" (57–58). Freedom's

Trust goes bankrupt, the injunction is suspended, and the land is purchased from the city at cost by a white realtor who will profit from building the proposed mall. Easy uncovers the collaboration of Clovis, a secretary at Freedom's Trust, and Mason LaMone, the white realtor. A second investigation has him looking for the witness who called the police on Mouse. Mouse is determined to kill someone in retaliation for his prison sentence, so Easy arranges for him to kill a friend whose illness has made him eager to die. Easy is a family man despite his failed marriage. Although his wife has left him, he has found a family, one made up of people who need and want each other: Easy says, "The only agreement between us was love and mutual need" (32). Easy's family consists of Jesus, or "Juice," a child rescued from prostitution, and Feather, whose white mother was murdered by her grandfather for "bearing a black child" (19). Easy brags about his found family, even going so far as to suggest it is superior to biologically determined families: "He was my son. A son of preference. We weren't blood, but he wanted to live with me and I wanted to have him—how many fathers and sons can say that?" (51). His concern for his business enterprises, his friends, and his family distinguishes Easy from most detectives. The detective in the dashiki is a community man whose story is told because it is typical. He frequently refers to the invisible poor and "men like me"—inserting them into history, recording their presence and explaining their lives:[3]

> Men like John and me didn't have lives like the white men on TV had. We didn't roll out of bed for an eight-hour day job and then come home in the evening for *The Honeymooners* and a beer.
>
> We didn't do one thing at a time.
>
> We were men who came from poor stock. We had to be cooks and tailors and plumbers and electricians. We had to be our own cops and our own counsel because there wasn't anything for us down at City Hall.
>
> We worked until the job was done or until we couldn't work anymore. And even when we'd done everything we could, that didn't mean we'd get a paycheck or a vacation. It didn't mean a damn thing. (188)

This life insists on its own telling. The episodic plot structure duplicates the multifarious quality of Easy's life. Not only will he write into history the story of a black detective, the "righter of wrongs," but he will make the effort to tell the whole story and include the untold stories of others. His story encompasses the stories of his friends and the stories of those who live in his neighborhood. The importance of this locus is not to be overlooked. Theodore O. Mason, Jr., notes that though the detective element and the search make Mosley's fiction of "a piece with a great deal of crime fiction," Mosley's decision to "present the black community as the dominant site of the novel's action rather than simply being the locus of exotic difference" makes his work unique to the genre of detective literature (173).

Easy assembles the pieces of an intricate puzzle to uncover Elizabeth's whereabouts and the murderers of her brother and two children. His act of deciphering the mystery of Elizabeth's whereabouts parallels the reader's act of deciphering text. Psychoanalytic readings of crime fiction explain this correspondence between reader and detective. According to Geraldine Pederson-Krag, the detective story is a nonthreatening replay of the primal scene (Most and Stowe 13). In this family drama, the reader identifies with the child who is cast in the role of detective. The parent is the victim of the crime, and the secret crime is the sex act. According to this analysis, the child learns of his or her parent's sexual activity via detective work. Easy's search for Elizabeth (or Betty) fits this pattern because she introduces him to sex, and he fantasizes about her. The rescue is interspersed with memories of his desire. His longing for her is transferred to her daughter. This act of incest is avoided by Gwen's murder, which recasts Easy as surrogate parent and nurturer to the grieving Elizabeth. The story allows for the vicarious resolution of the reader's oedipal complex. The identification with Easy takes the reader through the stages of the child-parent relationship, which begins with the desire for the parent and ends with the child assuming the role of the parent's guardian or protector. This transition is evident in the passage below:

For years after her kiss, I dreamed of it, yearned for it. And there she was, filled with passion and calling out for love. But not my love. Not me.

I held her and ran my flat palms over her back and head. We slid
down to the porch and she tucked up her legs so I could run my
hands from her head to her feet; not a lover's stroke but a mother's, a mother's whose child has come awake from a terrible
nightmare. (211)

In the closing scene, Easy chooses to obey protective impulses and
suppress sexual ones. Readers have been escorted through the oedipal complex and its resolution. Gwen's murder and his decision to
parent Elizabeth rather than act a lover toward her enable Easy to
maintain the "loner" stance typical of most detectives. Like most
detectives, Easy finds that women distract his attention from his
work.

As scholars of the African American detective novel note, race alters the genre in important ways. In his study of the ethnic detective,
Peter Freeze identifies a "cultural mediator," or a narrator who introduces the reader to an unfamiliar ethnic culture (9). This cultural
mediator allows the novel to "fulfill the function of anthropological
handbooks" by introducing readers to a foreign culture (10). Similarly, by relying on the theories of Bakhtin and Lukács, Theodore Mason describes the interplay of cultures in the Rawlins mysteries as an
act of *transgression*, a "crossing of categories or the violation of social protocols about social, cultural and historical identity" (178). In
his analysis, "cultural knowledge" becomes represented initially as
racial knowledge or, more precisely, "the negation of racial protocols" (179). Regardless of whether it is intended to challenge or educate, cultural knowledge affects the character of the detective and
the solution of the crime-story by precluding the return to order and
justice that serves as the standard close for detective fiction.[4] In
Black Betty, the police are criminals, the lawyers are motivated by
self-interest, and courts are at the disposal of those who have money.
In a two-page final chapter, Mosley describes the trial and its outcome. Some, but not all, of the police are indicted. The wealthy son,
an accomplice to murder, goes free. Elizabeth is destroyed by the
trial, and the accusation of her working as Cain's concubine is used
to break the will that made her heir to a fortune. Mofass wrests his
business from the hands of a conniving secretary, Clovis. Mouse

kills terminally ill Martin, and Easy signs on to the construction crew to lay the foundation for the shopping plaza. In this instance, Easy decides to do what the courts don't by taking justice into his own hands and enacting revenge: "No one ever suspected that it was me who put the extra sand in the cement that made it crumble only one year after the opening ceremonies" (255). This is revenge for being cheated out of Freedom's Plaza. The message isn't that the right will be victorious or that the system of justice will punish the guilty. Instead, Easy employs an Islamic code of justice that includes self-protection and retaliation. When laws fail to protect and punish, Easy accomplishes these things on his own. Mosley rewrites the message of the detective genre and makes it relevant to the lives of those who are denied power by the legal, judicial, and social institutions.

Easy says that though he had his foot on the chest and a shotgun pointed at the temple of the man who called him "nigger," he "didn't enjoy it" (42). Although this may seem a peculiar moment for genuflection, he adds: "One of the problems with so many oppressed people is that they don't have the stomach to give what they get. I hurt that simple white man because I was scared of him. If he'd called me boy or nigger one more time I might have started gibbering myself" (42). Mosley explains the fear that leads to violence—for those who haven't experienced it themselves—but this information is coupled with the observation that most oppressed people can't "give what they get," an implicit admonishment to toughen up. Its irony is evident, given that the genre is founded on the assumption that ethics is a virtue. Outside a boxing parlor, an old man approaches Easy, who has just been knocked down. The old man offers assistance and remarks: "It's always a black man out there hittin' another black man so all the white folks could laugh: 'look at that fool . . . beatin' the blood outta his own brother'" (95). Regardless of whether we agree with this sociology of "black-on-black" violence, remarks such as this alter the usual message of detective fiction, extending its scope beyond platitudes about crime and punishment, truth and justice, to encompass the complex realities of life.

In "Literature under the Table: The Detective Novel and Its Social Mission," Ernest Kaemmel argues that the genre is a "child of capitalism" (Most and Stowe 55). According to Kaemmel, the crime represents an attack on private property. Authorized institutions are incapable of bringing it to justice, but an individual representing the oppressed classes can. This interpretation is validated by Mosley's novel, which shows in the character of Easy and in the observations concerning oppressed classes that the hope for ethics resides in the lower classes and oppressed peoples. Although rooted in historical analysis rather than Marxism, Slotkin argues similarly when he says that the present-day detective hero is like Sam Spade, "a person who finally ends up doing the work of the law—but who stands finally outside the law as well" (99).

Like the real world, both our understanding and the events are colored by attitudes toward race, toward trying to second-guess people because of who they are and where they come from. Easy sees the cruelest forms of racism and oppression not just in the effects on the community—poverty, drugs, and gambling—but in the effects on individuals such as Elizabeth Eady (Black Betty), a servant sought by her affluent employers, the Cains. She has been employed by an affluent white man who attempts to make amends for his sexual exploitation of her by naming her his heir. His widow, son, and lawyer kill her son and daughter and will do anything necessary to claim the estate. They hire a detective, Saul Lynx, who in turn hires Easy, who is known "for finding people in the colored part of town" (15). Easy certainly seems to know everyone, but his investigation reveals that he has been hired by the master to punish the slave. The Cains want to murder Elizabeth to reclaim the estate that has been bequeathed to her by the repentant Mr. Cain.

While Easy's almost instinctual distrust of white people saves his life repeatedly, a message about blue-eyed devils and the evil inherent in whiteness is too simplistic for Mosley.[5] To erase whatever doubt the reader may have concerning Mosley's intent on this matter, he has Easy's life saved by the white detective who hired him. Saul Lynx puts himself between his buddy and the bullet intended for him. At the hospital, awaiting a report on his condition, Easy meets Saul's black wife and infant son, who, Rawlins says, "has very little of Saul in his dark features" (252). This episode complicates what Easy has learned about white people from Elizabeth's ordeal. The descendants of Cain are momentarily redeemed. What Easy says about the Horns, the neighbors who care for Juice and Feather, is further evidence of his stubborn, ironic disavowal of racial stereotypes: "The [Horns] were real people and so I rarely thought about them being white" (48).

Black Betty is told from the first-person point of view, and while there is no reference to the writing of the text or the assembling of the story for literary production, it is a "speakerly text," which reads as if it is being spoken. The cadence and inflection of Easy's speech reveal his character, and it is largely by his voice that we know him. Easy addresses an audience unfamiliar with the world he inhabits. His voice chaperons the reader on a guided tour through the "bad" part of town. This voice is that of the "cultural mediator" discussed earlier.[6] A clue to the fact that he is talking to outsiders is his repeated efforts to explain life on the street. Reference has already been made to his explanations of the working life of a "poor man." Additional examples provide insight into other aspects of a poor man's life: "Poor men are always ready to die. We always expect that there is somebody out there who wants to kill us" (44). Insight into his friendships: "One of the reasons I was broke is that I gave my money away to friends who had less than I did. That's a poor man's insurance: Give when you got it and hope that they remember and give back when you're in need" (65). And his attitudes toward war and death: "Behind every poor old man there's a line of death. Siblings and children, lovers and wives. There's disease and no doctor. There's war, and war eats poor men like an aardvark licking up ants" (93).

Easy serves as an interlocutor, a narrator who uses standard English to bracket dialogue in the vernacular. He even interrupts conversations among characters to instruct his readers in what is going on. When Jackson Blue opens the door with a mean "What the fuck you think you poundin' on, motherfucker?" Easy's "Who axin'?" is preceded by this explanation: "One of the things the street teaches you is that if you bend over you're bound to get kicked" (27). He interrupts another anecdote to explain his use of the expression "down home":

I always talk about down home like it really was home. Like everybody who looked like me and talked like me really cared about me. I knew that life was hard, but I hoped that if someone stole from me it would be because they were hungry and needed it. But some people will tear you down just to see you fall. They'll do it even if your loss is their own.

They will laugh at your misfortune and sit next to you at misery's table. (109)

In both passages the narrator's explanation of events illustrates his skill with both formal English and the vernacular. Easy moves easily from the language that he uses to address his audience to the language of the street. His explanation of "down home" provides the pick necessary to mine the rich vein of ironic street talk. Here Easy tells his uninitiated audience that things aren't really what they are said to be and that "down home" is a place where people don't act like family, but act instead out of malice and evil. Easy knows that words deceive and he knows how to use that to advantage. Moreover, he knows when to use the vernacular to his advantage in conversation with whites: "Marlon wasn't nowhere to be seen. I spoke in a dialect that they would expect. If I gave them what they expected then they wouldn't suspect me of being any kind of real threat" (72). Easy knows the power of language. He learned it when Elizabeth chided him for saying she was *almost* the prettiest woman he had ever seen. Easy remembers this lesson so well, he assumes the role of teacher with others. When Lynx refers to Elizabeth as a girl, Easy is quick to correct him: "She's almost fifty years old, man. She's a woman" (221). Education, language, and politics are interwoven in this conversation between Easy and Jackson:

"Did you ever get that degree from UCLA?"
"Shit. Motherfuckers wanted me to study some kinda language. Uh-uh, man. I walk on the ground an' I talk like my people talk."
"But you could do somethin', Jackson. You're smart."
"Naw, Easy, I cain't do nuthin'."
"Why not? Of course you could."
"Naw, man. I been a niggah too long." He said it as if he were proud of the fact.
"You think that Martin Luther King is down south marchin' an'

takin' his life in his hands just so you could be gamblin' and actin' like a niggah?"

"I ain't got nuthin' to do wit him, Easy. You know I be livin' my life the onliest way I can." (134–135)

Jackson's refusal to speak formal English, to enter the world outside the black community, is respected by Easy. Although Easy speaks whatever language is necessary, he respects the person who chooses to speak only in the vernacular. Hence passages like the above, rich in street talk, dwarf the bi-dialectism of Easy. What is usually represented negatively in detective fiction is presented as a positive here. The reader respects Jackson for his decision, just as he or she comes to respect Bruno, Mouse, and all the other characters who are part of Easy's world. This community is neither more nor less violent or irrational than the world that detective literature has traditionally portrayed as its apotheosis.

Easy tackles the subject of language and then moves on to the latest controversies in education and censorship. At the beginning of the second chapter, he picks up a copy of *Huckleberry Finn* and says, "A few liberal libraries and the school system had wanted to ban the book because of the racist content. Liberal-minded whites and blacks wanted to erase racism from the world. I applauded the idea but my memory of Huckleberry wasn't one of racism. I remembered Jim and Huck as friends out on the river. I could have been either one of them" (18).

The novel indulges this similarity. As first-person narrator, Easy resembles Huck, but when he puts a white sheet over his head and lies down in the back of his car so Lynx can gain access to a high-security Hollywood neighborhood, he evokes an image of Jim lying on the bottom of the canoe. Whereas the duke and king double-cross Jim by trying to sell him, the people who hire Easy—Lynx and the Cains—are the very people who wish to kill Elizabeth. Like Jim's floating down the Mississippi, Easy's involvement in the case proves increasingly dangerous as the police try to pin the murder on him. A final similarity is the episodic structure. Just as the first part of *Huckleberry Finn* contains repeated episodes of Huck and Jim interacting with people on land and retreating to the community of two aboard the raft, the first part of the novel contains repeated episodes of Easy pursuing information about Betty's location. Finding Elizabeth is like reaching Cairo. If, as Easy says, "Mr. Clemens knew that all men were ignorant and wasn't afraid to say so," Mosley knows it too (18). He shares Twain's cynicism when he observes the effects of racism. He addresses a favorite subject of Twain's when he writes: "Law is just the other side of the coin from crime . . . they're both the same and interchangeable. Criminals were just a bunch of thugs living off what honest people and rich people made. The cops were thugs too; paid by the owners of property to keep the other thugs down" (197).

Huckleberry Finn isn't the only work of literature implicated in the novel. If Easy is a composite of Huck *and* Jim, he is also the invisible man. This affinity is suggested in the opening pages of the novel when Saul Lynx approaches Easy asleep on his porch: "I didn't want him to see me with no clothes on. It was still in a dream, as if I was vulnerable if someone could see my skin. I wanted to linger in the shadows, but I'd learned that you can't hide in your own house— if somebody knows where you live you've got to stand up" (12). Like the invisible man, Easy realizes that he is invisible and that it is impossible to hide, even in his own home. Like the invisible man and his predecessors, he has tried to fit into white society but comes to realize that he can never be the successful businessman he aspired to be: "I had reached out for the white man's brass ring and got caught up short. . . . I knew the world wasn't going to let me be an upright businessman. It was just that I had worked so hard. Since I was a child I worked the daylight hours; sweeping, gardening, delivering, I'd done every kind of low job, and I wanted my success. I wanted it— violently" (59).

He also realizes that his life will be filled with "violence" and "insanity" and "that feeling of anger wrapped tight under [his] skin" (60). Like the invisible man, he realizes that, to the police, "all blacks were criminals" (248), and he is haunted by nightmares that reflect his fear:

I was running with a mob of black men. In pursuit of us were ravens and dogs followed by rabid white men and white women—the white people were naked and hairless. Horses with razor hooves

galloped among them and a searing wind blew. We were all running but every black man trying to get away was also pushing his
brothers down. And every man that fell was set upon by dogs with
hungry rats dangling down from between their legs. (138)

Toni Morrison concludes her theoretical treatise on American literature, "My project is an effort to avert the critical gaze from the
racial object to the racial subject; from the described and imagined to
the describers and imaginers" (90). Within this purview, the absence
of the African presence in American literature becomes as significant
as the presence of it. Elizabeth Eady epitomizes this absence. She is
the missing subject of the novel, the empty center that acts as a centrifugal force controlling characters and events. She explodes beyond
the boundaries in the imaginings of others. Although many of the
characters have nicknames (Bluto gets his from wearing the blue
shoes he won in a bet from a white man who was so angry about
having to give them up that he dyed them blue; Ed Sullivan for the
funny way his head sits on his shoulders—no neck), Elizabeth Eady's
nickname, Black Betty, makes her color and race the foremost thing
about her, a pronouncement that precedes her given name. Black
Betty may be a play on brown betty, a sweet, fruity dessert, for all
regard her as a "dish" to be consumed and discarded. Easy may correct Saul's word choice when he refers to her as a girl, but when he
mentions Elizabeth Eady to Easy her name strikes a "dark chord" in
the back of his mind, one that fit with "the humid September heat—
and with my dreams" (13). Saul presents a photograph to Easy, who
focuses on her blackness and sexuality:

Its colors were rose-brown and tan instead of black and white. It
wasn't a posed portrait, but a kind of snapshot. A young woman
on the front porch of a small house. She was smiling at the time,
leaning awkwardly against the doorjamb. She was tall and big-
boned and very dark, even the rose coloring couldn't hide Betty's
blackness. Her mouth was open as if she were smiling and flirting
with the photographer. It brought a sense of intimacy that few
amateur photographs have. Intimacy but not warmth. Black Betty
wasn't your warm sort of home-making girl. (13–14)

Easy's description begins with what he sees in the photograph, moves to what he imagines, and concludes with what he knows about Elizabeth from direct experience. All three of these ways of knowing contribute to his sense of her identity. Even his actual experiences with Elizabeth are affected by his imaginings and his memory. He knew her when he was a twelve-year-old boy growing up in the Fifth Ward of Houston, Texas. She was the woman every boy fantasized about. He followed her around and was flattered when she asked him to do errands for her. This childhood infatuation prompts Easy to pursue the case: he wants to be her rescuer. The protective feelings he has toward Elizabeth are identical to those he feels toward his orphaned children, Feather and Juice. This desire to protect, to father, is complicated by what he knows about the life of this beautiful woman. He knows that she will be used by men like Rufus, a Houston beau who assaults her on a mattress between two buildings, and Cain, the wealthy employer who exploited her and deprived her of her children.

Everyone is searching for her, and while her life illustrates to Easy the tragic fate of too many beautiful black women, it takes on a different significance for others. She is maid and servant to Mrs. Cain. She is concubine and means of redemption for Mr. Cain. She is friend in need to her brother, Marlon, who dies in an effort to save her. She is the unknown mother of Terry and Gwen, children who are murdered by those looking to kill her. Easy's remark—"Miss Eady is a black woman and there's a whole lotta people wanna see her"—suggests that she is the African "other" that Toni Morrison recognizes in American literature (198):

> This African other became the means of thinking about body, mind, chaos, kindness and love; provided the occasion for exercises in the absence of restraint, the presence of restraint, the contemplation of freedom and of aggression; permitted opportunities for the exploration of ethics and morality, for meeting the obligations of the social contract, for bearing the cross of religion and following out the ramifications of power. (48)

Elizabeth embodies sexuality and in so doing signals an absence of restraint for Cain and its presence for Easy. She serves as a means of sin and redemption for Cain and an opportunity for Easy to test his self-control. Finally, she represents freedom from Cain's wife and the unwritten and ongoing history of the black woman's bondage and persecution for Easy.

When Easy gives Elizabeth the news that her children have been murdered, he has to restrain her. In this scene, readers witness the confusion of paternal and sexual roles. The introduction of the mirror, a renowned symbol in detective literature and metafiction, further complicates the description:

> I was holding Betty in front of a long slender mirror that was attached to the door leading to her tiny bedroom. Both of her breasts were out and she struggled with the strength of a mother fighting to save her child. With a great heave she pulled one arm free and let fly with a china cup that she'd grabbed. The mirror shattered in place, our images froze for a second in a thousand slender shards, and then fell to the floor giving me the distinct impression that it was both of our lives that had been splintered and destroyed. (241)

The shattered mirror reflects the inseparability of Elizabeth and Easy, the victim and the rescuer. It also suggests the inseparability of the black man's and black woman's fates. The mirror does more than reflect the entanglement of two lives, however; it also reminds readers that the story is Easy's and that Elizabeth can never escape the role of the object. We never know her without his vision and understanding filtering her image. The postmodern symbol has added significance in detective fiction. Tani reads its presence as an indication of the relationship between the detective process and time. According to Tani, the mirror is the present distorted view of the crime, which occurred in the past (48). Easy's view of the past and his efforts to resurrect it culminate in the breaking of the mirror, asserting freedom from the past. The shattering of the mirror gives rise to a view beyond the boundaries of fiction, an acknowledgment of the stories that will go untold:

> In the early sixties nearly everybody was working. On the bus there were mainly old people and young mothers and teenagers coming in late to school.

Most of them were black people. Dark-skinned with generous features. Women with eyes so deep that most men can never know them. Women like Betty who'd lost too much to be silly or kind. And there were the children, like Spider and Terry Tonce were, with futures so bleak that it could make you cry just to hear them laugh. Because behind the music of their laughing you knew there was the rattle of chains. Chains we wore for no crime; chains we wore for so long they melded with our bones. We all carry them but nobody can see it—not even most of us.

All the way home I thought about freedom coming for us at last. But what about all those centuries in chains? Where do they go when you get free? (199)

This subtext on freedom transforms the genre of detective fiction, taking it one step beyond the hard-boiled detective story. If the trend has been to move from a simplistic good versus bad, law versus criminal, to a more complex vision that questions fixed definitions of these terms as well as their dialectical relationships, the African American detective novel projects the genre further down the path of ambiguity, so that the idea of right and wrong as fixed categories seems a distant memory. The interjection of race and class in Mosley's *Black Betty* illustrates the relativity of such terms as "good" and "bad" and demonstrates that different codes of behavior operate in different contexts. It topples the belief in universal values and encourages the audience to reconsider the role of the individual in taking justice into his own hands, in acting in socially responsible ways, in choosing not to interact with the alien, imperfect, dangerous world outside the black community.

Octavia E. Butler's *Parable of the Sower* also relies on social and political ideas to extend the boundaries of fantasy. In *Fantasy and Mimesis*, Kathryn Hume outlines four types of fantasy: escapism, expressive literature, didactic literature, and perspectivist literature (xiv). Butler's novel fits Hume's classification of didactic literature or "the literature of revision." This classification of fantasy literature "calls attention to a new interpretation of reality" as it "tries to force the readers to accept the proffered interpretation of reality and to revise their worlds to fit this interpretation." The authors of didactic fantasy literature offer "at least a token program of reform," which may be religious or moral, as in Bunyan's *Pilgrim's Progress*, or social and political, as in John Steinbeck's *The Grapes of Wrath* (xiii). Butler addresses moral, religious, social, and political themes. One lesson she teaches is that there is a continuum from personal to political, from religious to social and communal. As Mosley revises categories of the personal and collective, so does Butler. The second revision of genre is evident in Butler's use of positive and negative examples for instruction. She presents both utopia and dystopia, encouraging readers to imitate the actions of some and refrain from imitating the actions of others. Butler's heroine, Lauren, also defies classification. Hume distinguishes between "stories which center on a hero" and "stories which use a superhuman saint or messiah" (104). Lauren combines characteristics of both. Like the folk hero, she has imperfections and personal idiosyncrasies that make her human. Like the messiah, she espouses "new interpretations of the cosmos" and "assigns new meanings to life" (105). Through the introduction of a new religion, Lauren fits Northrop Frye's definition of a hero in the "high mimetic mode" (she is superior to other people but not to her environment), but the plot in which she appears is that of a romance. It commences with her living with her family as a member of a walled community. The dissolution of that society at the hands of villains who live outside the walls begins her journey and entry into a nonrational world governed by violence. She undergoes tests and trials, survives, and emerges a triumphant new leader (Hume 152). The story also fits the pattern of a tale of initiation. The novel traces Lauren's development from a fifteen-year-old girl living under the watchful eye of an overprotective father to an independent eighteen-year-old woman who is beginning her life's work and a mature relationship. The novel employs a variety of archetypes for the purpose of demonstrating that romances tell the story of the ego gaining control over the id. In Butler's novel, the unconsciousness is the world beyond the wall, outside the community, and the people residing on either side of the road that Lauren travels. The Satan worshipers in Butler's tale are cannibals, scavengers, thieves, and drug users whose survival depends on the destruction of others. Arrival at Bankole's farm represents a return to order, a celebration of community values and hope for future generations, and, of course, a subsuming of the id to the control of ego and superego.

Freedom is the subject of this, Butler's tenth science fiction novel. Like her earlier novels, it integrates historic elements to introduce this subject. There are references to slavery and to the African Diaspora. The novel can be read as an allegory of the slave narrative. In this apocalyptic tale, Lauren Oya Olamina, the daughter of a Baptist minister, leads a diverse group north to establish Earthseed. The story Lauren records in her diary begins in 2024 and describes the destruction of the walled community in Robledo, California. It describes the three-year journey north on Route 101 toward the freedom represented by the land owned by Taylor Franklin Bankole on the coastal hills of Humbolt County. Lauren describes her group as the "crew of the modern underground railroad" (268). She figures as a Sojourner Truth leading the way north, persevering because of her own stubborn refusal to live "as some kind of twenty-first century slave" (155).

Bankole's observation that the "country has slipped back 200 years" is validated by the histories of those who join the group (278). Emery's sons have been taken from her and sold for payment of debts owed to the company store. Allison and Jillian Gilchrist run away from a father who is trying to sell his daughters. Grayson Mora and Doe Mora are runaway slaves, as are Travis, Gloria, and Dominic Douglas, whose flight to Canada is assisted by the wife of the slavemaster who knows of her husband's desire for Gloria.

In her discussion of *Wild Seed* and *Kindred*, Butler's previous novels, Sandra Y. Govan observes that the writer "links science fiction to the Black American slavery experiences via the slave narrative" (79). In an interview, Butler explains how history affects her writing. She begins by recalling a visit to Mount Vernon, where she listened to the presentations of tour guides whose memorized speeches obscured the historical truth by referring to "slaves" as "servants." As preparation for writing science fiction, Butler read slave narratives but realized that she "was not going to come anywhere near presenting slavery as it was. [She] was going to have to do a somewhat cleaned-up version of slavery, or no one would be willing to read on" (497). Although she may refrain from portraying the African American experience of slavery as history, her cleaned-up science fiction version provides a frightening degree of verisimilitude. Govan describes Butler's references as follows: "Butler treats the reoccurring themes of casual brutality, forcible separation of families, the quest for knowledge, the desire to escape, the tremendous work loads expected of slaves as effectively as any of the narratives or documentary histories discussing the slavery experience" (91). Butler rescues the past from the obscurity that results from identifying "slaves" as "servants."

When Christopher Charles Morpeth Donner assumes the office of president in 2024, he dismantles the space program, suspends "overly restrictive worker protection laws" (26), and encourages foreign investments in company towns such as Olivar. This former middle-class suburb of Los Angeles has been purchased by Kagimoto, Stamm, Frampton, and Company, a Japanese-German-Canadian enterprise, which has taken control of municipal utilities such as the desalination plant that provides the town's water and corporate-owned power and agriculture industries. Because most people are unemployed, the company is able to staff its operations with highly qualified workers who soon become in debt to the company. This is what happens to the Solis family. Emery's husband, Jorge Francisco Solis, becomes ill with appendicitis and dies as a result of inadequate medical care. Emery must work to pay off the debt that her husband, a company-town employee, has incurred. Because she is unable to do so, her two sons are taken from her and sold into slavery. Afraid that her daughter will also be taken, she flees.

When Cory, Lauren's stepmother, urges her father to consider applying to Olivar, her father echoes the words of the Bible and the ex-coloured man who said he had sold his birthright for a mess of pottage when he crossed the color line: "This business sounds half antebellum and half science fiction. I don't trust it. Freedom is dangerous, Cory, but it's precious, too. You can't just throw it away or let it slip away. You can't sell it for bread and pottage" (112).

Unlike the ex-coloured man, Lauren's father, a dean, professor, and Baptist minister, knows the cost of freedom and is unwilling to relinquish it for the safety and security that company towns represent. This is Butler's special blend of fact and fiction, the historical past and the imagined future. Addressing this issue of fact and fiction in the creation of Olivar, Lauren says:

> Maybe Olivar is the future—one face of it. Cities controlled by big companies are old hat in science fiction. My grandmother left a whole bookcase of old science fiction novels. The company-city subgenre always seemed to star a hero who outsmarted, over-threw, or escaped "the company." I've never seen one where the hero fought like hell to get taken in and underpaid by the company. In real life, that's the way it will be. That's the way it is. (114)

Lauren distinguishes between science fiction and reality. Reference to the "company-city subgenre" sets the fictional world apart from the real world. Her plot summary develops a set of oppositions between "real" and "fictive" worlds. Fiction features a hero who out-smarts or escapes the company town. "Real" heroes succeed in gain-ing admittance to these towns. Cory, Lauren's stepmother, debuts for this role of hero when she urges her husband to apply to Olivar. Her daughter, Lauren, will fulfill the destiny of the fictional hero. *Parable of the Sower* sets up this dichotomy between real and fictive worlds, leading the reader to expect that once the definitions of "real" and "fiction" have been established, the novel will attempt to traverse the boundaries. Contrary to these expectations, the novel follows the plot outline of the subgenre. Lauren, the hero, establishes the first Earthseed community. This community, aptly named Acorn, is a co-operative rather than a corporate venture. The novel announces its "fictionality" and meets all the necessary criteria of the subgenre.

These definitions of fiction and reality are complicated by Lauren's own discussions of them. This hero-character, a writer and reader, defends the belief that imaginary and real worlds intersect. As an ini-tial effort to convert others to Earthseed, Lauren asks her followers to read and think about how what they read can assist them in im-proving their lives. Lauren agrees that the good old days that their parents discuss will never return, but she feels that the future is not devoid of hopeful possibilities. The past cannot occur again, but the future can be good. Joanne asks what can be done to prepare for the future. As if eagerly awaiting an opportunity to address this question, Lauren answers by instructing her to read all the books she can. Joanne scoffs, "Books aren't going to save us," and Lauren responds:

> "Nothing is going to save us. If we don't save ourselves, we're dead. Now use your imagination. Is there anything on your family bookshelves that might help you if you were stuck outside?"
>
> "No."
>
> "You answer too fast. Go home and look again. And like I said, use your imagination. Any kind of survival information from encyclopedias, biographies, anything that helps you learn to live off the land and defend ourselves. Even some fiction might be useful." (55)

Lauren reconciles fictive and real worlds by stressing the importance of imagination to survival: "Use your imagination," she tells Joanne. "*Even* some fiction might be useful" (italics for emphasis). Of course, fiction, as the previous passage suggests, is exactly what Lauren is engaged in, and it has already assisted her by providing her with important information about the character she is playing. Lauren defends her author and the genre of science fiction against the argument that it has no bearing on "reality." Even though we may know the story before we finish or even begin the book, because fiction engages our imaginations, it is useful to our individual and collective survival. Keith, Lauren's stepbrother, leaves the walled community to enter the real world outside. Before he is killed, he returns home several times with such valuable commodities as chocolate candy bars and currency. When Lauren inquires into his procuring of these items, he confides that he lives in an old, deserted building with thieves, prostitutes, and drug addicts and that he is valued by this group because he can read and write: "They stole all this great stuff and they couldn't even use it. Before I got there they even broke some of it because they couldn't read the instructions" (97). So, as Lauren correctly surmises, Keith reads for a living, helping his friends learn to use their stolen equipment (97). This would seem to suggest that reading—in and of itself—will not help us to survive. To be an effective tool in our salvation, reading must be accompanied by imaginative thought. The evidence that suggests this is Keith's brutal murder. Lauren teaches her traveling companions to read by way of the exercise book she created to explain Earthseed. This book—which we shall look at shortly—requires imagination to assist with survival.

After disclosing the meaning of Earthseed, Lauren says, "I've never felt I was making any of this up. . . . I've never felt that it was anything other than real: discovery rather than invention, exploration rather than creation. All I do is observe and take notes, trying to put things down in ways that are as powerful, as simple, and as direct as I feel them" (72). By referring to her discovery of something that already exists, Lauren advances the platonic descriptions of artistic invention. Earthseed is a component of Lauren's religion, and the title of a book she is writing on the subject. In this passage, she embellishes her ideas concerning the interplay of real and imaginary worlds:

> "You believe in all this Earthseed stuff, don't you?"
> "Every word," I answered.
> "But . . . you made it up."
> I reached down, picked up a small stone, and put it on the table between us. "If I could analyze this and tell you all that it was made of, would that mean I'd made up its contents?" (199)

Elsewhere she explains that she is discovering or imagining something that already exists. She says: "I never felt that I was making any of this up—not the name, Earthseed, not any of it. I mean I've never felt it was anything other than real: discovery rather than invention, exploration rather than creation" (72).

Imagination is a gateway to truth. And Lauren's book, *Earthseed: The Book of the Living*, exemplifies this idea. She contrasts it with the Tibetan and Egyptian Books of the Dead by saying that there may already be a book of the living, but she doesn't care (115). As a collection of verse, it explores the nature of God and the role of humankind. It is her own book of Psalms. Thirty-one excerpts are interspersed in the diary that serves as the frame.

According to Hume, literature is the product of two impulses: fantasy and mimesis. Although the mimetic has been celebrated and studied, while fantasy has been regarded with suspicion or trivialized (she reminds us that Plato banned it from the Republic)—Hume believes it is an equal component in the creation of literature and "an impulse native to literature and manifest in innumerable variations from monster to metaphor" (21). Butler's novel investigates these ideas about literature by transforming them into fiction.

Lauren never told her father that she was not a Baptist. He was a minister, and she didn't want to hurt his feelings, especially since the family jeopardized their lives by practicing their religion. When the novel opens, a group is traveling to a church outside the city wall in order to be baptized in a church rather than at home with bathwater. Although Lauren finds comfort and consolation in her religion, especially the community it fosters, she also takes issue with its portraiture of God. Rather than believe in "a big-daddy-God or a big-cop-God or a big-king-God, . . . a kind of superperson," she sees God as change (13). "From the second law of thermodynamics to Darwin evolution, from Buddhism's insistence that nothing is permanent and all of Ecclesiastes, change is a part of life" (25). Lauren believes that "God *is* change" and that humans can affect the changes that occur. She compares her beliefs to those of Benjamin Franklin, Thomas Jefferson, and the Deists. She says they believed God was something "that made us then left us on our own." Lauren disagrees with this image of God as "a big kid, playing with toys" (14–15). Instead, she believes that people have control over their lives and that "God exists to be shaped" (24). She calls this "godshaping," and when things don't go well she admonishes herself, "Poor Godshaping. Lack of Forethought" (145). Lauren's religion celebrates the role of the individual in shaping his or her destiny. In this context, prayer becomes a way of imagining things into occurrence:

> God can't be resisted or stopped, but can be shaped and focused. This means God is not to be prayed to. Prayers only help the person doing the praying, and then, only if they strengthen and focus that person's resolve. If they're used that way, they can help us in

our only real relationship with God. They help us to shape God and to accept and work with the shapes that God imposes on us. God is power, and in the end, God prevails.

But we can rig the game in our own favor if we understand that God exists to be shaped, and will be shaped, with or without forethought, with or without our intent. (24)

The supreme will of the individual is set against a backdrop of Agamemnon. As the reader travels with Lauren along Route 101, he or she sees the destruction of civilization: scavengers profit from the demise of others, children and women are victims of the lawless activities of men, three-year-olds and seventy-three-year-olds are raped to death by outlaws. The biggest threat are the paints, men and women who shave their heads and paint their faces blue, green, or yellow. Paints take a drug—pyro (also known as blaze, *fuego*, flash, and sunfire), which affects their neurochemistry and makes watching the "leaping changing patterns of fire a better, more intense longer-lasting high than sex" (133). Lauren says, "It's like they [the paints] were fucking the fire, and like it was the best fuck they ever had" (102). At the close of the novel, Lauren's tribe of converts cover their bodies with wet rags to protect themselves from the "orgy of burning" that is consuming "dry-as-straw Southern California" (133).

Cory compares the discord to Babylon, while Joanne compares the devastation to Jericho, but Lauren consoles herself with the parable of the widow and the story of Noah, focusing on the "two-part nature of this situation": "God decides to destroy everything except Noah, his family, and some animals. *But* if Noah is going to be saved, he has plenty of hard work to do" (63). This fictional world ends as the Bible predicts, and the salvation of humankind takes place with the birth of the Earthseed community and the resurrection of Bankole's farm.

Unlike the old world, where race was a barrier and interracial relationships were condemned, the world that Lauren creates welcomes people of all races and ethnicities. The children of Earthseed are part white, Mexican, Japanese, Black, and Black Latino. When Lauren looks at them she sees the future of humankind. Thelma Shinn discusses the role of race in Butler's utopian future. She says,

"By combining Afro-American, female, and science fiction patterns, she can reveal the past, the present, and a probable future in which differences can be seen as challenging and enriching rather than threatening and denigrating and in which power can be seen as an interdependence between leader and those accepting that leadership, each accepting those limits on freedom that still allow for survival of the self" (214).

The title of the novel announces its fictionality: it is a parable, a story with a religious or moral slant, but unlike the original biblical tale, it suggests hope for the future. The sower's seed doesn't bear harvest, but Lauren's Earthseed "falls on good ground," bearing "fruit a hundredfold" (299).

Both *Parable of the Sower* and *Black Betty* introduce history into genres that are often thought to be ahistorical. Both introduce black history, as "unrecorded history" or the history inspired by visits to Mount Vernon and reading slave narratives. By introducing the issue of race, Mosley and Butler transform genres traditionally viewed as entertainment for a general audience. Tani and Hume suggest that this audience can be educated while it is being entertained. Mosley and Butler take advantage of this opportunity, and the result is the modification of the detective and the science fiction genres. Formulas for detective fiction fail to account for Mosley's novel, and characterizations of science fiction and fantasy are unable to account for Butler's work. African American writers transform these genres by introducing inquiry and commentary about standard practices, formulas, and norms into the works themselves.

Conclusion

> When he uses his mind he is intelligent; when his
> theories use his mind he is stupid.
>
> —Jean Toomer, *Essentials*

This investigation of black metafiction shows the weakness of privileging theories that are based on elaborate systems of classification. One problem is that things—sometimes important ones—get lost between the cracks, in the gaps between categories. As a hybrid of mimetic and diegetic forms, voice evades the categories premised upon these classifications, yet it is an important component of metafiction. Because poststructuralist theories emphasize formal innovation, a disproportionate amount of attention goes into the analysis of diegetic techniques, often at the expense of disregarding or overlooking mimetic indices. Although theorists are painstaking in their attempts to describe linguistic maneuvers and narrative strategies of self-consciousness, they often treat thematic concerns superficially, as if they were self-evident and needed no explanation.

The thematization of art, discussions of the process of artistic creation, and the portraiture of the artist are important venues of metafiction. To overlook them is to exclude many relevant books from the discussion.

Similar problems result from theories that are based upon the artificial distinction of form and content. While such divisions may provide a valuable framework for dissecting and analyzing elements of fiction, they reduce the complexity of fiction to a single simple formula. Scholars of African American literature and scholars of Anglo-European literature have made this error. Donald Gibson warns against writers who pay too much attention to form at the expense of neglecting politics. The harlequin mask that serves as a metaphor in Gates' description of literary ancestry suggests that black writers are influenced by their white ancestors in all things having to do with form and influenced by their black ancestors in all things having to do with content. Gaines and Wright candidly reveal their own harlequin masks in discussions of writers who have influenced them. Those who continue to employ the form/content distinction are unpersuaded of the role of language in shaping thought. While many believe that we think in language, adherents of the form/content distinction believe thought is prelinguistic. Once we are fully satisfied with the formulation of our ideas, we search for the best way to express them.

This obsession with form is a response to new critics whose Eurocentric theories excluded African American literature from discussions of serious literature because it was not perceived as stylistically complex. Instead, it was dismissed as social realism and classified as propaganda tract rather than fiction. It served a useful, rather than artistic, purpose—that of educating readers to the effects of racism, oppression, and social injustice. The new critics continue to exert their influence by advocating restrictive definitions of art. Like many people seeking public office, none of these theorists knows the cost of half a gallon of milk or a loaf of bread, but they determine the definitions and standards, the blazing hoops through which a work must pass unscathed in order to be recognized as art.

These biases are also present in academe, where multiculturalists and African Americanists are regarded as exotics, extras who provide relief from the serious work done in the classrooms where the required courses in Shakespeare are taught. Because they are regarded as accessory, scholars of non-European literature are excluded from the forums and debates that determine requirements, curriculum, and educational objectives. Scholars of African American literature and ethnic literatures are often excluded from the tribe of specialists known as "Americanists." Such distinctions may have their origins in convenience rather than an overarching vision, but the consequences are apparent in hiring practices and scholarship. Scholars of African American literature are rewarded for keeping within the confines of their discipline, and like scholars of other ethnic literatures, they work in isolation. The result is a perpetuation of the status quo and their status as second-class citizens in departments of English. Scholars of Latina/o literature write and teach it, but like the African Americanists, many are discouraged from bringing what they know to bear on discussions of American literature. As a result, there is a scarcity of research that bridges ethnic subdisciplines to American studies. Houston Baker's *Modernism and the Harlem Renaissance* and Phillip Brian Harper's *Framing the Margins* are evidence of the original, informative work that can be accomplished when the boundaries that divide fields of study are overstepped.

In the essay "Postmodern Blackness" bell hooks laments the absence of scholarship on African American postmodernism. She is angered by scholars of African American studies who believe postmodernism has nothing to do with the black experience because this reinforces the idea that "blackness is associated with gut level experience and has no connection to abstract thinking" (510). Hooks suggests that scholars question "the idea that there is no meaningful connection between black experience and critical thinking about aesthetics" (510–511). After criticizing scholars of black studies for abruptly leaving the room when the subject of postmodernism arises, hooks shames scholars of postmodernism, including feminists, for excluding black writers from their discussions. She provides a "hands-on" example for everybody when she explains black nationalism as a school of modernism. Hooks concludes "Postmodern Blackness" with this call to action: "To change the exclusionary practice of postmodern critical discourse is to enact a postmodernism of resistance" (517).

John Barth and Raymond Federman are at the center of discussions of postmodernism. As writers of fiction and theory, they represent that peculiarity in postmodernism that blurs the distinctions between these disciplines. In recent essays, Barth and Federman assess the current state of postmodernism, tracing its lineage from the first generation of writers to the current, second generation. Barth traces a line of descent from Donald Barthelme, Robert Coover, William Gass, John Hawkes, and Thomas Pynchon to a second generation of early-Hemingway minimalists—Raymond Carver and Ann Beattie—and "traditional pigeons"—Joyce Carol Oates, Ann Tyler, and John Updike (*Further Fridays* 125). Federman traces the lineage from William Burroughs, Kurt Vonnegut, Jr., Thomas Pynchon, John Barth, and Donald Barthelme to Kathy Acker and William Vollman (*Critifiction* 132). To a longer list of originators, he adds John Coltrane and this parenthetical aside: "I include that name to remind us that John Coltrane's type of jazz was also postmodern" (*Critifiction* 111). Although the tribute does not go unappreciated, one musician is named among a dozen writers, and he stands out like the only uninvited guest at a dinner party. Canonizers take note: African American postmodernists—some of whom reproduce the techniques of jazz in their writing—abound. Postmodern writers like Ishmael Reed, Al Young, Albert Murray, Xam Cartiér, Leon Forrest, Reginald McKnight, Charles Johnson, Clarence Major, John Edgar Wideman, and Ntozake Shange must be included on any list. Their exclusion and the exclusion of other writers of race and ethnicity invalidate any such lists and all generalization originating from them.

Barth and Federman formulate a canon of postmodern writers whose exclusionary nature adds urgency to bell hooks' plea for a "postmodern resistance." Beginning with hooks' pronouncement of the aims of the resistance, critics, scholars, and students can outline a plan of action. Their agenda will weigh the ideas of Barth, Federman, and other theorists of postmodernism with Afrocentric and vernacular theories. Occasionally the temptation to dispense with

Western theory will seem nearly impossible to ignore, but this temptation should be resisted. To resist this temptation, hooks says, is to refuse to reinforce the negative stereotypes that perpetuate this exclusivity. Ishmael Reed suggests another reason for refusing to throw up our hands:

> The Afrocentric exploration of the black past only scratches the surface. A full examination of the ancestry of those who are referred to in the newspapers as black and African Americans must include Europe and Native America. The pursuit of this journey requires the sort of intellectual courage that's missing in contemporary, politically correct America, where certain words cannot be spoken and certain secrets cannot be unearthed and certain investigations are frowned upon. (*Dirty Laundry* 267)

At the conclusion of "Postmodern Blackness," hooks identifies another problem and solution. She says that many scholars are alienated by the language of postmodernism. She says she is accustomed to discussing her work with friends and family. The discourse of postmodernism is an intellectual hurdle but also, and more important, a political one. Like Jackson, who refuses to study "some kinda language," preferring instead to "walk on the ground an' talk like my people talk," hooks is not sure she wants to speak the language of postmodernism (Mosley 134). To adopt this language, even for the purpose of challenging it, is to cease speaking, at least momentarily, to "family, friends and comrades" (hooks 518). Speaking to people, speaking to everybody so that anybody who wants to can understand is, for many, including hooks, an uncompromisable position traceable to vernacular traditions. Hooks suggests a compromise: "cultivating habits of being that reinforce awareness that knowledge can be disseminated and shared on a number of fronts" (518). She suggests that scholars of African American postmodernism may participate in the resistance by making the ideas obscured by the rhetoric of postmodernism accessible and malleable.

African American writers of postmodern fiction are enacting this agenda. Many share hooks' commitment to address an audience of friends and family, and many depend heavily on the support and appreciation of this audience. Making the ideas accessible and entertaining is the call to action that makes many PowerBooks hum. If game playing is, as Federman, Barth, and other theorists of postmodernism suggest, one characteristic of the postmodern sensibility,[1] African American postmodernists rewrite the game. The goal is to entertain professionals, for whom reading is a way of life, as well as family and friends, for whom reading is a leisurely pastime. The game of pleasing diverse audiences is not new to the African American writer, nor is it better or worse than using only words that begin with the letter *c* in chapter 3 or requiring that the last two letters of each word be repeated as the first two letters of the next word.[2]

Reginald McKnight's short story "The Homunculus: A Novel in One Chapter" reflects the "playfulness" characteristic of postmodernism in a title that delights all readers. It plays with language, particularly literary terminology, while experimenting with the cross-germination of novel and short-story forms. McKnight's novel-story directs attention to the arbitrary nature of genre classifications, then proceeds to experiment with hybrid forms nevertheless. This amuses the hobbyist and indulges the specialist's penchant for theory-fiction.

In "Before Postmodernism and After," Federman paraphrases the tenets of the literature of exhaustion. Like Barth, the originator of the term, Federman acknowledges the effect of literature's "usedupedness" on postmodern writers. With all the possible stories already written, the only outlet for the contemporary writer's creativity is to remake the old: "Postmodern literature could no longer produce original works of art (**masterpieces**) nor could it have great artists (**masters**), it could only produce works which resembled one another, and writers who mostly imitated each other's work" (*Critifiction* 118). Many African American writers share this sense of literature's "usedupedness," and like the postmodernists Federman describes, their energies are engaged in making the old new. The oral tradition also prescribes the remaking of old stories. The storyteller who is also historian and educator refashions existing stories so that they are relevant to the circumstances and the audience. McKnight's novel-story acknowledges both traditions by telling a familiar story revised to meet the needs of his audience. Unlike the postmodernist who sees herself engaged in a last-ditch effort to keep a dying art alive, the storyteller aware of the oral storytelling traditions recognizes that she is one of many who tell this story and alter it to suit the circumstances. Like the minister citing a particular text, she knows that her audience expects her to remain faithful to the text and to embellish it. She is granted the latitude to do whatever is necessary to make the text meaningful to the congregation. McKnight refashions the fable and the quest, stories familiar to all audiences. He delights an audience of specialists with name-dropping, the assertion and negation (deconstruction) of literary self-consciousness, and the requisite literary jargon.

The "many, many years ago" with which the story begins signals the reinvention of the fable (3). The protagonist-hero is distinguished from the other inhabitants of the Realm by "the thumbprint of the Old One" (4). He is a "marvelous poet," an "adept fiction writer," a master of "lyre, lute, kleetello, guitar, dulcimer, fiddle, cello and vibraphone" (4). In this classic tale of unrequited love, his beloved, Nohla, refuses him. At the urging of his friends and family, the despondent artist departs from the Realm and journeys to the vanished Land of Light and Dark, where "five of the eight mysteries of the Ur-Realm" exist and there is "blood-freezing violence and beauty so profound that it is said the Old One actually slept there" (7). The Land of Light and Dark is an idyllic oasis. The land is inhabited by angels, "winged people with the skin of polished obsidian who speak only in proverbs" (7). As in Eden, the people and animals share the same language.

According to Federman, "the most significant innovations [of postmodernism] involve the self-conscious exploration of the nature, limits, and possibilities of art" (*Critifiction* 109). McKnight makes this the subject of his story. Fortified by the friendship of N'Thou and the other congenial inhabitants of the land, the artist begins a journal. What starts as a record of daily events becomes an all-consuming passion. Before long, it occupies every minute available to the artist, and as he works, it is transformed from journal to "a novel, a poem, a prayer, then a chant, then a one-act play, an opera—it actually made sound!—a painting, a sculpture and then, wonder of wonders the thing became flesh!: A miniature version of himself!" (9) Just when he realizes he is writing himself into existence, a homunculus steps off the page and begins talking to him: ". . . one day as he scribbled and chiseled and stitched upon the . . . text . . . we shall call it, he began to notice that fingers were clutching his throat, in a manner of speaking, and his thumbs were shaping his own, well . . . it wasn't a sentence anymore, he had to admit to himself. It wasn't a canvas or clay, it was—'My chin!'" (9) The homunculus and artist converse while the homunculus eats the journal and grows larger. The homunculus is metafiction brought to life. The artist has reproduced himself in his work, but he hasn't read it because he wouldn't understand it. In this exchange between the homunculus and the artist, "Skippy," the artist attempts to explain why he has refrained from reading his manuscript:

> "Tell me something, Skippy," he said. "Whycome you never stopped to read what you wrote?"
> The artist shrugged and sighed. "I don't know, exactly. Fear, perhaps? It's everything I've ever wanted to do, I've ever wanted to say. It's my whole life. It's about my lovely What's-Her-Name. It's . . . rather it could be—*could* have been, anyway, the greatest work ever created. Old One! There is something wonderful about it. And . . . and even if no one had ever liked it, why, even if no one had ever even read it, I know in my heart that it's changed me. It's done something to me. How all this has happened—how it resulted in you, I mean—I don't know but I have just known it was a great work. So great, perhaps, that I knew that even I wouldn't be able to understand it." (15)

The artist's reproduction of himself in his work suggests that writing is both a means of self-discovery and transformation. We write, paint, sculpt so that we can learn who we are by examining what we have produced. Art is an artifact of consciousness. From it, we reconstruct an image of that consciousness. When there is no other, when the beloved's gaze is diverted, art becomes the only mirror available. Not only does it allow us a glimpse at ourselves, it may be the only evidence of our existence. Unlike Dove's dancer, whose grace is destroyed by self-consciousness, unlike Narcissus, who is similarly destroyed, the artist in McKnight's novel-story suggests that artists can never know themselves by their work because the person they reconstruct is not the person they are. After reading the manuscript, the artist returns to the Realm, reads "the popular writers and poets of the day," "buys inexpensive art," "marries a young woman who had never heard of him," "raises seven sons and daughters," and dies "neither a happy man nor a sad man" (19). This metafiction is accessible. The reader does not have to be familiar with metafiction or its history to enjoy McKnight's novel-story. Experiments with numerology, naming, animation, and a homunculus who greets his maker with "Morning, blood," ensure entertainment for a general audience. An audience of specialists can also appreciate the homunculus, as a cautionary reminder of erroneous theories and as an allusion to the homunculus that appears in Laurence Sterne's highly self-conscious novel, *Tristram Shandy*. Addressing a dual audience produces "double-coding," simultaneous suggestions of illusion and anti-illusion in fiction.[3]

Even though McKnight and others are still writing postmodern fiction, stories that speculate about their own creation, theorists believe that postmodernism is dead. In "Before Postmodernism and After," Federman lists the twenty answers he received in response to the question "Do you think postmodernism is dead? If so, what killed it?" (*Critifiction* 121). All twenty responded that it was, indeed, dead, and many cited popular culture and the widespread commercialization of its tropes and figures as the cause.[4] Summarizing the responses he received, Federman says, "Though no one ever really felt comfortable with the term Postmodern, nonetheless for several decades it served to define a certain avant-garde activity played out on a high intellectual and artistic level, at times even accused of being elitist, until that activity was absorbed into mainstream culture by the economy and quickly turned into Pop-Art. And so now it is time, perhaps, to abandon the term Postmodern" (*Critifiction* 132).

Although he says it is dead, the characteristics that he identifies in his description of postmodernism flourish. Those characteristics include the ability to disorient, to create difference, and to present rather than re-present. Even though these characteristics aptly describe much current fiction, postmodernism is strictly "reserved seating" for a select few. Theorists would rather murder postmodernism than watch helplessly as it is fondled by the hands of strangers. The idea that its tropes are familiar to anyone watching prime-time television is an insult to their intelligence. McKnight's homunculus is an appropriate metaphor for these outdated theories of literary self-consciousness. Hooks' plea for resistance celebrates the popular culture that theorists of the postmodern are determined to exclude. Her essay concludes: "It's exciting to think, write, talk about, and create art that reflects passionate engagement with popular cultures, because this may very well be 'the' central future location of resistance struggle, a meeting place where new and radical happenings can occur" (518).

William Gass, the person credited with coining the term "metafiction," also writes about recent literary history. By shifting the focus from "postmodernism" to "experimental writing," he visualizes a different past and future. In "On Experimental Writing," he identifies several kinds of writing experiments but warns that not all originate from a "real dissatisfaction with existing knowledge" (3). He says that much experimental fiction resembles his childhood experiments with chemistry. Such experiments are not inspired to increase knowledge but to break rules, to be subversive. Other experiments produce something new by virtue of "minuscule and trivial additions" rather than genuine innovative problem solving (3). Like most contemporary theorists, Gass restricts his definition of innovation to formal concerns: "Real innovation is nearly always formal: it is an expression of style at the level of narrative structure and fictional strategy" (3). From this definition of literary innovation, Gass develops his ideas of "exploratory literature," which

> records an often painful and disappointing journey, possibly a discovery, possibly of empty sailing; yet never toward what may lie out of sight in the self but toward what lies unappreciated in the landscape of literature—implications unperceived, conclusions undrawn, directions everyone has failed to follow. Exploration is the work of the realist, however fanciful that reality may seem to those encountering it for the first time. (27)

Having put his money on the future of "exploratory realism" with a technical edge, art motivated by genuine scientific inquiry, the father of metafiction disowns his earlier brainchild as a second-rate experiment that indulged writers in solipsistic drivel: "Many times metafictions, because they caressed themselves so publicly, behaved more like manifestoes than stories. They were more 'explanatory' than 'experimental.' Instead of showing that something could be done by doing it, they became tutorial, emphasizing technique: teaching the reader how to read, admonishing him for his traditional bourgeois expectations and directing his attention to art instead of nature, to the reality of the work instead of the reality of the world" (27).

These dichotomies are as problematic as the form/content distinctions that Gass relies on to define innovation. The opposition of inner and outer worlds, the "work" and "the world," is reductive and inaccurate. Double-coded stories such as the one by McKnight illustrate the simultaneous exploration of inner and outer worlds. Barth reminds us that "even the artist who tries to hold a mirror *away* from life—toward another mirror, perhaps—is still mirroring life" (*Further Fridays* 142).

＞　＞　＞　＞　＞　＞　＞　＞　＞　＞

Notes

1. Introduction

1. See the preface to Henry Louis Gates, Jr.,'s *The Signifying Monkey*, in which he discusses his development as a critic and scholar. Also see "Criticism in the Jungle," the introductory essay to *Black Literature and Literary Theory*. In this essay he discusses the difficulties of imposing Western theory on black texts.

2. Houston A. Baker, Jr., in *Workings of the Spirit*, applies phenomenology to black women's writing. Deborah McDowell's "Boundaries: Or Distant Relations and Close Kin" (Baker and Redmond 51–70) and Mae Gwendolyn Henderson's "Speaking in Tongues" apply dialogics to black women's writing.

3. In this essay Zora Neale Hurston identifies the qualities of black expression. She describes the centrality of metaphor and simile, the double descriptive, and the use of verbal nouns in the vernacular (*The Sanctified Church* 49–68).

4. A recent contribution to the continuing discussion of language and speech in the novel is Maria J. Racine's "Voice and Interiority in Zora Neale Hurston's *Their Eyes Were Watching God*." Unlike most critics, who focus on the speech and language of the female characters, Racine analyzes both male and female speech patterns to conclude that "the evolution of male voices seems to parallel the evolution of Janie's" (283).

5. James A. Mellard's *The Exploded Form* and Robert Alter's *Partial Magic* argue that postmodernism is not the exclusive proprietor of metafiction. Like Linda Hutcheon and Patricia Waugh, they argue that literary self-consciousness can be traced at least as far back as the eighteenth century.

6. For a thorough discussion of the death of the novel and its causes and consequences, see the collection of essays edited by Raymond Federman, *Surfiction*.

7. Gates founds his definition of signifyin(g) on work done in linguistics by Thomas Kochman, Claudia Mitchell-Kernan, and Geneva Smitherman. In accordance with the findings of these researchers, Gates

defines signifyin(g) as "the black rhetorical difference that negotiates the language user through several orders of meaning" (*Signifying Monkey* 79). Like Mitchell-Kernan, Gates distinguishes between signifying and signifyin(g) by explaining that the latter is "the black term for what in classical European rhetoric are called figures of signification" (81). In other words, signifying "denotes meaning" and signifyin(g) "denotes ways of meaning" (81). Hereafter I use these terms as Gates has defined them.

8. Waugh's assertion of the political nature of metafiction is a counter-argument to the assertion that such fiction is solipsistic and apolitical. Critics of such literature argue that raising questions about the nature of reality presupposes an apolitical stance. They also believe that questions about the effectiveness of language as a vehicle of communication and questions about the relationship between sign and signified, *langue* and *parole*, are unalterably linked to fatalism. Advocates and practitioners of metafiction have defended their work against such accusations by pointing to experimental writing or unrealistic fiction as a challenge to the reality from which such fictions issue. This has been especially true for black writers, who are often viewed as neglecting their social responsibility through their preference for nonrealistic fiction.

9. This is the important contribution that critics such as Gates and Baker would make. They would also demonstrate that an understanding of the significance of aesthetic interests requires a careful examination of a specific work: its meaning is variable.

10. McDowell sees Celie as a revision of Iola Leroy. See her essay "'The Changing Same'," 99.

11. New realism has been used by critics (among whom are Waugh) to identify the school of writing that follows postmodernism (hence it is sometimes called post, postmodernism). Unlike the postmodernists, who questioned objective reality, new realists view reality as a social construct built on a consensus of opinion.

2. Mimesis of Process

1. Hutcheon notes that "aside from parody . . . the two most frequently used devices in this thematization process are the *mise en abyme* (a term for which there is no convenient English equivalent) and a kind of more extended allegory, two devices which are often hard to distinguish from one another" (*Narcissistic Narrative* 53–54).

2. Reed's Law defines parody as a form of signifyin(g). Parody that issues from the black vernacular is not a consequence of literature's exhaustion but is instead a consequence of the abundance of stories, the interplay of storyteller and audience, and the continuously evolving form of the story itself. Unlike the parody prompted by the literature of exhaustion, parody that often culminates in satire, signifyin(g) culminates in a "mutation which renders the original obsolete." Gates describes it as parody "minus the negative critique" (xxvi). Signifyin(g) is founded on the shared knowledge of a story. It is effective when the audience appreciates its improvisations. The pleasure of signifyin(g) is founded on the fact that the story is "exhausted" and that the storyteller's version can improvise on the existing one, making it relevant to the specific audience to which it is told. Gates discusses this pleasure in his analysis of intertextuality and the Monkey poems:

> It is as if a received structure of crucial elements provides a base for poeisis, and the narrator's technique, his or her craft, is to be gauged by the creative (re)placement of these expected anticipated formulaic phrases and formulaic events rendered anew in unexpected ways. Precisely because the concepts represented in the poem are shared, repeated, and familiar to the poet's audience, meaning is devalued while the signifier is valorized. Value, in this art of poeisis, lies in its foregrounding rather than in the invention of a novel signified (*Signifying Monkey* 61).

3. Classical theories form the basis for Hutcheon's argument for the reintroduction of "mimesis of process." She observes that "the concept of mimesis of process is a constant in literature" and that "even Aristotelian mimetic theory allowed room for the imitation of the creative process" (40). She cites M. H. Abram's *The Mirror and the Lamp* as evidence that "the mimetic concept in art and in criticism after Plato and Aristotle became restricted, focusing on the product of artistic endeavor rather than on the artistic process of creation: 'It is not that the emphasis has shifted *from* mimesis *to* the creating imagination, but rather that the critical terms in which we discuss that which is imitated in fiction must be opened again to make room for the new novels being written and read'" (41).

4. Charles Johnson credits Herbert Spiegelberg and his essay "Phenomenology through Vicarious Experience" for an intellectual exercise that assists actors and writers in imagining the lives of others. See Johnson, "Being and Fiction," for an outline of the procedure (*Being and Race* 43).

5. In "Ishmael Reed—A Self-Interview," the author discusses the influences of telepathy, synchronization, and HooDoo on his work. He discusses the novel *Mumbo Jumbo* as an exercise in automatic writing, which was assisted by voices from his heritage (*Shrovetide* 158).

6. Nullification is defined as "an extremist doctrine of States Rights holding that a state can declare null and void any federal law it deems unconstitutional. The principle was invoked by South Carolina in 1832, at the instigation of Senator John C. Calhoun to protest federal tariffs favoring Northern interests at the expense of the South. Nullification was a forerunner of the doctrine of secession" (Levey and Greenhall 614).

7. Johnson apologizes for sounding "cranky" and "harping at this late hour in American literary history" on the priority of character and then proceeds to do just that. In "First Philosophy" he says that "everything in first-rate fiction as well as in film, or in all narrative forms of entertainment, hinges on this matter" (*Being and Race* 40).

8. McDowell borrows these classifications from Susan Lanser's *The Narrative Act*. Lanser uses "public" to refer to "narrative acts designed for public readership" and "private" for those "designed for reception only by the other characters and textual figures" (McDowell 93). McDowell uses the distinction to differentiate between novels by black women "that imply a public readership, or one outside the black cultural community, and those that imply a private readership, or one within that cultural matrix" (93). She notes the use of similar distinctions in essays by Richard Wright and Robert Bone (111).

9. She traces the evolution of black women's writing from the turn of the century to the present. She suggests that black women's novels of the eighties "pose the question concerning what community black women must belong to in order to understand themselves most effectively in their totality as blacks *and* women" (180).

10. In his course on contemporary American literature, Neil Schmitz distinguished between "happy metafictionists" and "unhappy metafictionists." The former recognize the distinction between sign and signified as a site for humor; the latter regard it as a site for despair and inescapable solipsism. Vladimir Nabokov, Robert Coover, Donald Barthelme, and Ishmael Reed can be viewed as happy metafictionists, John Barth and John Hawkes as unhappy ones.

11. See Felipe Smith's "Alice Walker's Redemptive Art," Ikenna Dieke's "Toward a Monistic Idealism," and Thomas F. Marvin's "'Preachin' the Blues'" for discussions of spiritualism in Walker's novels.

3. The *Künstlerroman* and the Blues Hero

1. Laura Sue Fuderer's *The Female Bildungsroman* and David Williams' *Confessional Fictions* are evidence of this kind of research. Scholars of neglected literatures are revising the definition of the bildungsroman to make it more inclusive. This work contributes to the advancement of theory and the study of postcolonial and feminist literature. There is an abundance of such work to be done; however, it can be successful only if one makes the literature the foremost consideration and the theory only a point of departure. The following investigation of the blues hero and African American *künstlerroman* is an attempt at this.

2. The "bildungsroman" is defined as a novel, often autobiographical, that portrays a character's development from adolescence to maturity (Holman 55).

3. In *Fabulation and Metafiction* Robert Scholes says, "Both the conditions of being and the order of fiction partake of a duality which distinguishes existence from essence" (100). He uses this distinction as a basis for the classification of metafiction.

4. This is beginning to change as studies such as Craig Hansen Werner's *Playing the Changes* and Keith E. Byerman's *Fingering the Jagged Grain* explore the interplay of aesthetic traditions.

5. I borrow the term "self-definition" from Barbara Christian, who traces the history of African American women's fiction as a movement toward self-definition.

6. In the interview with Mohamed B. Taleb-Khyar, Rita Dove speaks about Du Bois' idea of double-consciousness as the "binocular vision" that results from growing up as a member of a minority (350).

7. This idea of parodying parody or "loa-making" is a form of signifyin(g). It is also, more generally speaking, a trope or strategy drawn from the "vernacular" as defined by Baker in "Belief, Theory, and Blues." Baker says, "By the vernacular I want to suggest not only the majority of Afro-Americans, but, in both an economic and a political sense, the American majority. An image from a resonantly vernacular tradition of Afro-American expression serves to capture my notion of the vernacular. The picture is drawn from the black blues and sung by Howlin' Wolf" (9). Virginia's sense of herself as a black mime is disconnected from the history of "loa-making" in black theater and more generally, from the aesthetics of the black vernacular.

8. Dove explains her feelings about writing and politics in her interview with Taleb-Khyar:

When I walk into my room to write, I don't think of myself in political terms. I approach that piece of paper or the computer screen to search for—I know it sounds corny—truth and beauty through language. As an artist, I shun political consideration and racial or gender partiality; for example, I would find it a breach of my integrity as a writer to create a character for didactic or propaganda purposes, like concocting a strong Black heroine, an idealized so-called role model, just to promote a positive image. I'm interested in truth. (358)

9. See Gates, *Signifying Monkey*, pp. 170–216, and Baker, *Workings of the Spirit*, pp. 69–101, for discussions of "speakerly texts" and narrative voice in Zora Neale Hurston's fiction.

10. Robert Stepto's *From behind the Veil* traces the history of the African American narrative from its origins as slave narrative to the self-determination and self-definition of modern narratives such as Ralph Ellison's *Invisible Man*. Barbara Christian discusses the development of black women's writing as a movement toward self-definition. Valerie Smith's *Self-Discovery and Authority in Afro-American Narrative* is a third study that traces the history of the movement toward autonomy in fiction.

4. Revision, Dialogism, and Intertextuality

1. See Caesar R. Blake's "On Richard Wright's *Native Son*" for a discussion of the genre of African American crime fiction (192).

2. For an example of feminist "revisionism" see Alicia Ostriker's "The Thieves of Language." For a discussion of dialogism and feminism, see Dale M. Bauer and S. Jaret McKinstry, eds., *Feminism, Bakhtin, and the Dialogic*, and Anne Herrmann's *The Dialogic and Difference*.

3. In "Canon Formation and the Afro-American Tradition," Gates contradicts his theory of the "harlequin mask" of influence, arguing that black art never adopted "white form": "The very fact that the Negro, by nature of his environment was deprived of education, prevented his art form from ever becoming purely imitative. Even where he adopted the white man's substance, as in the case of religion, he never adopted his form" (Baker and Redmond 34).

4. McDowell distinguishes between influence in works by men and in those by women. She agrees with Gates' recognition of the "adversarial and parodic" relationships among Richard Wright, Ralph Ellison, and Ishmael Reed. However, the absence of parody, particularly in her study

of Frances Harper and Alice Walker, is, for McDowell, the "fundamental distinction between Afro-American male and female literary relations" ("'The Changing Same,'" 107).

5. See Herrmann and Ostriker for discussions of influence among women writers. See McDowell, Henderson, and Awkward for discussion of influence among black women writers.

6. Bakhtin defines "double-voiced discourse" in "Discourse in the Novel":

> Heteroglossia, once incorporated into the novel (whatever the forms for its incorporation), is *another's speech in another's language*, serving to express authorial intentions but in a refracted way. Such speech constitutes a special type of double-voiced discourse. It serves two speakers at the same time and expresses simultaneously two different intentions: the direct intention of the character who is speaking, and the refracted intention of the author. In such discourse, there are two voices, two meanings and two expressions. And all the while these two voices are dialogically interrelated, they—as it were—know about each other (just as two exchanges in a dialogue know of each other and are structured in this mutual knowledge of each other); it is as if they actually hold a conversation with each other. Double-voiced discourse is always internally dialogized. Examples of this would be comic, ironic or parodic discourse, the refracting discourse of a narrator refracting discourse in the language of a character and finally the discourse of a whole incorporated genre—all these discourses are double-voiced and internally dialogized. A potential dialogue is embedded in them, one as yet unfolded, a concentrated dialogue of two voices, two world views, two languages. (*The Dialogic Imagination* 324–325)

7. See Keneth Kinnamon's introduction to *New Essays on* Native Son for a discussion of the impact the Robert Nixon and Earl Hicks case had on *Native Son* (5–6). In an interview with Marcia Gaudet, Gaines discusses visits to local prisons in preparation for writing *A Lesson before Dying* (*Porch Talk* 133).

8. This observation invites comparison with Donald Gibson's discussion of *Native Son* as an example of literary modernism.

9. Jay Clayton and Eric Rothstein discuss influence and intention in the introductory essay of *Influence and Intertextuality*.

10. For a discussion of literacy and freedom, see Gates, "The Trope of the Talking Book" (*Signifying* 127–169).

11. See John M. Reilly's "Giving Bigger a Voice." Reilly argues that "Wright's decision to use a narrative point of view closely identified with Bigger's, though not identical to it . . . accounts for readers' taking his side" (45).

12. Tanner discusses the difference between the narrator's language and Bigger's language, the narrator's use of a master language, and the distinction between symbolic and experiential discourses.

13. Gaines discusses the importance of the first-person point of view with Carl Wooton. He tells his students, "What we've [Americans] done with the first person . . . is as great . . . as anything else we have done— any of the characters that we have created, any of the stories we have told, or anything else" (*Porch Talk* 14). He discusses the different points of view used in each of his novels with Marcia Gaudet (*Porch Talk* 25–29).

14. André Malraux says, "'Stylization . . . is the supreme objective of the creative process.' He also maintains that the artist derives not from nature itself but from other artists" (65). Albert Murray quotes Malraux in *The Hero and the Blues* (65–107).

15. Ishmael Reed's poem "The Neo-HooDoo Aesthetic" uses cooking as a metaphor for the creative process. Unspecified quantities and varied ingredients attest to the necessity for improvisation (*Conjure* 26).

16. Harris, *Uncle Remus or Mr. Fox, Mr. Rabbit, and Mr. Terrapin.* For a different transcription of this version, see Henry D. Spalding's *Encyclopedia of Black Folklore and Humor* 9–11.

17. Sources of this version are Daryl Cumber Dance's *Shuckin' and Jivin'* 195; Richard M. Dorson's *American Negro Folktales* 75–76; and Langston Hughes and Arna Bontemps' *The Book of Negro Folklore* 1–2.

18. For a fuller description of Son as trickster, see Harris 119–124.

19. See Karla F. C. Holloway and Stephanie A. Demetrapoulos 118–142; and Barbara Christian 65–69.

20. Shlomith Rimmon-Kenan provides an overview of implied writers and readers, theories and constructs in chapter 7 of *Narrative Fiction* (86–105). Summarizing the work of Wolfgang Iser, Wayne C. Booth, Menakhem Perry, and Seymour Chatman, she defines the implied author as "a construct inferred and assembled by the reader from all the components of the text" (87).

21. See Deborah McDowell's "The Self and the Other." See her response to Hortense Spiller's treatment of the subject in "A Hateful Passion, A Lost Love," *Feminist Studies* 9 (Summer 1983): 296, quoted in McDowell 80.

5. Voice, Metanarrative, and the Oral Tradition

1. See Zora Neale Hurston's *Dust Tracks on a Road*, particularly chapter 14, "Love," which Hurston concludes with her own advice on the subject:

Love is a funny thing; Love is a blossom;
If you want your finger bit, poke it in a possum. (265)

2. According to Smitherman, "Harmony in nature and the universe is provided by the complementary, interdependent, synergic interaction between the spiritual and the material." This provides a "paradigm" in which "opposites . . . constitute interdependent, interacting forces which are necessary for producing a given reality" (75). In "Earthly Thoughts on *Divine Days*," John Cawelti discusses this synthesis in cultural traditions in the interplay of W. A. D. Ford and Sugar-Groove (433–437).

3. In her discussion of the interrogative text, Catherine Belsey defines the split subject that originates in Lacanian theory as "the division between the subject of the enunciation and the subject of the *énoncé*, the 'I' who speaks and the 'I' who is represented in the discourse." She argues that "it is in the interest of the stability of a class society to suppress this "contradiction in the subject" and that "this process of suppression characterizes the classic realist text" (84). The split subject should not be confused with the fragmented subject, which is discussed in Phillip Brian Harper's *Framing the Margins*.

6. Metafiction as Genre

1. In his study of the postmodern anti-detective novel, Stephano Tani identifies the metafictional anti-detective as one of the three types. Like Hutcheon, he reads this type of detective story hermeneutically. The relationship between the writer and the reader is an enactment of the detective story with the writer "deviously hiding his own text" and the reader-as-detective trying "to make sense out of it" (43).

2. Richard Alewyn recognizes it as a descendant of the German Romantic movement and the Gothic; Tani sees it as a product of the Enlightenment, evidence of reason triumphing over the irrational.

3. These descriptions of poverty suggest Easy's affinity to Chester Himes' detectives, Coffin Ed and Grave Digger, who, according to Peter Rabinowitz, "have strong identification with the poor black people

among whom they work" and "do what they can to alleviate the pain and suffering in the black community" (22).

4. Freese says the message of detective fiction is that the "disturbed order of the world can be restored by the eventual discovery and punishment of any criminal" (8).

5. He says things that might make some call him a racist and, like Coffin Ed in Himes' *All Shot Up*, he beats up everyone who calls him "nigger." The opening scene of Himes' novel is repeated several times in the first half of Mosley's novel.

6. Peter Freese uses this term, "cultural mediator," to describe the narrator who "introduces the reader to an unknown ethnic culture" (9). According to Freese, the ethnic detective stories are illustrations of "ethnic friction and cultural confrontation" and "comment on the challenges of everyday life in a 'multicultural' society'" (9–10). In this way the ethnic mystery "fulfills the function of anthropological handbooks" (10). In contrast to this is Mason's analysis of the interplay of cultures in the Rawlins Mystery Series. Relying on theories of M. M. Bakhtin and Georg Lukács, Theodore Mason sees this as an act of *transgression*, a "crossing of categories or the violation of social protocols about social, cultural and historical identity" (178). He says, "Cultural knowledge within the universe of *Devil in a Blue Dress* becomes represented initially as racial knowledge, or more precisely, the negotiation of racial protocols" (179).

7. Conclusion

1. In "Before Postmodernism and After," Federman says, "Postmodern fiction offered itself as a playful object and even as an object of pleasure, a toy, a game with which the reader was asked to play" (*Critifiction* 126).

2. Walter Abish introduces a new letter in each chapter of *Alphabetical Africa*. In chapter 3, he introduces the letter *c* and uses a vocabulary of words which begin with *a*, *b*, or *c*. A sentence from chapter 3: "Coming by car colonialists avoid anthills, but are confronted by curious cannabis chewing custom, but colonists avoid customs, by checking charts containing African cattle crossing captions" (5). In his book review of Ross Eckler's *Making the Alphabet Dance: Recreational Wordplay*, Douglas Hofstadter describes similar patterns for determining word choice, such as repeating the last two letters of a word at the beginning of the following word.

3. Barth explains the narrative strategy of double-coding in "Postmodernism Revisited": "When Donoso declares elegantly and elaborately to us from time to time in *A House in the Country* (1984) that he has no wish to trick us into believing that his characters are real or that their joys and sufferings are any more than ink marks on paper—and then immediately beguiles us back into the gorgeous, monstrous reality of his fable—he is 'double-coding' like Umberto Eco's lovers; he is having it both ways with illusionism and anti-illusionism" (*Further Fridays* 123).

4. Federman says the exact date of the death of postmodernism is December 22, 1989, when Samuel Beckett "changed tenses," or died (*Critifiction* 105).

Works Cited

Abish, Walter. *Alphabetical Africa*. New York: New Directions, 1974.

Addison, Gayle, Jr. *The Way of the World*. New York: Doubleday, 1975.

Alter, Robert. *Partial Magic: The Novel as a Self-Conscious Genre*. Berkeley: University of California Press, 1975.

Andrews, William L. *To Tell a Free Story: The First Century of Afro-American Autobiography, 1760–1865*. Urbana: University of Illinois Press, 1986.

Attebery, Brian. "Fantasy as an Anti-Utopian Mode." In *Selected Essays from the Fourth International Conference on the Fantastic in the Arts*, edited by Michael R. Collins, 3–8. New York: Greenwood Press, 1983.

Awkward, Michael. *Inspiriting Influences: Tradition, Revision, and Afro-American Women's Novels*. New York: Columbia University Press, 1989.

Babb, Valerie Melissa. *Ernest Gaines*. Twayne United States Author Series, edited by Frank Day. Boston: Twayne Publishers, 1991.

———. "Old-Fashioned Modernism: 'The Changing Same' in *A Lesson before Dying*." In *Critical Reflections on the Fiction of Ernest J. Gaines*, edited by David C. Estes. Athens: University of Georgia Press, 1994.

Baker, Houston A., Jr. "Belief, Theory, and Blues: Notes for a Post-Structuralist Criticism of Afro-American Literature." In *Studies in Black American Literary Criticism*, edited by Joel Weixlmann and Chester J. Fontenot, 5–30. Greenwood, Fla.: Penkeville Publishing Company, 1986.

———. *Black Studies, Rap, and the Academy*. Chicago: University of Chicago Press, 1993.

———. *Blues, Ideology, and Afro-American Literature: A Vernacular Theory*. Chicago: University of Chicago Press, 1984.

———. *Modernism and the Harlem Renaissance*. Chicago: University of Chicago Press, 1987.

———. *Workings of the Spirit: The Poetics of Afro-American Women's Writing*. Chicago: University of Chicago Press, 1991.

Baker, Houston A., Jr., and Patricia Redmond, eds. *Afro-American Literary Studies in the 1990s*. Chicago: University of Chicago Press, 1989.

Bakhtin, M. M. *The Dialogic Imagination: Four Essays*. Austin: University of Texas Press, 1981.

Barth, John. *The Floating Opera*. New York: Bantam, 1972.

———. *Further Fridays: Essays, Lectures, and Other Nonfiction, 1984–1994*. Boston: Little, Brown, 1995.

———. *The Last Voyage of Somebody the Sailor*. Boston: Little, Brown, 1991.

———. "Life-Story." In *Lost in the Funhouse*, 113–126. New York: Bantam, 1969.

———. "The Literature of Exhaustion." In *Surfiction: Fiction Now and Tomorrow*, edited by Raymond Federman. Chicago: Swallow Press, 1975. Originally published in *Atlantic* (August 1967): 19–33.

Barthelme, Donald. *Snow White*. New York: Atheneum, 1978.

Bauer, Dale M., and S. Jaret McKinstry, eds. *Feminism, Bakhtin, and the Dialogic*. Albany: State University of New York Press, 1991.

Belsey, Catherine. *Critical Practice*. London: Methuen, 1980.

Bérubé, Michael. "Hybridity in the Center: An Interview with Houston A. Baker, Jr." *African American Review* 26, no. 4 (Winter 1992): 547–564.

Blake, Caesar R. "On Richard Wright's *Native Son*." In *Rough Justice: Essays on Crime Literature*, edited by M. L. Friedland. Toronto: University of Toronto Press, 1991.

Bloom, Harold. *Agon: Towards a Theory of Revisionism*. New York: Oxford University Press, 1982.

———. *The Anxiety of Influence: A Theory of Poetry*. New York: Oxford University Press, 1973.

Butler, Octavia E. *Parable of the Sower*. New York: Four Walls Eight Windows, 1993.

Butler-Evans, Elliott. *Race, Gender, and Desire: Narrative Strategies in the Fiction of Toni Cade Bambara, Toni Morrison, and Alice Walker*. Philadelphia: Temple University Press, 1989.

Byerman, Keith E. *Fingering the Jagged Grain: Tradition and Form in Recent Black Fiction*. Athens: University of Georgia Press, 1985.

Cawelti, John G. "Earthly Thoughts on *Divine Days*." *Callaloo* 16, no. 2 (Spring 1993): 431–447.

Christensen, Inger. *The Meaning of Metafiction: A Critical Study of Selected Novels by Sterne, Nabokov, Barth, and Beckett*. Bergen, Norway: Universitetsforlaget, 1981.

Christian, Barbara. *Black Feminist Criticism: Perspectives on Black Women Writers.* New York: Pergamon Press, 1985.

Clayton, Jay, and Eric Rothstein, eds. *Influence and Intertextuality in Literary History.* Madison: University of Wisconsin Press, 1991.

Cooper, J. California. *The Matter Is Life.* New York: Doubleday, 1991.

Dance, Daryl Cumber. *Shuckin' and Jivin': Folklore from Contemporary Black Americans.* Bloomington: Indiana University Press, 1978.

de Weever, Jacqueline. *Mythmaking and Metaphor in Black Women's Fiction.* New York: St. Martin's Press, 1991.

Dieke, Ikenna. "Toward a Monistic Idealism: The Thematics of Alice Walker's *The Temple of My Familiar.*" *African American Review* 26, no. 3 (Fall 1992): 507–514.

Dorson, Richard M. *American Negro Folktales.* Greenwich, Conn.: Fawcett, 1956.

Dove, Rita. *Through the Ivory Gate.* New York: Pantheon, 1992.

Ellison, Ralph. *Invisible Man.* 1947. Reprint, New York: Vintage, 1972.

Federman, Raymond. *Critifiction: Postmodern Essays.* Albany: State University of New York Press, 1993.

———. ed. *Surfiction: Fiction Now and Tomorrow.* Chicago: Swallow Press, 1975.

Folks, Jeffrey J. "Ernest Gaines and the New South." *Southern Literary Journal* 24, no. 1 (Fall 1991): 32–46.

Forrest, Leon. *Divine Days.* New York: Norton, 1993.

———. *Relocations of the Spirit.* Emeryville, Calif.: Asphodel Press, 1994.

Field, Trevor. *Form and Function in the Diary Novel.* Totowa, N.J.: Barnes and Noble Books, 1989.

Foucault, Michel. "The Order of Discourse." Inaugural lecture at the Collège de France, 2 December 1970. In *Untying the Text: A Post-Structuralist Reader,* edited by Robert Young, 48–78. Boston: Routledge and Kegan Paul, 1981.

Freese, Peter. *The Ethnic Detective: Chester Himes, Harry Kemelman, Tony Hillerman.* Essen, Germany: Verlag die Blaue Eule, 1992.

Fuderer, Laura Sue. *The Female Bildungsroman: An Annotated Bibliography of Criticism.* New York: Modern Language Association, 1990.

Gaines, Ernest J. *The Autobiography of Miss Jane Pittman.* New York: Bantam, 1971.

———. *A Lesson before Dying.* New York: Knopf, 1993.

Gass, William H. *Fiction and the Figures of Life.* New York: Knopf, 1970.

———. "On Experimental Writing: Some Clues for the Clueless." *New York Times Book Review*, 24 August 1994.

Gates, Henry Louis, Jr. *Loose Canons: Notes on the Culture Wars*. New York: Oxford University Press, 1992.

———. *The Signifying Monkey: A Theory of African-American Literary Criticism*. New York: Oxford University Press, 1988.

———, ed. *Black Literature and Literary Theory*. New York: Methuen, 1984.

———, ed. *"Race," Writing, and Difference*. Chicago: University of Chicago Press, 1986.

———, ed. *Reading Black, Reading Feminist: A Critical Anthology*. New York: New American Library, 1990.

Gaudet, Marcia, and Carl Wooton. *Porch Talk with Ernest Gaines: Conversations on the Writer's Craft*. Baton Rouge: Louisiana State University Press, 1990.

———. "Talking with Ernest J. Gaines." *Callaloo* 11, no. 2 (Spring 1988): 289–243.

Georgoudaki, Ekaterini. "Rita Dove: Crossing Boundaries." *Callaloo* 14, no. 2 (1991): 419–433.

Gibson, Donald B. *The Politics of Literary Expression: A Study of Major Black Writers*. Westpoint, Conn.: Greenwood Press, 1981.

———. "Wright's Invisible Native Son." In *Richard Wright: A Collection of Critical Essays*, edited by Richard Macksey and Frank M. Moorer. Englewood Cliffs, N.J.: Prentice Hall, 1984.

Giovanni, Nikki. *Racism 101*. New York: William Morrow, 1994

Govan, Sandra Y. "Homage to Tradition: Octavia Butler Renovates the Historical Novel." *MELUS* 13, nos. 1–2 (Spring–Summer 1986): 79–96.

Graff, Gerald. *Literature against Itself: Literary Ideas in Modern Society*. Chicago: University of Chicago Press, 1979.

Harper, Phillip Brian. *Framing the Margins: The Social Logic of Postmodern Culture*. New York: Oxford University Press, 1994.

Harris, Joel Chandler. *Nights with Uncle Remus*. New York: Riverside, 1881.

———. *Uncle Remus or Mr. Fox, Mr. Rabbit, and Mr. Terrapin*. New York: G. Routledge and Sons, 1881.

Harris, Trudier. *Fiction and Folklore: The Novels of Toni Morrison*. Knoxville: University of Tennessee Press, 1991.

Hawthorn, Jeremy. *A Concise Glossary of Contemporary Literary Theory*. New York: Routledge, Chapman, and Hall, 1992.

Henderson, Mae Gwendolyn. "Speaking in Tongues: Dialogics, Dialectics, and the Black Woman Writer's Literary Tradition." In *Changing Our Words: Essays on Criticism, Theory, and Writing by Black Women*, edited by Cheryl A. Wall, 16–37. New Brunswick, N.J.: Rutgers University Press, 1989.

Herrmann, Anne. *The Dialogic and Difference: "An/Other Woman" in Virginia Woolf and Christa Wolf*. New York: Columbia University Press, 1989.

Himes, Chester. *A Case of Rape*. New York: Carroll and Graf Publishers, 1994.

Hofstadter, Douglas. Review of *Making the Alphabet Dance: Recreational Word Play*, by Ross Eckler. *New York Times Book Review*, 10 March 1996.

Holloway, Karla F. C. "The Lyrical Dimension of Spirituality: Music, Voice, and Language in the Novels of Toni Morrison." In *Embodied Voices: Representing Female Vocality in Western Culture*, edited by Leslie C. Dunn and Nancy A. Jones, 197–211. Cambridge: Cambridge University Press, 1994.

Holloway, Karla F. C., and Stephanie A. Demetrapoulos. *New Dimensions of Spirituality: A Biracial and Bicultural Reading of the Novels by Toni Morrison*. Westport, Conn.: Greenwood Press, 1987.

Holquist, Michael. *Dialogism: Bakhtin and His World*. New York: Routledge, 1990.

Homan, C. Hugh, and William Harmon. *A Handbook to Literature*. 5th ed. New York: Macmillan, 1986.

hooks, bell. "Postmodern Blackness." In *A Postmodern Reader*, edited by Joseph Natoli and Linda Hutcheon, 510–518. Albany: State University of New York Press, 1993.

Hughes, Langston, and Arna Bontemps, eds. *The Book of Negro Folklore*. New York: Dodd, Mead, 1958.

Hume, Kathryn. *Fantasy and Mimesis: Responses to Reality in Western Literature*. New York: Methuen, 1984.

Hurston, Zora Neale. *Dust Tracks on a Road: An Autobiography*. Philadelphia: Lippincott, 1942. Reprint, Urbana: University of Illinois Press, 1984.

———. *The Sanctified Church*. Berkeley: Turtle Island Press, 1983.

Hutcheon, Linda. *Narcissistic Narrative: The Metafictional Paradox*. Waterloo, Ontario: Wilfrid Laurier University Press, 1980. Reprint, New York: Methuen, 1984.

———. "'The Pastime of Past Time': Fiction, History, Historiographic

Metafiction." In *Postmodern Genres*, edited by Marjorie Perloff. Norman: University of Oklahoma Press, 1988.

Johnson, Barbara. "The Re(a)d and the Black." In *Richard Wright: Critical Perspectives Past and Present*, edited by Henry Louis Gates, Jr., and K. A. Appiah, 149–155. Amistad Literary Series. New York: Penguin, 1993.

Johnson, Charles. *Being and Race: Black Writing since 1970*. Bloomington: Indiana University Press, 1988.

——. *Middle Passage*. New York: Atheneum, 1990.

——. *Oxherding Tale*. Bloomington: Indiana University Press, 1982.

Johnson, James Weldon. *The Autobiography of an Ex-Coloured Man*. New York: Hill and Wang, 1960.

Jones, Gayl. *Liberating Voices: Oral Tradition in African American Literature*. Cambridge: Harvard University Press, 1991.

Jones, Leroi (Amiri Baraka). *Blues People: Negro Music in White America*. New York: Morrow Quill Paperbacks, 1963.

Kenan, Randall. "An Interview with Octavia E. Butler." *Callaloo* 14, no. 2 (Spring 1991): 495–504.

Kinnamon, Keneth. "How *Native Son* Was Born." In *Richard Wright: Critical Perspectives Past and Present*, edited by Henry Louis Gates, Jr., and K. A. Appiah, 110–131. Amistad Literary Series. New York: Penguin, 1993.

——. "*Native Son*: The Personal, Social, and Political Background." In *Richard Wright: A Collection of Critical Essays*, edited by Richard Macksey and Frank E. Moorer, 87–94. Englewood Cliffs, N.J.: Prentice Hall, 1984.

——. ed. *New Essays on* Native Son. Cambridge: Cambridge University Press, 1990.

Kontje, Todd. *Private Lives in the Public Sphere: The German Bildungsroman as Metafiction*. University Park: Pennsylvania State University Press, 1992.

Lanser, Susan Snaider. *The Narrative Act: Point of View in Prose Fiction*. Princeton: Princeton University Press, 1981.

Levey, Judith S., and Agnes Greenhall, eds. *The Concise Columbia Encyclopedia*. New York: Columbia University Press, 1983.

Lyotard, Jean-François. *The Postmodern Condition: A Report on Knowledge*. Translated by Geoff Bennington and Brian Massumi. Minneapolis: University of Minnesota Press, 1984.

McDowell, Deborah E. "'The Changing Same': Generational Connections and Black Women Novelists." In *Reading Black, Reading Femi-*

nist: A Critical Anthology, edited by Henry Louis Gates, Jr., 91–115. New York: Penguin, 1990. Originally published in *New Literary History* 18 (Winter 1987): 281–302.

———. "The Self and the Other: Reading Toni Morrison's *Sula* and the Black Female Text." In *Critical Essays on Toni Morrison*, edited by Nellie Y. McKay, 77–90. Boston: G. K. Hall, 1988.

McKay, Nellie Y. "An Interview with Toni Morrison." *Contemporary Literature* 24, no. 4 (Winter 1983): 413–429.

McKnight, Reginald. "The Homunculus: A Novel in One Chapter." In *The Kind of Light That Shines on Texas: Stories by Reginald McKnight*. Boston: Little, Brown, 1992.

Major, Clarence. *The Dark and Feeling*. New York: Joseph Okpaku Publishing Company, Third World Press, 1974.

Marvin, Thomas F. "'Preachin' the Blues': Bessie Smith's Secular Religion and Alice Walker's *The Color Purple*." *African American Review* 28, no. 3 (Fall 1994): 411–421.

Mason, Theodore O., Jr. "Walter Mosley's Easy Rawlins: The Detective and Afro-American Fiction." *Kenyon Review* 14, no. 4 (Fall 1992): 173–183.

Mellard, James A. *The Exploded Form: The Modernist Novel in America*. Urbana: University of Illinois Press, 1980.

Morrison, Toni. *Beloved*. New York: Knopf, 1987.

———. *Playing in the Dark: Whiteness and the Literary Imagination*. Cambridge: Harvard University Press, 1992.

———. *Tar Baby*. New York: New American Library, 1981.

———. "Unspeakable Things Unspoken: The Afro-American Presence in American Literature." *Michigan Quarterly Review* 28, no. 1 (Winter 1989): 1–34. Originally presented as the Tanner Lecture on Human Values at the University of Michigan, 7 October 1988.

Mosley, Walter. *Black Betty*. New York: Norton, 1994.

Most, Glenn W., and William W. Stowe, eds. *The Poetics of Murder: Detective Fiction and Literary Theory*. New York: Harcourt Brace Jovanovich, 1993.

Murray, Albert. *The Hero and the Blues*. Columbia: University of Missouri Press, 1973. Originally presented as three lectures in the Paul Anthony Brick Lecture Series, University of Missouri, 7–9 October 1972.

Naylor, Gloria. *Bailey's Cafe*. New York: Harcourt Brace Jovanovich, 1992.

Neal, Larry. "And Shine Swam On." In *Black Fire: An Anthology of Afro-American Writing*. New York: William Morrow, 1992.

Neely, Barbara. *Blanche among the Talented Tenth*. New York: St. Martin's Press, 1994.

Ostriker, Alicia. "The Thieves of Language: Women Poets and Revisionist Mythmaking." In *Feminist Criticism: Essays on Women, Literature, and Theory*, edited by Elaine Showalter, 314–338. New York: Pantheon, 1985. Originally published in *Signs* 8 (1981).

Rabinowitz, Peter J. "Chandler Comes to Harlem: Racial Politics in the Thrillers of Chester Himes." In *The Sleuth and the Scholar: Origins, Evolution, and Current Trends in Detective Fiction*, edited by Barbara A. Rader and Howard G. Zettler, 19–29. Westport, Conn.: Greenwood Press, 1988.

Racine, Maria J. "Voice and Interiority in Zora Neale Hurston's *Their Eyes Were Watching God*." *African American Review* 28, no. 2 (Summer 1994): 283–292.

Reed, Ishmael. *Airing Dirty Laundry*. Reading, Mass.: Addison-Wesley, 1993.

———. *Conjure: Selected Poems, 1963–1970*. Amherst: University of Massachusetts Press, 1972.

———. *Japanese by Spring*. New York: Atheneum, 1993.

———. *Mumbo Jumbo*. New York: Avon Books, 1972.

———. "Shrovetide in Old New Orleans." In *Shrovetide in Old New Orleans*. New York: Avon, 1978. Originally appeared as "Voodoo in New Orleans" in *Oui* (January 1977).

———. "You Can't Be a Literary Magazine and Hate Writers." In *Shrovetide in Old New Orleans*. New York: Avon, 1978. Originally published in *Yardbird* 5 (1976).

Reilly, John M. "Giving Bigger a Voice: The Politics of Narrative in *Native Son*." In *New Essays on* Native Son, edited by Keneth Kinnamon, 35–62. Cambridge: Cambridge University Press, 1990.

Rimmon-Kenan, Shlomith. *Narrative Fiction: Contemporary Poetics*. New York: Methuen, 1988.

Rushdy, Ashraf H. A. "The Phenomenology of the Allmuseri: Charles Johnson and the Subject of the Narrative of Slavery." *African American Review* 26, no. 3 (Fall 1992): 373–394.

Sanchez, Sonia. *Wounded in the House of a Friend*. Boston: Beacon Press, 1995.

Scholes, Robert. *Fabulation and Metafiction*. Urbana: University of Illinois Press, 1979.

Scott, Nathan. "Black Literature." In *The Harvard Guide to Contempo-

rary Writing, edited by Daniel Hoffman. Cambridge: Harvard University Press, 1979.

Shange, Ntozake. *Liliane: Resurrection of the Daughter*. New York: St. Martin's Press, 1994.

Shaw, Harry. *Dictionary of Literary Terms*. New York: McGraw-Hill, 1972.

Sherman, Charlotte Watson. *One Dark Body*. New York: HarperCollins, 1993.

Shinn, Thelma J. "The Wise Witches: Black Women Mentors in the Fiction of Octavia E. Butler." In *Conjuring: Black Women, Fiction, and Literary Tradition*, edited by Marjorie Pryse and Hortense J. Spillers, 203–215. Bloomington: Indiana University Press, 1985.

Simpson, Anne K. *A Gathering of Gaines: The Man and the Writer*. Lafayette: University of Southwestern Louisiana, 1991.

Sitter, Deborah Ayer. "The Making of a Man: Dialogic Meaning in *Beloved*." *African American Review* 26, no. 1 (1992): 17–29.

Slotkin, Richard. "The Hard-Boiled Detective Story: From the Open Range to the Mean Streets." In *The Sleuth and the Scholar: Origins, Evolution, and Current Trends in Detective Fiction*, edited by Barbara A. Rader and Howard G. Zettler. New York: Greenwood Press, 1988.

Smith, Felipe. "Alice Walker's Redemptive Art." *African American Review* 26, no. 3 (Fall 1992): 437–451.

Smith, Valerie. *Self-Discovery and Authority in Afro-American Narrative*. Cambridge: Harvard University Press, 1987.

Smitherman, Geneva. *Talkin and Testifyin: The Language of Black America*. Detroit: Wayne State University Press, 1977.

Spalding, Henry D., comp. and ed. *Encyclopedia of Black Folklore and Humor*. New York: Jonathan David Publishers, 1972.

Stepto, Robert. *From behind the Veil: A Study of Afro-American Narrative*. Urbana: University of Illinois Press, 1979.

Swales, Martin. *The German Bildungsroman from Wieland to Hesse*. Princeton: Princeton University Press, 1978.

Taleb-Khyar, Mohamed B. "An Interview with Maryse Condé and Rita Dove." *Callaloo* 14, no. 2 (1991): 347–366.

Tani, Stephano. *The Doomed Detective: The Contribution of the Detective Novel to Postmodern American and Italian Fiction*. Carbondale: Southern Illinois University Press, 1984.

Tanner, Laura E. "Uncovering the Magical Disguise of Language: The Narrative Presence in Richard Wright's *Native Son*." In *Richard*

Wright: Critical Perspectives Past and Present, edited by Henry Louis Gates, Jr. and K. A. Appiah, 132–148. Amistad Literary Series. New York: Penguin, 1993.

Tate, Claudia, ed. *Black Women Writers at Work.* New York: Continuum, 1983.

Toomer, Jean. *Essentials.* Chicago: Lakeside Press, 1931. Reprint, edited by Rudolph P. Byrd. Athens: University of Georgia Press, 1991.

Traylor, Eleanor. "The Fabulous World of Toni Morrison: *Tar Baby.*" In *Critical Essays on Toni Morrison,* edited by Nellie Y. McKay, 135–150. Boston: G. K. Hall, 1988.

Walker, Alice. *In Search of Our Mothers' Gardens.* New York: Harcourt Brace Jovanovich, 1983.

———. *The Temple of My Familiar.* New York: Harcourt Brace Jovanovich, 1989.

Wall, Cheryl A., ed. *Changing Our Words: Essays on Criticism, Theory, and Writing by Black Women.* New Brunswick, N.J.: Rutgers University Press, 1989.

Warren, Kenneth W. "The Mythic City: An Interview with Leon Forrest." *Callaloo* 16, no. 2 (Spring 1993): 392–408.

Waugh, Patricia. *Metafiction: The Theory and Practice of Self-Conscious Fiction.* New York: Methuen, 1984.

Werner, Craig Hansen. "Bigger's Blues: *Native Son* and the Articulation of Afro-American Modernism." In *New Essays on Native Son,* edited by Keneth Kinnamon, 117–152. Cambridge: Cambridge University Press, 1990.

———. *Playing the Changes: From Afro-Modernism to the Jazz Impulse.* Urbana: University of Illinois Press, 1994.

Williams, David. *Confessional Fictions: A Portrait of the Artist in the Canadian Novel.* Toronto: University of Toronto Press, 1991.

Wright, Richard. *Native Son.* 1940. Reprint, New York: Harper and Row, 1966.

Zaki, Hoda M. "Utopia, Dystopia, and Ideology in the Science Fiction of Octavia Butler." *Science Fiction Studies* 17, no. 2 (July 1990): 239–251.

Index